FV

St. Louis Community College

Forest Park
Florissant Valley
Meramec

Instructional Resources
St. Louis, Missouri

From Margin to Mainstream

FROM MARGIN TO MAINSTREAM

The Social Progress of Black Americans

Second Edition

Sethard Fisher

Rowman & Littlefield Publishers, Inc.

ROWMAN & LITTLEFIELD PUBLISHERS, INC.

Published in the United States of America
by Rowman & Littlefield Publishers, Inc.
4720 Boston Way, Lanham, Maryland 20706

British Cataloging in Publication Information Available

Library of Congress Cataloging-in-Publication Data

Fisher, Sethard.
    From margin to mainstream : the social progress of black
Americans / Sethard Fisher. — 2nd ed.
    p.   cm.
    Includes bibliographical references and index.
    1. Afro-Americans—Civil rights.   2. Afro-Americans—Social
conditions—1975–   3. Afro-Americans—Social conditions—
1964–1975.   4. United States—Race relations.   I. Title.
E185.615.F53   1992
305.896'073—dc20   92–8557 CIP

ISBN 0–8476–7749–4 (cloth : alk. paper)
ISBN 0–8476–7750–8 (pbk. : alk. paper)

Printed in the United States of America

 TM The paper used in this publication meets the minimum requirements of
American National Standard for Information Sciences—Permanence of
Paper for Printed Library Materials, ANSI Z39.48–1984.

To those of its victims who no longer understand racism as an unlucky and inevitable stamp of fate but who have come to view it as a man-made historical circumstance to be changed.

Contents

List of Tables and Figures ix

Foreword, second edition xi

Foreword, first edition xv

Acknowledgments, second edition xix

Acknowledgments, first edition xxi

1 Traditions of Protest 1

2 Analytic Approaches to Oppression: 21
Park, Marx, And Weber

3 From Caste to Ethnicity to Class 51

4 Transition in California I 89

5 Transition in California II 101

6 Political Gains 127

7 Wage and Employment Gains 141

8 Educational Gains 163

9 Black Pride and the Decline of Colonialism 179

10 Proletarian Vanguard or Interest Group 217

11 Nonwhite Equality and Social Transition 245

Appendix A: Blacks and the Radical Left 273

Appendix B: The Meaning of Third World 281

Appendix C: The Significance of Race Controversy 289

Appendix D: Tactics and Strategy 299

Index 305

About the Author 315

List of Tables and Figures

Tables

11.1   Nonwhites and Whites in the Upper Class   254

11.2   Nonwhites and Whites in the Middle Class   255

11.3   Nonwhites and Whites in the Lower Class   255

11.4   Percent Distribution of the Population, by   259
       Color within Socioeconomic Status
       Categories for the United States, 1960

Figures

3.1   Oscillating Phases of Black History   54
       in the United States

3.2   Oscillation of Black History and   55
       Class Confinement

3.3   Socioeconomic Status and Color, 1960   56

11.1   Social Distance Pyramid   260

FOREWORD, second edition

This second edition of *From Margin to Mainstream* has been expanded and chapters have been changed around a bit. This was in the interest of making it a user-friendly text for upper-division undergraduate students without distortion of the sometimes harsh reality with which it deals. The idea of a text for introductory ethnic studies courses seems timely and appropriate as ethnic studies consolidates itself as a respected discipline on campuses throughout the nation.

This second edition accomplishes two important purposes. First, it incorporates recent research on aspects of black-white relations. Second, it introduces more of the empirical reality of racism as a balance against the rather extensive and important theoretical treatment. For example, the caste concept becomes more starkly clear by inclusion of the adaptation that deals with a recent episode of caste-based brutality and death in India.

Though much has changed in the world since the first edition appeared, none of the new developments have caused radical change in the theoretical thinking that went into the volume originally. My assumptions for the most part have been grandly supported by much that has happened in the interim.

Collapse of the communist world has been, perhaps, the most startling recent change. In 1982 when the book first appeared, the communist world and the capitalist world were pitted against one another as if in mortal combat. Today, as this is written, the president of the United States is in Moscow as a welcome guest. For better or worse, the communist world is rapidly turning to capitalism as a preferred and dominant form of socioeconomic organization. So startling has been this development that communist parties around the world that linked their hopes and aspirations for human betterment on Marxism appear paralyzed and as yet without coherent and meaningful response. What is the importance of this astounding development for black-white relations in the United States and the world? It says something about the much touted emphasis in sociology on the rise of technological society and the decline of ideology as a dominant way of being in, and of looking at, the world. But that is another story, one that surely intersects this one but that has been well and more fully developed elsewhere.

Another major change in recent years has been the growth of the middle class among blacks in the United States, and the novel spectacle of blacks playing significant roles at very high levels of industry, government, and politics. Although these events clearly do not mean the end of racism, they do suggest change in that direction. But, this discussion gets us ahead of the story.

The first three chapters of the book are introductory. They tell of the outrage and outcry caused by the slave trade and slavery, and of the transformation of this dissatisfaction into a social movement. They tell of serious social science conceptualization that allows understanding of racism in terms of the interplay of class and caste phenomena. Chapter 3 introduces a distinctive approach to black American history that depicts it as central to broader social processes operating in the society.

Chapters 4 through 8 are data chapters. They present information designed to substantiate the fact that there has been significant positive change in the resources of black Americans over time. The evidence is not to be taken to mean the end of racism but as the operation of a process that other ethnic groups encountered at an earlier time in their history as Americans.

Chapter 9 discusses two important elements that have been instrumental in initiating and accelerating the rate of gain to black Americans: a new pride in blackness and in self-identity among blacks, and the decline of colonialism. Chapter 10 focuses on strategy and attempts to assess the relevance of Marxism, which has continually utilized the grievances of black Americans for the specific interest of a general proletarian rise to power in the society. The final chapter of the book assesses the meaning of a distinctively black agenda as articulated in prior chapters for change in the wider society.

The four appendixes deal with aspects of the book that deserve special comment but which seemed out of place in earlier discussion.

FOREWORD, first edition

The social habits and prejudices of an era, especially those that have a functional tie to social systems as does racism, only die slowly and with struggle. This, in part, is because they are deeply embedded in the consciousness of several interdependent generations. Their demise causes distress, pain, and confusion as a new order gradually emerges. The progressive growth of civilized life itself occurs in just that way: discarding of old and emergence of new patterns of human relatedness. So it is with racism in the United States today. A new racial order is emerging and an old one dying. This is an unmistakable trend amid the chaos and confusion of contemporary race relations. Frederick Douglass, John Brown, W.E.B. Du Bois, Martin Luther King, Jr., to name but a few, have had a cumulative impact on our society and time. The assault on racism continues and with decisive success.

Yet, the confusion, pain, and stress of the change process remain predominant characteristics of our time. The death of the old racial order is by no means complete. Groping efforts in many directions are apparent. Black separatist tendencies, white vigilante efforts, apathy and indifference among many—all can be seen as aspects of the change process. Nevertheless, the emergence of an active and intelligent opposition to racism as a way of life can now be seen as both possible and necessary. This suggests a new phase in the struggle against racism, a phase similar to one that briefly appeared once before. Reconstruction lasted only a few short years, ending long before its work of securely establishing a nonracist society was finished. The "second reconstruction," as Vann Woodward has referred to the 1960s, proceeds apace, reviving this unfinished process that had a spurious prosperity more than 100 years ago.

There are many academic statements on the horror and tragedy of racism in the United States, yet only a few of these are working documents of social change directed to the demise of racism and to the emergence of a new racial order. My search through the social science literature revealed rich accounts of incidents, episodes, and events reflecting racism; analytic efforts that bear some link to one or another conceptual view of it; ethnographic accounts; and some rather massive empirical studies. Yet, today, in a time of demand for intelligent action and reconstruction, these works have proved woefully insufficient. They do not provide theoretical or conceptual interpretations of different strategic and tactical options that effective struggle against racism might adopt. A more direct source of this kind of literature was to be found in radical bookshops rather than in conventional academic places.

The radical literature seems a strained effort to fit the problem of racism into conceptual schemes designed for other purposes. In this literature blacks and other nonwhites are regularly exhorted to action, the essential outcome of which is to promote the interest of a social class or a political party, but not the distinctive interest of the victims of racism themselves. Much of this literature incorporates the assumption that racism cannot be dealt with until the inequalities of class stratification are eliminated. This does not provide a rationale and direction for action against racism but against the privileges of social classes and political parties.

I have concluded from my study, and from my preoccupation with racism, that there is now underway a fundamental change in relations between white and nonwhite Americans. Conceptually, this change can be characterized as a transition from the condition of a castelike group to that of a class entity proper. There is, I argue, an intervening necessary condition recently achieved by nonwhites in the transition process, namely, ethnic status. This volume is an attempt to substantiate the relevance of this vision and to spell out some of its consequences for social reconstruction and some of its implications for class analysis and change in the broader social system. I have drawn on both academic and nonacademic literature and have attempted to develop a view of racism that can facilitate meaningful and effective action against it.

ACKNOWLEDGMENTS,
second edition

There are several persons to whom thanks is due for their invaluable assistance in preparation of this second edition. A constant source of support, of creative suggestion, as well as actual craft in formatting the volume has been my son, Gregor R. Fisher. Denise Hurtado, Andrea Frommer, Lucy Casale, and Ann Wainwright did most of the word processing and much of the editing of the volume. Acknowledgment is also due to several offices on my own campus of the University of California at Santa Barbara, which provided small grants to assist with research and with preparation of the book. The Academic Senate's Research and Travel Committee, the College of Letters and Science, and the Office of Research and Development were all helpful at one time or another with small amounts of financial assistance.

Grateful acknowledgment is also made of permission by Dr. James. P. Smith and Finis R. Welch to use their previously published research, and to the Joint Center for Political Studies.

Finally, I want to acknowledge the inspiration and the rich discussion and debate on the race issue provided by my undergraduate students. Many of the ideas in this book at one time or another have been the subject of debate, discussion, and often spirited exchange in my race relations class. We all have grown immensely from the excitement of discovering new ways of thinking about and viewing ourselves and the world.

ACKNOWLEDGMENTS, first edition

I want to express my appreciation to a number of people whose support and encouragement were important to me in writing this book. Robert Wenkert and I carried on discussions of the central idea of the book some years ago in Syracuse, New York. Marnie Lynn Sayles, Victoria Smith, and Stephen Stumpf were of invaluable assistance with the sections on black elected officials. Peter Rose, Harry Specht, and Colin Jones read prior versions of the manuscript and made helpful, insightful, suggestions.

Special mention and appreciation go to Robert Blauner as well as to my late friend and colleague Richard Frucht. My understanding of the race problem has benefited enormously from their work and thinking. Though we maintain important theoretical differences, their example has taught me an important lesson: humanist scholarship that seeks both to know the world as well as to change it must take initiative and understanding from the firing line and trenches of everyday life rather than from the isolation of the academy alone.

Of course this book, as well as any academic work I may produce, owes much to those who, advertently or inadvertently, willing or unwillingly, served as academic and intellectual mentors. Among those to whom I owe thanks in this regard are Herbert Blumer, Tamotsu Shibutani, Seymour Martin Lipset, Reinhard Bendix, and David Matza. At one time or another these scholars contributed to the exciting and creative intellectual atmosphere of the University of California at Berkeley where I spent many, perhaps too many, graduate and undergraduate years.

I hasten to add that none of those mentioned here can be held accountable for the shortcomings of the book. It is entirely my own creation and responsibility. Yet, it must be recognized and acknowledged that any positive value the book may have is explained in considerable part by their influence.

Acknowledgment should be made of the vital assistance of small grants provided by my own campus to assist with various phases of the book. Also, the Ford Foundation generously supported my research on black elected officials, portions of which appear in this volume.

Appreciation is due to Dr. Nathan Hare, R and E Associates, the Vikas Publishing House, and the *American Journal of Sociology* for their permission to use segments of previously published work.

1

TRADITIONS OF PROTEST

The roots of modern American racism reach deep into the historical past of the Western world. Their delineation is a common preoccupation of scholarly effort. Less commonly noted, and studied, is the fact that the roots of opposition to racism in the Western world lie equally deep reflecting an astounding tenacity and vitality. This means that the social forces in opposition to racism in the United States, and in the Western world today, are based on a high degree of legitimacy, or basic agreement that racism is a social evil that should be eliminated. Some of the confluent historical episodes that reveal this strong antiracist tradition are discussed in this chapter. I shall portray the opposition to racial inequality as a social movement, and suggest the depths to which its roots extend. That these roots should be both sacred and secular should come as no surprise, as both traditions have frequently been seminal sources of creative ferment and change in the Western world.

From the very beginning of the slave trade and slavery, there was widespread moral indignation and protest. It came from organized religions, intellectuals, and from conscience-stricken individuals, among others. Eventually, these protests became widespread and gave rise to a social movement that has been the motive force undergirding the drive to racial equality in the United States. Characteristic of the accomplishments of this movement are abolition of the slave trade and slavery, passage of various constitutional amendments in the interest of racial equality, abolition of separate but equal social arrangements of races, and abolition of racial restrictions on voting. This is not to suggest that racist oppression in the United States no longer exists, but that some major changes have occurred that must be viewed in broad historical perspective. They are not independent of people and events in other parts of the world.

Historically, the national consciousness of several countries of the Western world has been troubled by racism, and this happened at the very time that racist practices were in full flourish. Out of the turmoil was generated a widespread, militant, and triumphant social movement that has had enormous effect as an opposition to racism. This movement toppled the slave trade and slavery itself; it essentially overthrew by military force an encysted, oppressive, racist economy and way of life in the American South; and it has destroyed subsequent attempts to reinstate racial oppression through legislative and/or terroristic tactics. This movement continues today as a vital force in the cultural life of American society.

The social and political history of blacks as Americans begins with Emancipation and Reconstruction in the South. This is not to imply that no blacks had voted before Emancipation or that black people before then were not objects of political concern in the United States. In several states, the free black population had voted before Emancipation. However, as an oppressed people, the massive movement into, and participation in, the political and social life of the country as equals first occurred just after slavery was destroyed by the Civil War and the passage of several constitutional amendments. Only then did millions of black Americans first become registered voters, first vote, first become elected on a large scale to political office, and first entertain the idea of equality on a large scale. The year in which this process began was 1867.[1]

This formal incorporation into the social and political life of the country was the result of many years of effort by different people variously located in this society and in the Western world generally. Their collective efforts leading to the destruction of slavery as a social institution reflect a social movement,[2] the effects of which have been profound. It has affected the lives and loyalties of generations of Americans young and old, black and white, rich and poor. The social movement against black oppression developed in those same countries that were themselves most actively involved in slavery and the slave trade. In what countries was this movement most apparent?

World reaction against black slavery and slave trading had made itself felt in policy by 1807, when Great Britain and the United States outlawed the slave trade. The ideological impetus of the abolitionist movement was diverse, coming from Spain, England, and eighteenth-century France. The French Enlightenment spawned a broad network of progressive ideas and enthusiasts that sought to destroy all existing forms of inhumanity. Although their primary target was the organized church, in Spain and England the organized church itself was central to the antislavery effort.

Spain

Sixteenth-century Spain produced one of the most dramatic and influential controversies over the oppression of slavery ever to appear among a conquering people. One Sunday morning in 1511, a Dominican friar, Antonio de Montesinos, spoke to his congregation on the island of Hispaniola:

> In order to make your sins against the Indians known to you I
> have come up on this pulpit, I who am a voice of Christ crying
> in the wilderness of this island, and therefore it behooves you
> to listen, not with careless attention, but with all your heart
> and senses, so that you may hear it; for this is going to be the
> strangest voice that ever you heard, the harshest and hardest
> and most awful and most dangerous that ever you expected to
> hear. This voice says that you are in mortal sin, that you live
> and die in it, for the cruelty and tyranny you use in dealing
> with these innocent people. Tell me, by what right or justice do
> you keep these Indians in such a cruel and horrible servitude?
> Are these not men? Have they not rational souls? Are you not
> bound to love them as you love yourselves? [3]

Henceforth there grew within the church, slowly but
perceptibly, formidable opposition to the cruelties and inhu-
manities instigated by the conquistadors.[4] Particular objec-
tion was taken to the assumption that the native inhabitants
of the New World (and later the imported black slaves) were
inhuman and without souls. Bartolomé de Las Casas became
the foremost proponent of the viewpoint that the captured
and oppressed peoples were the equals of their captors in the
sight of God. This meant that they, therefore, must be treated
as human beings rather than as objects or things. He was
vehemently opposed in this view by his fellow countryman,
the influential and respected scholar, Juan Ginés de
Sepúlveda; but Las Casas' argument persuaded the Crown
and was influential among his fellows. The widespread
propagation of this view had an important influence in miti-
gating the severity of oppression of nonwhites in Spanish
areas of the New World.

Serious discussion of the basis for Spanish rule in America and of the right of Spaniards to profit from Indian labor,
took place in Spain in 1503. Theologians, canonists, and
members of the royal council all took part in these discussions. From them grew a broad concern for the moral legitimacy of conquest in the New World. A council was formed

that drew up the first comprehensive code of Indian legislation called the Law of Burgos (on December 27, 1512). The sermons of Friar Montesinos, in 1511, had come at a strategic time and had had some effect. The conflict of the two viewpoints (Montesinos and Las Casas on one side and Sepúlveda on the other) was at its height in the great debate that took place in the middle of September 1550 before the Council of Fourteen whose job it was to determine what laws and government would best ensure extension of Roman Catholicism in the New World.

Sepúlveda's argument was taken indirectly from St. Thomas Aquinas, who had argued centuries earlier that wars may be fought justly when their cause is just and when the authority behind the war conducts it in the right spirit and way. Sepúlveda gave four reasons for conducting war against natives in the New World: their sins and idolatries against nature; the rudeness of their nature, which obliged them to serve persons of more refined natures such as the Spaniards; a means of more effectively spreading the faith; and protection of the weak among the natives themselves. Las Casas presented a quite different picture of the Indian to the council. He characterized the Indians as prudent and rational beings with ability and judgment as good as those of other men. It was his opinion that conquests of the New World should be undertaken by preachers rather than soldiers. He advised winning over the natives to Christianity by peace, love, and good example. Of this fateful debate, Lewis Hanke comments,

> The disputation at Valladolid in 1550 and 1551 stands forth clearly, not as a personal struggle between a friar and a scholar, not merely as a loud argument to approve or disapprove the printing of Sepúlveda's treatise, but as the passionate record of a crucial event in the history of humanity. Because Sepulveda's ideas failed to triumph, Spain through the mouth of Las Casas made a substantial contribution to-

ward the development of one of the most important hypotheses ever set forth, the idea that the Indians discovered in Spain's onward rush through the lands of the New World were not beasts, not slaves by nature, not childlike creatures with a limited or static understanding, but men capable of becoming Christians, who had every right to enjoy their property, political liberty, and human dignity, who should be incorporated into the Spanish civilization rather than enslaved or destroyed. One more painful and faltering step was thus taken along the road of justice for all races in a world of many races, spoke at Valladolid for the American Indians. His argumentation had another usefulness: it strengthened the hands of all those who in his time and in the centuries to follow worked in the belief that all the people of the world are human beings with the potentialities and responsibilities of men.[5]

Herbert Klein points out that this debate over slavery in the New World and over the legitimacy of the Spanish conquest committed the crown to a fundamental approach to Indian equality. This commitment was testimony to the effect that the tremendously vital humanitarian forces of Spain's golden century *(Siglo de Oro)* had upon imperial policy. He continues: "Nor did the fervor of reform stop with the Indian. Many even carried it to the question of Negro slavery as well, and it was in sixteenth century Spain that the first abolitionists of modern history gave voice to the question of Negro rights and Negro freedom."[6]

England

In England a similar humanitarian tradition emerged that also had a decisive impact on slavery. England was of major importance in the development of the abolitionist movement. The Society for Effecting the Abolition of the Slave Trade was organized by Thomas Clarkson, William Wilberforce, and others in 1787. Largely due to the pressure of this organization the slave trade in England was terminated in 1807. Then antislavery leaders began agitation and action for complete abolition. A number of religious and humanitarian organizations and associations emerged in both England and the colonies. The Society for the Mitigation and Gradual Abolition of Slavery Throughout the British Dominions, founded in London in 1823 by Thomas F. Boxton, was one of these. Shortly after its founding, several hundred branch societies came into existence.[7]

Frank Klingberg notes a right-about change of English opinion on slavery and the slave trade that took place over a hundred-year period. At first, the British legislature encouraged the trade, but later the courts outlawed slavery in the British Isles and slave trading became first a felony and finally a capital crime. This dramatic shift in viewpoint reflects the radical forces at work in society.[8]

During the first half of the eighteenth century, English government was in the hands of the old middle class and the landed aristocracy. The king had essentially abdicated, yet the new entrepreneurial and industrial middle classes were not powerful. Eventually, achievements in science, industry, agriculture, and literature led to and reflected accelerated social and economic changes that ushered in a new middle class to greater power. With this development came a more clear demarcation between the capitalist and the laboring classes and, of course, new social problems. Consequently, public debate in England became widespread concerning a number of issues, such as the distress and poverty caused by new industry or overseas usurpation of the rights of Asians and Africans. Debates on such issues were stimulated, conducted, and propagated by a wide range of reform-oriented individuals and groups inspired by new concepts of human nature, by the belief in human perfectability, and by the conviction that Christian principles should apply to everyday life.

Although earlier philosophic thought in England was

generally favorable to slavery, a marked change occurred in the eighteenth century. An expression of antislavery sentiment in an influential work addressed to the literate and learned stratas of society was John Locke's *Two Treatises on Government*.[9] Locke declared emphatically against slavery arguing the necessity of freedom from absolute arbitrary power. Such freedom, he stressed, was basic to man's preservation. Adam Smith and Jeremy Bentham were critical of slavery on economic grounds arguing that the work done by free men is more productive, or less costly, than the work of slaves.[10] There were other less well-known people who greatly influenced public opinion in eighteenth-century England. John Wesley, William Paley, and Granville Sharp were among them.[11]

Contrary to antislavery action and sentiment in France, the movement in England was built largely on sacred rather than secular foundations. The British antislavery tradition rested in large measure on evangelical elements in British Protestantism.[12] Pressures against slavery emanated from the conception of slavery as a sin and evangelical techniques were urged as means to end it. The effects of such influential antislavery figures as William Wilberforce and Thomas Clarkson were greatly accelerated when British ministers busied themselves in the cause. Thomas Harwood claims that the direct influence of the British evangelical message on their American counterparts was decisive in the 1880s in the outcome of secession and the Civil War. British Baptists and Methodists were foremost among the religious groups influential in the struggle, but the work of Quakers, Wesleyans, and Presbyterians was also important.

In the British West Indies slavery was abolished by a government-introduced bill in 1833. This bill, forced by the British antislavery lobby, reflected a high level of antislavery agitation and organization in England. In fact, controversy still exists over the extent to which American antislavery agitation and action are indebted to the movement in England.[13]

France

The French Enlightenment stressed that all human beings are rational, humane, and reasonable and that their actions could show these qualities. Men, being endowed with these qualities, could build a world that would embody them. In the Enlightenment view the tradition of blind faith in an afterlife, and of guidance by religious intermediaries, was objectionable, unnecessary, and unwise. The eighteenth-century French intelligentsia fought the organized institutions of their time that they felt condoned or promoted ignorance and inhumanity. As J. Salwyn Schapiro describes them,

> The French intellectuals of the eighteenth century waged uncompromising and relentless war against the Old Regime on the grounds that its institutions, its ideas, its traditions, and its methods were violations of the rights of man. This wholesale repudiation was revolutionary; it plainly implied that if an existing order did not conform to the principles of the rights of man, it must be destroyed, and a new one set up on the basis of these rights. The strange and concentrated glow that burns in the pages of Rousseau's Social Contract came from the newly lighted fire of social revolution which, in the French Revolution, was to burst into devouring flames.[14]

Slavery was among the conditions that aroused lively opposition among the Philosophes. One of these men was the mathematician-philosopher Condorcet, who was actively opposed to slavery. Schapiro writes,

> Slavery and the slave trade shocked the humanitarian conscience of the eighteenth century. Anti-slavery societies were formed in England and in France that agitated in favor of the

emancipation of the Negro. Condorcet was active in this agitation, and became the president of a French anti-slavery association, the Friends of the Negro. In 1781 he published a pamphlet, *Reflections on Negro Slavery*, which was an eloquent and devastating indictment of slavery. When the elections for the Estates-General were taking place, Condorcet issued an appeal to the voters to demand the abolition of slavery in San Domingo, then a French possession. When the National Assembly was organized, he appealed to that body to exclude the representatives from San Domingo on the ground that they, as masters, could not represent their slaves.[15]

Some of the drama surrounding this time is found in C.L.R. James' account of events during the French Revolution. He described Paris in the period between March 1793 and July 1794 as one of the supreme epochs of political history. For during this time the French masses had more influence on government than at any other time during the Revolution. James comments,

> In these few months of their nearest approach to power, they did not forget the Blacks. They felt towards them as brothers, and the old slave owners, whom they knew to be supporters of the counter-revolution, they hated as if Frenchmen themselves had suffered under the whip.[16]

Many of the common people of France were so moved by the suffering of slaves that they stopped drinking coffee, because it was produced only with the blood and sweat "of men turned into brutes."

He continues,

> Cambon drew the attention of the House to an incident which had taken place among the spectators. "A citizeness of colour who regularly attends the sittings of the Convention has just felt so keen a joy at seeing us give liberty to all her brethren that she has fainted (applause). I demand that this fact be mentioned in the minutes, and that this citizeness be admitted to the sitting and receive at least this much recognition of her

civic virtues." The motion was carried and the woman walked to the front bench of the amphitheater and sat to the left of the President, drying her tears amidst another burst of cheering.[17]

Clearly, the reaction against slavery and the slave trade in the West originated and grew within the very countries that were central in instigating and perpetuating these practices. The effects of this mobilized resistance were extensive throughout the Western world.

This fateful time for black people was a product of the idealistic efforts of the rationalists of the eighteenth century who hoped to end tyranny and oppression everywhere.

One important effect was to stimulate resistance to slavery and the slave trade in the New World also. Haiti was the first country to outlaw slavery and this was because in 1793 France proclaimed universal freedom for everyone living under the French flag. In the following year this proclamation was ratified by the National Convention marking the first instance in which a legislative assembly decreed the abolition of human slavery.[18]

The "New World"

Throughout Latin America the sentiment against slavery grew along with the sentiment for independence. Bolivia emancipated its slaves in 1831, Uruguay in 1842, Colombia and Argentina in 1851 and 1853 respectively. Though the abolition movement was widespread and many antislavery societies existed in Brazil, it was the last country in the New World to abolish slavery. Not until May, 1888, was emancipation complete.

In the United States a civil war was required to settle the issue of slavery. Organized opposition to emancipation of slaves was so formidable that the federal government was required to put an end to slavery through force and military occupation of the South. The impetus to end slavery in the United States arose from the same forces that so valiantly resisted slavery in Spanish, in English, and in French dominions. The abolitionists included a wide range of persons in many different countries and conditions throughout the Western world. Only when the incremental growth and prosperity of the tradition of opposition and resistance to black oppression is understood as a social movement and only when its growth, development, and successes are analyzed can one fully understand the decline of slavery. Then can one understand the prosperity of the current movement toward racial equality in the United States.

Abolition and the Liberal Tradition

Being an abolitionist in England in the 1840s was quite a different experience from being an abolitionist in the United States. The British antislavery effort was mild compared with the American effort. In American eyes the British experience was seen as drawing room philanthropy. As Frank Thistlethwaite reports,

> To be an Abolitionist in Boston, Philadelphia, or Cincinnati meant courting social ostracism, business ruin and physical assault: it called for qualities of personal courage and character which should not be minimized, however foolhardy and short-sighted the single-mindedness which went with it. For Americans, slavery was in the backyard and the color problem in the kitchen and the meeting house.[19]

In North America slaveholding was widespread; it was nearly nonexistent in England. Thus, the extent of direct social investment in the institution was much less in England than in the United States, and this made for much more formidable opposition to antislavery efforts in the United States than in England. The widespread violence against both blacks and white advocates of black freedom in America was never faced by English abolitionists. It is, perhaps, the rise of such opposition that distinguishes what is sometimes referred to as internal colonialism from some of its other forms.[20]

Opposition to black oppression in the United States is something of an amalgam of these above-cited traditions. The broader perspective, of which this opposition is an integral part, encompasses resistance to a range of conditions and circumstances that are seen as major obstructions to human progress and well-being. Colonial rule has historically been one of these. Major advocates and activists in this progressive and change-oriented tradition were prominent during the American Revolution. Representative individuals at this juncture of American history were Thomas Paine and Benjamin Franklin. They regularly visited the European continent and were caught up in the main currents of advanced liberal thought, which were at that time centered largely in France.

Paine, a self-made intellectual and crusader for social change, was influential in two major social upheavals during his lifetime: the French and the American revolutions. He was instrumental in the effort of the colonists to secure independence from Great Britain. Though he did see combat, his main influence was that of advocacy of the principles and moral issues that underlay the independence movement. No one had so forthrightly, and in print, demanded independence before Paine's *Common Sense.* In this work he distinguished between society and government considering the latter a necessary evil. He attacked monarchy and the dream of a glorious British Empire, proposed a new American government, and prescribed a republic. *Common Sense,* had great influence in preparing the minds of plain men for independence and in shifting their loyalty from the British Crown to the American Republic.

Its influence later extended far beyond the continental boundaries of America. Paine himself considered it a defense of the natural rights of man and argued that many of its circumstances are universal. The cause of America, he proclaimed, was in great measure the cause of all mankind. Silas Deane reported in August 1776 that in France it had been translated and had had a greater run, if possible, than in America. And later during the Revolution of 1789 it was reissued into Spanish to vindicate the new French Republic. In Latin America, where it was re-translated and circulated, it became highly influential in the independence movements of Venezuela, Mexico, and Ecuador.[21]

Throughout the American Revolution, Paine published a series of influential papers on important issues of the war. The first, *Crisis*, which began with the still celebrated words "These are the times that try men's souls," had an invigorating effect on the American spirit. In 1791 the influential *Rights of Man* was published. This book contains his notorious attack against monarchy and aristocracy as well as his support for their overthrow. *The Rights of Man* was intended as Paine's reply to the widely read *Reflections on the Revolution in France*, written by conservative philosopher, Edmund Burke, who eloquently championed hereditary rights and the principle of monarchy. Burke wrote abusively of theories of abstract right and government. Paine wrote in defense of the French Revolution and against monarchy in the tradition of the French Enlightenment.[22]

In 1775, Paine published the tract *African Slavery in America* in the city of Philadelphia. In this work he pointed to the inconsistency of Americans loudly resisting English efforts to hold blacks in involuntary servitude while they themselves (the Americans) held many thousands of blacks in slavery. A month after this tract appeared the first American antislavery society was formed. The next year the Revolutionary Congress resolved that no slaves be imported into any of the thirteen colonies. By 1778 laws prohibiting slave importation had been passed in Rhode Island, Connecticut, Pennsylvanaia, Delaware, and Virginia.

In his day the talented, versatile Benjamin Franklin was widely known as a scientist, philosopher, and revolutionary hero. Contrary to Paine, whose role in the American Revolution was primarily propagandist and agitationist, Franklin's was closer to that of tactician, strategist, and rebel diplomat. Verner Crane characterizes him as a shrewd and subtle politician with a philosophical bent, and as one sharing the liberal doctrines of trade presented by his friend, Adam Smith, in *The Wealth of Nations*. Rather than being focused on morale and extensive public pamphleteering, Franklin's goals were independence, complete and unlimited, within ample boundaries; peace, friendship, and reciprocal commerce with Britain, but also, for counterinsurance (if Anglo-American friendship should fail), continued close relations with the Continental powers.[23]

Franklin spent some time in France as a diplomat, and successfully encouraged French support of the colonial movement for independence. His international reputation as scientist, philosopher, and man of learning, greatly assisted the success of his mission. He became familiar in circles of the most advanced progressive thought of his day. As Crane describes it,

> He was most nearly French, no doubt, in his gallantries. At Passy, feminine neighbors charmed him by their various attentions and civilities and then sensible conversation! The Comtesse d'Houdetat (Rouse ais Sophie) arranged for "our dear Benjamin" in 1781 the memorable fete champetre at Sanois, when verses were sung in his honor and he planted a Virginia locust tree in her park. More intimate, less theatrical, were his friendships with Madame Helvetries, widow of the wealthy Farmer-general and celebrated philosopher, herself a femme savante and the friend of Voltaire and Turgot; and with youthful, affectionate Madame Brillon.[24]

Franklin met the famous Voltaire, who was much older than he, on several occasions. They reportedly embraced at the Academy of Sciences in 1778.[25] Clearly, Franklin was deeply immersed in the progressive thought of eighteenth-century France. He, too, though American, was an enlightenment figure of major influence.

By 1727, Franklin had founded the Junto, a club in Philadelphia, that was proclaimed the best school of philosophy, morale, and politics that then existed in the province. It was organized the year after his return from London where similar societies and clubs were operating. Membership required of each prospect a declaration of love for mankind in general no matter what his profession or religion. Discussions of history, morality, and poetry were among the wide-ranging topics taken up by the Junto. The club became widely influential in Philadelphia: "The Junto grew, spawned other such clubs, promoted civic and cultural institutions. The Junto brought the Enlightenment, in a leather apron, to Philadelphia."[26]

In 1787, Franklin was named president of the antislavery society founded in Pennsylvania in 1775.[27]

The world movement against racial oppression has varied in intensity over time. Sometimes vitally alive and influential, and at other times latent. Yet the historical drift of this movement has been toward increased effectiveness such that today racial oppression is seriously and permanently challenged. As E. Digby Baltzell, in *The Protestant Establishment*, put it,

The authority of the white race, largely built up by the Anglo-Saxon gentlemen of England between the Ages of Francis Drake and Benjamin Disraeli, is now being called into question around the world. The optimistic and imperialistic ideology of the white man's burden, materially based on the Anglo-American lead in the Industrial Revolution, has now turned into a nightmare, frighteningly fed by the demon dreams of the racists in our midst.[28]

Baltzell argues that in the event of racial conflict moral authority throughout the world may die out and chaos reign:

> The central question in the second half of this century may well be whether the white Western world, led by America, will be able to retain its traditional freedoms in an overpopulated world, and at the same time, succeed in sharing the fruits of an industrial scientific civilization with the rising races which make up the rest of mankind. In this process, white Western man must, above all, learn to share the leadership of some sort of new world community with his nonwhite peers, many of them now educated in the West, before a stable world establishment with moral authority can be recreated.[29]

Baltzell accurately identifies an important part of the current crisis in the modern world as "due to the White-Anglo-Saxon-Protestant establishment's unwillingness, or inability, to share and improve its upper class traditions by continuously absorbing talented and distinguished members of minority groups into its privileged ranks."[30]

The remaining objective of the movement for racial equality in the United States, then, is clear: to continue and intensify the assault on the authority and legitimacy of racist imperatives in society and to strengthen and expand the sociopolitical forces working for this goal. This important process is now well underway.

Some indication of the broad range of persons, nations, events, and circumstances that have contributed to the movement for racial equality has been given in this chapter. Clearly, this movement was not an amorphous assembly of people, events, and ideas. Antislavery efforts were guided by moral outrage festering in several social institutions of the West. Inquiry, debate, and study by scholars has led to analyses and theories that help us understand how moral outrage was transformed into effective action for social change. Attention now turns to selected theoretical possibilities.

Questions for Review and Further Study

1. What was the nature of the disputation between Bartolomé de Las Casas and Juan Ginés de Sepúlveda?

2. What has been the impact of the Las Casas/Sepúlveda debate on race relations in the Americas according to Lewis Hanke?

3. What was Spain's *Siglo de Oro* and how is it connected with the idea of racial equality according to Herbert Klein?

4. What were the structural bases underlying the British and Spanish antislavery movements and how did they differ from those operating in France?

5. What was the issue of controversy between Edmund Burke and Thomas Paine regarding the French Revolution? What were some pertinent publications of each man on the issue?

Notes

1. Kenneth G. Goode, *From Africa to the United States and Then* (Atlanta: Scott, Foresman, 1969), p. 8.

2. Herbert Blumer, "Social Movements," in Alfred Lee (ed.), *The Principles of Sociology* (New York: Barnes & Noble, 1951), pp. 199-222.

3. Lewis Hanke, *The Spanish Struggle for Justice in the Conquest of America* (Philadelphia: University of Pennsylvania Press, 1949), p. 17.

4. Subsequent discussion of sixteenth-century Spain draws on Lewis Hanke (1949).

5. Ibid., pp. 131-32. Las Casas viewed the enslavement of blacks to be unjust as, he argued, was true of Indian slavery, and for the same reasons. These were that all people have the capacity for civic virtues, for humanity, and for reason. See p. 125.

6. Herbert Klein, *Slavery in the Americas* (Chicago: University of Chicago Press, 1967), p. 12.

7. John Hope Franklin, *From Slavery to Freedom* (New York: Knopf, 1967), p. 346.

8. Frank Klingberg, *The Anti-Slavery Movement in England* (Hamden, Conn.: Archon Books, 1968), p. 22.

9. John Locke, *Two Treatises on Government* (1764 edition), Bk.II, Ch.4 Cited in Klingberg, p. 34.

10. Adam Smith, *Wealth of Nations* (London: Strahan, 1791); and Jeremy Bentham, *Principles of the Civil Code, I,* p. 345.

11. John Emory, *The Works of the Reverend John Wesley* (New York, 1825); William Paley, *Complete Works* (New York, 1824); Prince Hoare, *Memoirs of Granville Sharp* (London, 1820).

12. Thomas F. Harwood, "British Evangelicalism: a Divisive Influence on Protestant Churches," in Richard O. Curry (ed.), *The Abolitionists* (New York: Holt, Rinehart & Winston, 1965), pp. 66-76.

13. Ibid.

14. J. Salwyn Schapiro, *Condorcet and the Rise of Liberalism* (New York: Harcourt, Brace, 1934), p. 33.

15. Ibid., p. 148.

16. C.L.R. James, *Black Jacobins* (New York: Random House, 1963), p. 139.

17. Ibid., pp. 140-41.

18. Ibid., p. 141.

19. Richard O. Curry (ed.) , *The Abolitionists* (New York: Holt, Rinehart & Winston, 1965), p. 64.

20. William K. Tabb, "Race Relations Models and Social Change," *Social Problems* 18, No. 4 (Spring 1971), p. 431.

21. Alfred Owen Aldridge, *Man of Reason: The Life of Thomas Paine* (Philadelphia: Lippincott, 1959), p. 43.

22. Tom Paine's involvement with this tradition is attested to by his acquaintance with Condorcet. Their acquaintance dated from his second visit to Paris in the winter of 1789-1790. They had become ardent admirers of each other's works, Condorcet going so far as to say that all the friends of liberty, truth, and reason, venerated Paine for the independence of his character, the disinterestedness of his conduct, and the profound reason and energy in his works. Aldridge, Ibid., p. 145.

23. Verner W. Crane, *Benjamin Franklin and A Rising People* (Boston: Little, Brown, 1954), pp. 184-85.

24. Ibid., p. 192.

25. Ibid., p. 180.

26. Ibid., p. 22.

27. August Meier and Eugene Rudwick, *From Plantation to Ghetto* (New York: Hill and Wang, 1970), p. 53.

28. E. Digby Baltzell, *The Protestant Establishment: Aristocracy and Caste In America* (New York: Random House, 1964), p. viii.

29. Ibid., p. ix.

30. Ibid., p. x.

2

ANALYTIC APPROACHES TO OPPRESSION: PARK, MARX, AND WEBER

Theories attempting to explain inequalities between black and white people make up a voluminous and varied literature. Most of this literature seeks to legitimate racial inequality. A wide variety of causal elements are put forth as explanatory, many of which blame the victims of racism themselves. Racism is said to be a "natural" phenomenon, a product of human nature and thus outside the province of human choice to remedy. For others, racism is mandated by God himself. It is seen as part of his divine plan for humankind. There are others who consider historical inevitability to be the basis for racial domination and inequality. Amid this profusion of assorted biases and opinions stands a relatively small number of studies of racial inequality that are linked to theoretical traditions in social science and constitute a source for serious analysis.

To my knowledge, neither Karl Marx nor Max Weber directly addressed the issue of racism as part of their extensive theoretical writings, though followers of Marx have found considerable explanatory value in his general analysis of capitalism. I know of no similar efforts by followers of Weber, which is surprising in view of the rivalry of ideas between these two scholars. Weber's work on capitalism, particularly his conception of the role of the economic substructure under capitalism, is commonly viewed as a challenge to, and a recasting of, the Marxist viewpoint. That this challenge and recasting can be applied to specific problems such as racism, as suggested in this chapter should hardly be surprising.

Another theorist whose writings address the problem of race is Robert E. Park, who spent a good deal of his life as an active advocate for racial equality. His writings and teaching at the University of Chicago influenced several generations of thoughtful efforts by his followers to understand racial inequality.

The work of these three scholars provides provocative beginnings and directions for the study of racial inequality. I have singled them out not only because of the value of their writings to useful ways of understanding the problem, but also because doing so reminds us that valued scholarly traditions do, in fact, have relevance to the volatile issues of our time.

Two theoretical traditions in sociology that bear on racial oppression in the United States will be discussed. These approaches share a common origin in the history of Western social thought, though subsequent elaborations of them have led to different suggestions about the nature of racism. These suggestions could not have been formulated, however, until the history of social thought arrived at a means of explaining change in the social world.

Progress and Change

For a long historical period, Western social thought was dominated by the idea that civilization began to decline with the decline of ancient Greece and Rome. The theory of world cycles was widely current among the Greeks and was passed on by them to the Romans. This view suggests that history always repeats itself. In essence, that nothing ever changes. This perspective envisions a fixed order in the universe. An order that keeps things in their proper places. As to why the Greeks never adopted the idea of progress, John B. Bury explains it thus:

> In the first place, their limited historical experience did not easily suggest a synthesis (of ideas); and in the second place, the axioms of their thought, their suspiciousness of change, their theories of Moira, or degeneration and cycles, suggested a view of the world which was the very antithesis of progressive development.[1]

Social thought during the the Middle Ages was also essentially incompatible with the idea of progress. Christian theory stressed that history's purpose was to secure happiness for the "saved." A happiness to be achieved in another world. History was seen as a series of events decreed by a divinity. The idea of original sin also mitigated against a highly developed idea of progress. The idea of cycles, popular among ancient Greeks, was abandoned during the Middle Ages though the belief in degeneration was maintained.

About 300 years were required for the climate of thought of the Middle Ages in Europe to begin to change to that of the modern world. During this long period the intellectual milieu in which the idea of progress could appear was slowly developing. Machiavelli, an influential thinker of the fifteenth century, held that man would always have the same passions, desires, weaknesses, and vices.[2] For Machiavelli, change, as with Plato, meant corruption. It was not until the sixteenth century that expressions of rejection of the hold of antiquity began to appear, expressions that became increasingly frequent, articulate, and bold. One of the first clear expressions of a doctrine of progress in knowledge was provoked by the controversy, during the seventeenth century, concerning the ancients and moderns. According to Bury, these were the crucial questions raised by this controversy:

> Can the men of today contend on equal terms with the illustrious ancients, or are they intellectually inferior? This implied the larger issue, has nature exhausted her powers; is she then no longer capable of producing men equal in brains and vigor to those whom she once produced; is humanity played out, or are her forces permanent and inexhaustible? [3]

Bernard le Bouier de Fontenelle was the first to formulate progress in knowledge as a full doctrine. Yet he did not expand the doctrine into a general theory of human progress that it later became. It was Abbé de Saint-Pierre who was the first to proclaim the new revolutionary creed of indefinite social progress. He enlarged the idea of intellectual progress into the idea of the general progress of man. The thought of the later eighteenth century concentrated on social problems and on the obstacles to achieving man's destiny of indefinite happiness.

The central figures of the eighteenth-century Enlightenment, the Encyclopedists, nurtured and propagated the idea of progress. They viewed human nature not as fixed, but as plastic; not as unchangeable, but as indefinitely malleable by education and social institutions. Helvétius proclaimed that in a well-organized society, all persons can rise to points of high mental development. He saw moral and intellectual inequalities as arising from unequal education and social circumstance. Another influential philosopher of this era, d'Holbach, wrote,

> The savage man and the civilized; the white man, the redman, the black man; Indian and European, Chinaman and Frenchman, Negro and Lapp, have the same nature. The differences

between them are only modifications of the common nature produced by climate, opinions, and the various causes which operate on them.[4]

While Enlightenment thought did embrace a unilinear view of history and the idea of the perfectibility of man in society, the eighteenth-century idealistic intellectuals failed to specify the means by which their ideas could be realized. This failure was due to the fact that they did not systematically articulate the dynamics of social change. This development, however, was but a few years away.

Social Change

In the transition in social thought from Immanuel Kant to the romantic idealists, George Mead[5] argues: "we proceed from a conception of static forms which are originally given, and which serve as a whole basis of Kant's transcendental philosophy, to an idea of the development of the form through a process, an evolutionary process." For Kant (and social thought generally up to this time) the forms for understanding the world of experience existed prior to actually having an experience of the world. His particular contribution to this tradition was to locate the forms of experience in the mind of the experiencing person. It is to Hegel that we are indebted for patterning the basic orientation of social thought after Kant. He is depicted by Mead as the primary figure among the romantic philosophers.

Hegel showed that institutions arose through a social process. During the medieval era social institutions were conceived of as given by God. Forms of social organization were given in advance of man, in the mind of God. They were fixed and static. The Hegelian viewpoint begins with three interrelated concepts that are aspects of a process: Being, Not-Being, and Becoming. Becoming represents a synthesis arising from the conflict between the two previous phases of the process, Being and Not-Being. This dialectical process Hegel saw as universal and as operative throughout the entire range of physical and social phenomena. It was reflected in the unfolding of history. It was applicable to analysis of any object of knowledge. Thus, for the forms of things that Kant located in the mind Hegel characterized as emerging and as ongoing products of a universal process. At a very general level this is a statement of social change based on evolutionary principles.

Evolutionary philosophy, especially that of Hegel, but also that of Fichte and Schelling, made up the general background out of which came the theory of evolution proper. The theory itself rests on the assumption of an organic life process that shows itself in different forms. Variation in the forms of this process is accounted for by what happens between specific embodiments of this process and their given environments. The work of Lamarck and Darwin presented a means by which this process could be seen as operating among certain life forms.

The Darwinian View

In *The Origin of Species,* Darwin depicted a life process that was reflected in various forms or species. He attempted to show that the difference in these forms could be explained by differences in the way the life process expressed itself in different environments, and he was able to show the emergence of new forms better suited to given environments. These emerged through "natural selection." At this historical time Western thought had arrived at an explanation of social change. There remained the task of applying this formula to the study of society. Social institutions came to be seen as another area in which the organic life process was in interaction with its environment this being, however, a social environment. As Jacques Barzun comments: "The idea of progress created the need for a science of society which would test the idea and show how conscious change and natural fact cooperated." [6]

Publication of *The Origin of Species* in 1859 reflected the existence of a climate of thought in which a conception of change through a natural and organic process was embedded. It was the absence of such a view that had blunted the thrust of Enlightenment ideals and relegated classical and medieval thought to relatively static or cyclical visions of society. It was only a short time after the publication of Darwin's great work that a tradition of scholarly efforts followed, which attempted to apply the Darwinian model of change to social phenomena. This effort was most pronounced in the United States where American scientists were prompt not only to accept the principle of natural selection, but also to make important contributions to evolutionary science. The American reading public became fascinated with evolutionary speculation, and gave a handsome reception to philosophies and political theories built, in part, upon Darwinism.[7]

In the United States Darwinism as a social philosophy was used in the interest of "the conservative mind." The age in which Darwin's thought became popular in the United States was soon after the Civil War and was politically conservative. Richard Hofstedter notes,

> The characteristic feeling was that the country had seen enough agitation over political issues in the period before the Civil War, that the time had now come for acquiescence and acquisition, for the development and enjoyment of the great continent that was being settled and the immense new industries that were springing up.[8]

Evolutionary theory served the interests of conservatives. It legitimated their actions and justified their dominance in the social and political life of the country. The main concern here, however, is to emphasize that evolutionary philosophy provided the first systematic theoretical means by which change in social institutions and social conditions could be envisioned. It might be noted that change theory did not remain either evolutionary or subservient to the interests of political conservatives. Yet the evolutionary vision was central to the social and political atmosphere in which Robert Ezra Park and the Chicago School developed and elaborated a distinctive understanding of racism. Park's approach to racism was "scientific sociology," which had fundamentally different implications for social change than a second major approach, "scientific socialism," to be discussed subsequently.

Robert E. Park (1864-1944)

In an introductory text by Robert E. Park and Ernest Burgess, published in 1921, care is taken to distinguish history from sociology. In doing so they reveal their view of the proper objective of sociology as a science. Historical location and events are never repeated. History deals with "individual events, persons, institutions." Natural science, on the other hand, is concerned with ". . . classes, types, species." As with any other species of animal man too has a natural history. Historical study, they argue, seeks to reproduce and interpret concrete events as they actually occurred in time and space. Sociology, however, seeks to arrive at natural laws and generalizations in regard to human nature and society, irrespective of time and place.

In other words history seeks to find out what actually happened, and how it all came about. Sociology, on the other hand, seeks to explain, on the basis of a study of other instances, the nature of the process involved.[9]

For Park and Burgess, as well as others of this tradition, the sociologist properly seeks laws of human nature or "natural" laws. These are statements that describe the behavior of an object in terms of the character of a class. In their words,

> Natural law may be distinguished from all other forms of law by the fact that it aims at nothing more than a description of the behavior of certain types or classes of objects. A description of the way in which a class, i.e., men, plants, animals, or physical objects, may be expected under ordinary circumstances to behave, tells us what we may in a general way expect of any individual member of that class. If natural science seeks to predict it is able to do so simply because it operates with concepts or class names instead, as is the case with history, of with concrete facts and to use a logical phrase, "existential propositions."[10]

Clearly, the emphasis in this approach is on the discovery of that which is generic in human experience and distinctive of specific social species. Sociology with its distinctive subject matter, namely culture and social institutions, can lead to the revelation of basic laws of human nature. Thus, in their approach to human society Park and Burgess make considerable use of the imagery and jargon deriving from the organic and naturalistic approaches developed by Darwin. This is particularly revealed in their approach to the study of race relations.

Park believed that wherever interethnic contacts occur they uniformly set in motion a certain social process of conflict and competition. It begins with the arrival of new immigrants in an established community. Since the new immigrants cannot compete for jobs on an equal basis they are relegated to the bottom of the stratification order. In subsequent generations, the immigrant group rises to higher levels within the society and is absorbed into the general population. The process by which this occurs constitutes for Park a "natural history" no less regular than that of the biologist who designates stages through which a plant or animal grows in its development .

There are distinctive stages in Park's "race relations cycle" that constitute a "natural history of the contact of peoples." The first stage is that of contact between two or more ethnic groups that results from migration.[11] Next comes the stage of competition. The usual objects of competition between the groups are land and jobs. The third stage is accommodation, which means the two groups have realized some relatively stable patterns of relations. A modus vivendi is reached. During this stage certain long-lasting patterns are established in the division of labor that carry attendant levels of prestige and esteem within the society. The fourth stage in the cycle is called assimilation. At this point members of the minority ethnic group have acquired the dominant culture and are absorbed into it. The race relations cycle is then completed

Though it is seldom referred to in the literature, Robert Park also developed a theory of the origin of racial groups.[12] He suggested that the races originated when men and women (along with other creatures) lived in direct dependence on the natural environment. Pressure from the need for food and a secure place continually pushed them to new and different places. He refers to this as the time of the great dispersion. Thus,

The first movements of mankind seem . . . to have been like the migrations of plants and animals . . . it was as if they were engaged in a general recognizance and exploration in order to spy out the land and discover the places where the different species might safely settle. It was, presumably, in the security of these widely dispersed niches that man developed, by natural selection and inbreeding, those special physical and cultural traits that characterize the different racial stocks.[13]

In Park's view, migration of peoples is to be taken as a starting condition for contact between different cultural and racial groups. This process, which he sees as operating at an accelerated pace today due to increase in the means of transportation, seeks a "permanent biotic equilibrium," which is yet to be seen. Migration by primitive peoples was within a kinship group, and it was the basis for group solidarity. The isolation of primitive life was eventually broken down by war and by intertribal trade. The development of trade relations and the marketplace introduced among primitive peoples a different type of social relationship that has had profound effects on human nature. It is largely from the growth and prosperity of the marketplace that secondary, or impersonal, relations became influential in human affairs. Park views this growth as central to the rise of cities. As he argues,

> The rise of the city state gave a new direction to the historical process which profoundly affected and presently transformed tribal and racial relations.[14]

The transformation was one of the dissolution of autonomous ethnic territories as they were incorporated into the territory of the city-state wherein a pattern of dominance and subjection emerged. This pattern eventually assumed the hierarchical form of caste and class domination. Another consequence of this transformation was to accelerate the process of ethnic amalgamation, which to that time had taken place largely by incorporating women and children into the tribes of conquerors. Park describes it this way: "In short, the contrast and conflict of ethnic groups were still the basis of the new social and political, as they were of the tribal, society."

But race consciousness and race conflict were in process of supersession by class consciousness and class conflict.[15] For Park, the point at which ethnic conflict is superseded by class conflict seems to represent the end of a developmental cycle that began with migration. Park illustrates the operation of this cycle among the ancients and goes on to say that the modern race problem is a product of the expansion of Europeans:

> In the modern world, wherever race relations . . . have assumed a character that could be described as problematic, such problems have invariably arisen in response to the expansion of European peoples and European civilization.[16]

This modern mass migration of Europeans, probably the largest and most consequential in human history, has had drastic consequences for the peoples and cultures affected. The Europeans disturbed existing population balances; imposed upon native peoples forms of political, judicial, and social control that superseded then existing customs; inoculated subject peoples with new and devastating diseases. Park views all this as part of the same cycle of events. As he argues,

> All this disorganization and demoralization seem to have come about . . . in the modern world as it did in the ancient, as an incident of ineluctable historical and cultural processes; the processes by which the integration of peoples and cultures have always and everywhere taken place, though not always and everywhere at a pace so rapid or on so grand a scale.[17]

Thus, Park believed race relations arose as a result of migration and conquest both in the ancient and modern worlds. The interracial adjustments that follow must be seen as "efforts of a new social and cultural organism to achieve a new biotic and social equilibrium." These adjustments involve, he argues, racial competition, conflict, accommodation, "and eventually assimilation."

For Park, over time, minority ethnic communities eventually lose their ethnic distinctiveness and are absorbed into the dominant culture. Several variations of this general scheme have been suggested by scholars in this tradition. They generally begin with a migratory movement of peoples, though questions have been raised about Park's assumption of ultimate assimilation.[18] Black people as an ethnic minority in the United States are to be understood in the same analytic terms as other ethnic groups. They are viewed as in the process of being assimilated into American society though certainly confronting conditions unique from those of other ethnic groups.

Karl Marx (1818-1883)

The *Communist Manifesto* was published more than ten years before Darwin's *The Origin of Species;* yet both works are built upon and reflect the evolutionary philosophy of Hegel. Both approaches envision a social process through which social forms arise. Both approaches are cast as natural or built into the human condition. Both approaches offer a set of dynamics of social change that has as central a process of interaction between humans and their surrounding environment.

Marx claimed Hegelian philosophy to be upside down. His point, which became a central tenet of Marxist thought, was that one must look at the conditions of existence in order to understand social life rather than studying the ideas about existence. Hegel's emphasis on the idea as a determiner of experience was reversed by Marx, who argued it is not the content of consciousness that determines existence, but existence that determines the content of consciousness. In analyzing the social world, priority must be given to the means of production and to those who own the productive machinery of society. The pattern of ownership discovered, he argued, will reveal the pattern of social classes. Social class is the hallmark of the Marxist approach, or of "scientific social-ism." As Marx and Engels stated in the *Communist Manifesto*,

> The history of all hitherto existing society is the history of class struggles. Free men and slaves, patrician and plebeian, lord and serf, guildmaster and journeyman, in a word, oppressor and oppressed, stood in constant opposition to one another, carried on an uninterrupted, now hidden, now open fight, a fight that each time ended either in a revolutionary reconstitu-tion of society at large, or in the common ruin of the contend-ing classes.[19]

This process of class antagonism is also, according to Marx, a salient feature of modern society:

> The modern bourgeois society that has sprouted from the ru-ins of feudal society, has not done away with class antago-nisms. It has but established new classes, new conditions of oppression, new forms of struggle in place of the old ones.[20]

Fundamental problems confronting modern society, such as poverty and war, are viewed in a Marxist perspec-tive as basically related to social class. The objective of social change must be to eradicate class antagonisms by creating a classless society. This is the primary task of those currently oppressed by the ruling bourgeoisie, namely the proletariat. On this point Marx and Engels argue,

> When in the course of development, class distinctions have disappeared, and all production has been concentrated in the hands of a vast association of the whole nation, the public power will lose its political character. Political power, properly so called is merely the organized power of one class for op-pressing another. If the proletariat during its contest with the bourgeoisie is compelled by the force of circumstances, to or-

ganize itself as a class; if, by means of a revolution, it makes itself the ruling class, and, as such sweeps away by force the old conditions of production, then it will along with these conditions, have swept away the conditions for the existence of class antagonisms, and of classes generally, and will thereby have abolished its own supremacy as a class. In place of the old bourgeois society, with its classes and class antagonisms, we shall have an association, in which the free development of each is the condition for the free development of all.[21]

Scientific socialism emphasizes that social ills are a product of oppressive patterns of socioeconomic organization. Such patterns are seen as varying over time as given oppressed classes overthrow their oppressors and set new directions.

One version of the condition of black Americans stemming from the radical, or Marxist, perspective is that blacks are subjects of colonial rule.[22] Colonization of the African continent created conditions and circumstances of oppression of black people by white people that are essentially the same conditions that currently confront black Americans.

Robert Blauner cites four basic components of colonization. First, there must be forced or involuntary entry. Second, the colonizer constrains, transforms, or destroys indigenous values, orientations, and ways of life. Third, the colonized group is administered by representatives of the dominant power. The final component cited is racism defined as "a principle of social domination by which a group seen as inferior or different in terms of alleged biological characteristics is exploited, controlled, and oppressed socially and physically by a superordinate group."[23] Thus stated, the black American community is essentially an oppressed colony being illegitimately ruled by white oppressor/colonialists. This view implicitly conceives of a kind of territorial autonomy based on race or ethnicity.[24]

Albert Memmi has expressed a similar view in *The Colo-*

nizer and the Colonized. Memmi's writings explore some of the problems of identity, of legitimacy, and of authority that arise in multiethnic social systems. In the introduction to Memmi's volume, Jean-Paul Sartre states clearly the key conditions and consequences of colonization:

> Colonialism denies human rights to human beings whom it has subdued by violence, and keeps them by force in a state of misery and ignorance that Marx would rightly call a subhuman condition. Racism is ingrained in actions, institutions, and in the nature of the colonialists methods of production and exchange. Political and social regulations reinforce one another. Since the native is subhuman, the Declaration of Human Rights does not apply to him; inversely, since he has no rights, he is abandoned without protection to inhuman forces—brought in with the colonialist apparatus, and sustained by relations of production that define two sorts of individuals—one for whom privilege and humanity are one, who becomes a human being through exercising his rights; and the other, for whom a denial of rights sanctions misery, chronic hunger, ignorance, or in general, "subhumanity."[25]

The black American struggle, then, is seen to be part of the worldwide struggle against colonial domination of one colonized group by another, a process that originated with the rise of capitalism as a dominant form of socioeconomic organization. It is the task of the oppressed to establish their independence from the colonialists, which presumes an effort toward territorial autonomy.

Followers of the Chicago School conceptualize the oppression of black Americans as a pattern of accommodation between racial groups. At any given point in time, depending on the specific characteristics of black/white relations, this pattern could be said to be changing toward greater or lesser conflict, or cooperation. Depending on the overall assessment of the amount and kind of cooperation and of the amount and kind of conflict over time, determination of how much assimilation and eventually amalgamation has occurred between the two groups could be made. The underlying polarities in this approach are separation and amalgamation; the amount of cooperation and conflict indicates the general direction along this polarity the two groups are developing. It is assumed that the history of black/white relations is part of a "natural history" of relations between different racial and ethnic groups that inhabit the same polity.[26]

From a Marxist viewpoint this is an insufficient explanation. The important missing consideration is the failure to recognize the meaning of immigration and initial contact for existing patterns of class relations in the society. Because diverse racial and ethnic groups have diverse meaning, in this regard, racism is not to be seen in terms of a set of all-encompassing or universal categories though they may be generic to the human condition. Such an approach is too general. Rather, the independent variable in understanding racism is social class patterns and class dynamics within the society.

The great merit of the approach to racism of Marxism and that of Park is that they bring to the study of social change and racism a capability that links change in specific institutional areas with more comprehensive processes in the society. This has the important advantage of viewing social phenomena as part of an interdependent societal system that we know to be true. These approaches to racism are both theoretically relevant and show cognizance of a broad range of social factors on which given social problems are dependent.

A major weakness of both approaches is that the specific variable that each has taken as independent in the change process (culture, or status, in the case of Park and economic organization, or class, in the case of Marx) is clearly too limited to constitute a sufficient explanation. In other words the independent variable in both approaches is certainly necessary in explaining American racism, but not sufficient. It is clearly inadequate to approach racism in the United States without fully considering social classes, and class dynamics, as the Park approach attempts to do. Likewise, it is impossible to properly analyze American racism on the assumption that class factors alone suffice. An approach that combines these and other important elements in a flexible way is required. Such a direction can be found in the writings of Max Weber.

Max Weber (1864-1920)

Weber serves as a reminder that status position and class position are both important concepts, and are intertwined in complex ways. He defines a status group, or status position, as having to do with the distribution of honor, regard, and esteem in a society. Class position or class, on the other hand, has to do with the distribution of economic goods and services in a society. Class and status distributions may be related in a number of ways. There is no single and invariant patterning between them.

Weber argues that the logical extreme of the status-producing process is formation of closed hierarchical groupings in a society known as castes. One form in which differentiated groups, including ethnic or racial groups, may exist in a society is as a caste patterning. One group of high prestige and honor becomes dominant over the other groups, which are ordered hierarchically by different degrees of low and demeaning status. According to Weber, the distinctive feature of this patterning is that caste groups agree that the differential distribution of status is legitimate and appropriate.[27] That is, the dishonored groups agree to their own demeaned position. As Park has suggested, this characterization is somewhat applicable to black Americans.

Strains Toward Caste

Clearly, the process of absolute oppression lasting over three hundred years has had an important effect on black Americans as a social group. This effect is consistent, *though not completely so*, with the condition cited by Weber as caste. Considerable documentation of the phenomenon of identification with the oppressor (high status group) by the oppressed (low status group) exists.[28] For example, E. Franklin Frazier writes of the black bourgeoisie and its lack of identity with the black masses:

> The entire history of the Negro in the United States has been of a nature to create in the Negro a feeling of racial inferiority. During the more than two centuries of enslavement by the white man, every means were employed to stamp a feeling of natural inferiority in the Negro's soul. Christianity and the Bible were utilized both to prove and to give divine sanction to his alleged racial inferiority or, as some contended, his exclusion from the races of mankind. When the system of slavery was uprooted in a Second American Revolution, it appeared for a brief period that the Negro might receive recognition as a man. But the result of the unresolved class conflict in which the democratic forces in the South were defeated, the demogogues who became the leaders of the disinherited whites but really served the interests of the propertied classes made the Negro the scapegoat . . . living constantly under the domination and contempt of the black bourgeoisie. The element which has striven more than any other element among Negroes to make itself over in the image of the white man exhibits most strikingly the inferiority complex of those who would escape their racial identification.[29]

In a similar view, Nathan Hare's impressionistic account of black Americans considers a segment called black Anglo-Saxons. This group is distinguished by its identification with whites. As he argues,

> Black Anglo-Saxons are chiefly distinguishable in that, in their

struggle to throw off the smothering blanket of social inferiority, they disown their own history and mores in order to assume those of the biological descendants of the white Anglo-Saxons. They relate to, and long to be a part of, the elusive and hostile white world, whose norms are taken as models of behavior. White society is to most of them a "looking-glass self," an image they must keep on grooming to make what they think white society imagines itself to be, in accord with what they themselves would like to be: like whites.[30]

One function of racial low status groups, stressed by Park and Burgess, is to reduce competition and conflict between racial and ethnic groups. They argue the case as follows:

Caste, by relegating the subject race to an inferior status, gives to each race at any rate a monopoly of its own tasks. When this status is accepted by the subject people, as is the case where the caste or slavery systems become fully established, racial competition ceases and racial animosity tends to disappear. That is the explanation of the intimate and friendly relations which so often existed in slavery between master and servant. It is for this reason that we hear it said today that the Negro is all right in his place. In his place he is a convenience and not a competitor. Each race being in its place, no obstacle to racial cooperation exists.[31]

Weber describes another pattern of existence for diverse groups as differentiated entities with varying rather than fixed status position. In this instance, Weber argues, each group maintains within itself a set of criteria by which its members are held to be more worthy and more highly esteemed than, for example, members of other ethnic groups independent of objective class position in the wider society.

For hundreds of years blacks occupied the very bottom rungs of the stratification system and indeed during these years, as a caste system would require, many did adopt the demeaning vision of themselves they learned from oppressive whites. This element of black history reflects powerful caste-like strains in the society. Yet, a fully developed caste system never emerged in America in spite of strong tensions generated by vigilante and terroristic whites. As discussed earlier, the dominant social forces in opposition to racism militated against caste. The ideals of freedom and democracy for all were never completely extinguished among Americans. Fidelity to its liberal and humanist roots, though questionable at times, has remained intact. Black Americans, then, have been one among a series of other differentiated ethnic entities, of the kind fitting the Weberian description. The crucial and distinctive feature of black history is not caste, but severe prejudice, discrimination, and segregation, which have been in continual interplay with democratic and equalitarian ideals.

The racist oppression of black Americans, and resistance to it, may be characterized as an oscillating movement leading alternately from castelike status toward that of a differentiated ethnic enclave. A brief sketch of black American history seems to bear out this characterization.[32]

Oppression of black people in the United States began as a process of indenture from which release to freedom could ultimately be secured. This condition was initially shared with some whites. Over time the indenturing of whites ceased and the absolute oppression of black people developed. The earliest developments are described by Kenneth Goode:

> In August 1619, the colonial government at Jamestown, Virginia, purchased twenty blacks from a Dutch frigate and thus commenced the importation of black people into North America for the purpose of service labor that was to last some 250 years. During the first forty years some Afro-Americans were accorded the status of indentured servants (a status given to whites who had bound themselves for a number of years to work for those who had paid for their passage to the New

World). Some of these Afro-Americans served out their terms of indenture, became free men, acquired property, and became the owners of indentured servants and slaves. From 1640, however, there is evidence that some Afro-Americans in Maryland and Virginia were being held as slaves.[33]

As the colonists found that their greed for profits could be more readily satisfied by blacks under chattel conditions the institution of absolute slavery became the characteristic condition of black people in the colonies. Each of the colonies began to give recognition to this deflation in the social status of blacks by customary demeaning treatment that came to be legislatively recognized. Slaves became essential to the prosperous agricultural economy of the deep South where crops of rice, indigo, tobacco, and cotton were developed.

Slave Codes

With the widespread legalization of slavery, and the concomitant increased numbers of slaves and profitability of their labors, harsh codes regulating the slave populations appeared in the slave colonies. Goode cites some of the common features of these codes as follows:[34]

❖ Slaves were declared to be chattel.
❖ Opportunities for manumission were greatly restricted.
❖ Business dealings of slaves had to be conducted through their white masters.
❖ Slaves could not bear firearms, consume alcoholic beverages, or vote.
❖ Slaves were denied the right of free assembly, free speech, fair and impartial trial, and education.
❖ The right of travel was restricted.

Provisions of the various slave codes were enforced with "brutal discipline."[35]

Resistance to Caste

Although the degree of devastation and inhumanness of oppression against black people in the United States was severe, there is evidence that the desire for freedom and the spirit of resistance were never totally extinct. That is, the logical endpoint of caste formation was never completely reached.[36] Nevertheless, the degree of brutality, subordination, and subjugation was probably greater in the United States than in colonial Africa or in most of the colonized West Indies. Even where the amount of oppression may have been the same as in the United States, the means available for insulation against this brutality were not as extensive or as effective.[37] Black Americans were decimated and brutalized as a group much more severely than blacks elsewhere in the New World. In the United States white racism effectively dismantled blacks as ethnic entities and reduced them to a condition much closer to that of caste than in other countries.

The oppression of black people in slavery died out in the nineteenth century. Emancipation was a widely celebrated event signaling a major step away from caste oppression toward the beginning of ethnic status for black Americans. Yet, after a brief period of prosperity—Reconstruction—black Americans were again victims of another virulent form of racist oppression referred to as Jim Crow. A hateful system grew from the principle of separate but equal. Fearful of the contamination by "impure" blacks, white racists opted for and attempted to impose a system of dual social development for the two racial groups. During this time attempts to reenslave, or to return black Americans to a caste status, were legion. Lynchings and intimidation were widespread, and access to the political process was almost entirely cut off. White racists who returned to power after emancipation attempted to initiate a social process that would completely wipe out the gains made by black people during Reconstruction.

All former Confederate states passed laws segregating blacks and whites, as well as laws cutting off access to political and social influence by black people. Vann Woodward says:

> We have seen that in the eighteen seventies, eighties, and nineties, the Negroes voted in large numbers. White leaders of opposing parties encouraged them to vote and earnestly solicited their vote. Qualified and acknowledged leaders of Southern white opinion were on record as saying that it was proper, inevitable, and desirable that they should vote. Yet after the disenfranchisement measures were passed around 1900 the Negroes ceased to vote. And at that time qualified and acknowledged leaders of white opinion said that it was unthinkable that they should be permitted to vote. In the earlier decades Negroes still took an active, if modest, part in public life. They held offices, served on the jury, the bench, and were represented in local councils, state legislatures, and the national congress. Later on these things were simply not so and the last of the Negroes disappeared from these forums.[38]

Yet the gradual buildup of some defensive capability among black Americans was not completely destroyed. Around the turn of the century this capability became a significant ingredient in the struggle to abolish racism. At this time, the influence of W.E.B. Du Bois began to be felt. The National Association for the Advancement of Colored People was formed, and a small cadre of blacks was becoming educated and thus better able to defend black people against the exploitative, racist, actions of American whites. The historic protest movement thus continued, but now with more influence and initiative by blacks themselves. It was only a few years later that the new, militant voice of Adam Clayton Powell joined that of W.E.B. Du Bois. One voice operated out of Atlanta and the other out of New York City. At this point the transition of black Americans from a castelike condition, at least in terms of the aspirations of blacks, was nearly complete.[39] Yet the efforts by racist whites to force blacks into caste conditions remained strong, though formidably challenged by a coalition of white and black activists who began a movement that became known in the 1960s as the civil rights movement.

Oscar Handlin discussing discriminatory practices against nonwhites since the end of World War II, admits the continuation of injustice, but nevertheless contends that great and decisive change in the status of black Americans has taken place:

> North and South, they still suffer from injustice and still have legitimate grievances. But the integrity of the patterns of segregation has decisively been broken; and it is a matter of time before equality of status and opportunity is within reach.[40]

It was during the decade of the 1960s that a major change in what appears to be an oscillating cycle was reached by black Americans. It is largely on the basis of gains made during this period that I rest my claim of a transition from caste to ethnic to class status for blacks. Clearly, there is room for debate over the extent of gains made by black Americans since the 1960s, as well as over the exact nature and durability of these gains. It is equally clear that some of these issues cannot be definitively determined a priori. For this reason my hypothesis of a transition process from castelike status to ethnic status must be viewed in probabilistic terms. The theoretical assumptions and data base on which this claim rests are discussed in the next three chapters.

Questions for Review and Further Study

1. What is "scientific socialism" and what is its suggested connection with racial oppression?

2. What is a "natural history" and what is its suggested connection with racial oppression?

3. What two analytic elements does Max Weber combine in his therorizing that are said to be of value in the study of racism?

4. Of what relevance is the caste concept in the study of racism in America?

Notes

1. John B. Bury, *The Idea of Progress* (New York: Dover, 1932), p. 19.

2. Machiavelli's much celebrated *The Prince* is illustrative of this view.

3. Bury, p. 79.

4. Ibid., p. 167.

5. George Herbert Mead, *Movements of Thought in the Nineteenth Century* (Chicago: University of Chicago Press, 1936), p. 153.

6. Jacques Barzun, *Darwin, Marx, and Wagner* (Garden City, N.Y.: Doubleday, 1958), p. 39.

7. Richard Hofstedter, *Social Darwinism in American Thought* (Boston: Beacon Press, 1955), p. 4.

8. Ibid., p. 5.

9. Robert Park and Ernest Burgess, *Introduction to the Science of Sociology* (Chicago: University of Chicago Press, 1921), p. 11.

10. Ibid., pp. 12-13.

11. Robert Park, *Race and Culture* (Glencoe, Ill.: Free Press, 1950), Ch. 9.

12. Ibid., Ch. 7.

13. Ibid., p. 85.

14. Ibid., p. 91.

15. Ibid., p. 92.

16. Ibid., p. 100.

17. Ibid., p. 104.

18. For criticisms of the Park approach to race relations particularly his cycle, see Milton Gordon, *Assimilation in American Life* (New York: Oxford University Press, 1964); and Tamotsu Shibutani and Kian M. Kwan, *Ethnic Stratification* (New York: Macmillan, 1965).

19. Karl Marx and Friedrich Engels, *The Communist Manifesto* (New York: Washington Square Press, 1965).

20. Ibid., p. 8.

21. Ibid., p. 21.

22. See Appendix A. Some discussion of this view is presented by William K. Tabb, "Race Relations Models and Social Change," *Social Problems* 18, No. 4. (Spring 1971).

23. See Robert Blauner, "A Caribbean Social Type: Neither Peasant nor Proletarian," in Richard Frucht (ed.), *Black Society in the New World* (New York: Random House, 1971), p. 367.

24. Interestingly, the suggestion of territorial autonomy as a legitimate aim of oppressed ethnic groups represents a return to the very condition that Park claims to have been the original state of primitive man. Park claims that before the wide development of trade, barter, and commerce, ethnic or racial groups lived in separate communal enclaves. See Park's, *Race and Culture*, ch. 7.

25. See Albert Memmi, *Colonizer and the Colonized* (New York: Orion Press, 1965), pp. xxiv, xxv. This volume by Memmi (the American edition) is dedicated "to the American Negro, also colonized."

26. Park and Burgess, pp. 578-79.

27. See Max Weber, *Social and Economic Organization*

(New York: Free Press, 1964). Several works by social scientists employ the concept of caste in their study of nonwhites, especially Afro-Americans. Notable among these is Gunnar Myrdal's massive study, *An American Dilemma* (New York: Harper & Row, 1962); and John Dollard, *Caste and Class in A Southern Town* (New York: Doubleday, 1949). Note is taken of the arguments opposing the use of caste to conceptualize the social situation of Afro-Americans. See Oliver C. Cox, "Race and Caste: A Distinction," *American Journal of Sociology*, No.3, (November 1944), pp. 360-68; and Charles S. Johnson, *Growing Up in the Black Belt* (New York: Schocken Books, 1967).

Myrdal contends that "Caste . . . consists of such drastic restrictions of free competition in the various spheres of life that the individual in a lower caste cannot . . . change his status." See *An American Dilemma*, Volume 2, pp. 674-75.

> When we say that Negroes form a lower caste in America, we mean that they are subject to certain disabilities solely because they are "Negroes" in the rigid American definition and not because they are poor and ill-educated. It is true . . . that their caste position keeps them poor and ill-educated on the average, and that there is a complex circle of causation, but in any concrete instance at any given time there is little difficulty in deciding whether a certain disability or discrimination is due to a Negro's poverty or lack of education, on the one hand, or his caste position, on the other (p. 669).

I am in essential agreement with the caste concept and its applicability to the black/white situation in the United States. Yet, most treatments miss the functional significance of caste for class relations and class stability. For example, consider Myrdal's comments regarding the relation between caste and class in relation to the Afro-American:

> The Marxian concept of "class struggle" with the basic idea of a class of proletarian workers who are united by a close bond

of solidarity of interests against a superior class of capitalist employers owning and controlling the means of production, and in between there is a middle class bound to disappear as the grain is ground between two millstones—is a superficial and erroneous notion in all Western countries. It minimizes the distinctions that exist within each of the two main groups . . . In America it is made still more inapplicable by the traversing systems of color caste. The concept of "caste struggle" is much more realistic (p. 676).

From this it is clear that Myrdal missed the essential meaning of caste for patterns of class relations. It is this connection that I shall continually stress and attempt to substantiate. It is a key consideration in understanding nonwhite oppression in the United States. The persistence of this condition rests essentially on its functional significance in thwarting the development of social change in the interest of the lower class generally.

28. See Franz Fanon, *Wretched of the Earth* (New York: Grove Press, 1968); Nathan Hare, *The Black Anglo-Saxons* (London: Collier-Macmillan, 1970).

29. See E. Franklin Frazier, *Black Bourgeoisie* (London: Collier-Macmillan, 1969), pp. 130-31.

30. Hare, p. 15.

31. Park and Burgess, pp. 620-21.

32. This characterization is also mentioned in Park's *Race and Culture.* See Chapter 3 for a more extensive and systematic treatment of the phases of black history.

33. Kenneth Goode, *From Africa to the United States and Then* (Atlanta: Scott, Foresman, 1969).

34. Ibid., p. 31.

35. Ibid., p. 32.

36. See Herbert Aptheker, *Slave Rebellions* (New York: Humanities Press, 1966) for valuable documentation on black slave insurrections and rebellions in the United States.

37. This is, I believe, partly because blacks as a propor-

tion of the total population differed greatly in these different areas. In the United States blacks were a smaller proportion of the population and thus more vulnerable to white brutality than in either the Caribbean or Africa.

38. See C. Vann Woodward *The Strange Career of Jim Crow* (New York: Oxford University Press, 1966), pp. 105-6.

39. Robert Park appears to designate this transitional beginning with emancipation and as continuing therefrom. See Ch. 12 of his *Race and Culture.*

40. Oscar Handlin, *Race and Nationality in American Life* (Boston: Little Brown, 1957), p. 178.

3

FROM CASTE TO ETHNICITY TO CLASS

One may reasonably wonder why blacks in the United States today seem so very slow in achieving levels of prosperity achieved long ago by other ethnic groups. Many ethnic groups, especially those of European and Asian origin, have achieved gains far in excess of those made by blacks, yet many Europeans and Asians are more recent arrivals. To some this would seem to suggest some kind of personal inadequacy or incapacity characteristic of blacks that is not shared by other racial and ethnic groups. It mistakenly is taken by many to mean black inferiority, and is the bottom line of a wide range of racist arguments.

A proper understanding of this lack of achievement among blacks requires a clear recognition of the virulence of racism in U.S. society. One also has to appreciate the utter devastation of the many years of slavery during which blacks were brutalized by abject poverty and servility, sanctioned by law and by the force of arms. We know, of course, that slavery disappeared over a hundred years ago, which may seem long enough for a group to make up for past historical losses. While this may be a reasonable time under conditions of free competition and equality of initial conditions, it neglects the fact that until quite recently gains made by blacks have not been cumulative and continuous as they have been with other ethnic groups. Rather, black history reveals periodic devastation as a result of white vigilante terror and/or legislative fiat. Blacks have served a scapegoat function in American society, easy victims for the wrath of white supremacists, and defenseless targets for the aggressions of militant racists.

What makes black gains, today, of special interest is that racism and the malevolent efforts of white supremacists are no longer the formidable obstacle they once were in victimizing the black population. The historical time has now arrived where gains by the black population are no longer subject to the whims of those who still cling to a white racist outlook. Although racism surely still exists, it is ever more constrained and circumscribed as the United States begins the unfamiliar task of accommodating itself to the new reality of a dependency on autonomous and independent nations of the Third World, essentially nonwhite, peoples. This new world reality exercises a major influence on the demise of racism as it casts racist practices as decidedly against the national interest. This new emerging reality means greater stability for gains achieved by blacks and accelerated upward mobility.

This chapter focuses on the process of gain and loss to blacks over historical time. Five periods of black history are suggested and discussed, each being a phase of an oscillation that, for the most part, is confined to the lower rungs of the stratification hierarchy. However, as the discussion of Phase 5 indicates, a qualitative change in this oscillating pattern is now taking place. The pattern is becoming more unilinear, thus more closely corresponding to the historical process characterizing other ethnic groups in the United States.

The history of black Americans can be characterized as distinctive, meaning that it differs significantly from the history of white ethnic groups in the United States. This is because the social process that this history reveals does not show the progressive, upward movement of the group within the social system as with white ethnics, such as German Americans, Polish Americans, Jewish Americans, and others. This is not to argue that no gains have been made by blacks, for clearly they have made enormous gain over historical time. It is, rather, to argue that the gains-producing process has been periodically and systematically manipulated to the detriment of black Americans, manipulation that has considerably slowed the process of gain and has often caused significant losses of what had been achieved.

Black history reveals an oscillation between gain and loss of a depth not shared by white ethnic groups. An important feature of the oscillation is its confinement for the most part to the boundaries of the lower class. This confinement, clearly, has not been total. There are a few upper-class blacks if one judges by the usual criteria of education, jobs, and income. Yet, upper-middle and upper-class representation of blacks has never been proportional, always being lower than that of white ethnic groups. The very large concentration of blacks at the very bottom of the stratification hierarchy has always been a larger proportion of the group than it has been for any of the white ethnic groups. A graphic representation of this oscillation, and the class confinement of the process, are illustrated by the figures below.

Figure 3.1 shows the ebb and flow of gain to blacks and associated historical periods. Subsequent discussion provides a brief descriptive account of each period that stresses some of the signal events reflecting gain or loss to blacks. Reviewing black history this way allows me to substantiate the claim of oscillation and to illustrate how the class confinement has been held more or less secure for a very long time. Figure 3.2 shows the constraints within which the oscillation of black history has fluctuated.

FIGURE 3.1

Oscillating Phases of Black History in the United States*

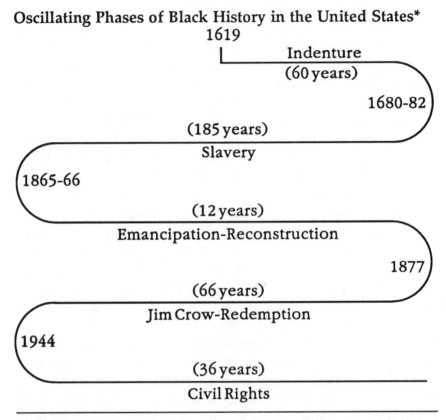

* Dates are rough approximations and are intended to capture a time period within which there are qualitative differences in the historical experience of American blacks.

As Figure 3.3 suggests, blacks today continue to be heavily concentrated in the bottom level of the class hierarchy. This was also the case at the very beginning of Afro-American history. The difference today is that some degree of spread throughout the class spectrum has started. Achieving even the limited degree of spread indicated here represents major and chronic struggle between the forces of white

FIGURE 3.2

Oscillation of Black History and Class Confinement*

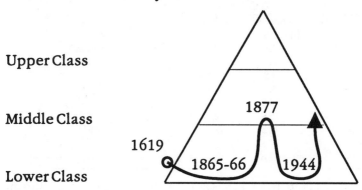

Upper Class

Middle Class

Lower Class

---

* This figure represents the general idea of the relationship between black history and the class structure in the United States. It is not constructed to a scale of actual events or realities for any given time period. Greater precision is found in Chapter 8, where the actual class structure is discussed in terms of race for 1960.

supremacy and the forces of humanism, enlightenment, and equality. Relatively speaking, white ethnic groups have been exempt from this struggle. Progress for them has been essentially unfettered by chronic racist confrontation. Consequently, their achievements over time have been considerably greater.

A more detailed consideration of the several historical phases of black history follows. Some of the more blatant race-based obstacles to black upward mobility will be clear in this brief review.

Phase 1 (1619-80): Indenture. This first phase of Afro-American history begins with the first arrival of blacks to the English colonies and extends to 1680, the year of the first major slave codes in Virginia. These codes of 1680 became

FIGURE 3.3

Socioeconomic Status and Color, 1960*

Socioeconomic Status Score		Color†	
		Nonwhite	White
90-99	(High)	1.5	98.5
80-89		2.1	97.9
70-79		3.5	96.5
60-69		3.8	96.2
50-59		5.6	94.4
40-49		10.2	89.8
30-39		15.9	84.1
20-29		21.5	78.5
10-19		27.6	72.4
0-9	(Low)	41.6	58.4

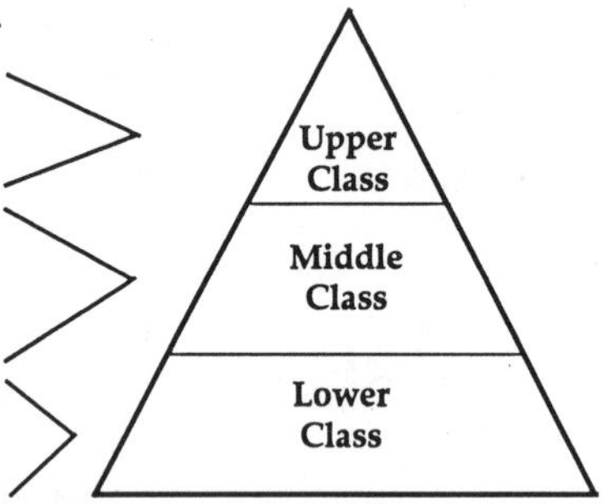

(Pyramid diagram: Upper Class, Middle Class, Lower Class)

* Figures taken from U.S. Department of Commerce, Bureau of the Census, "Socioeconomic Characteristics of the Population," Current Population Reports, Technical Studies, Series P-23, no. 12, July 1964.

† Blacks constitute more than 90 percent of the "nonwhite" represented in the figure.

the model of repression throughout the South for the next 180 years.[1]

The presence of Afro-Americans in the New World goes back to the wanderings of the early Spanish explorers, though some evidence from Indian carvings suggests the presence of blacks at an even earlier date. Columbus's ship, the *Santa María*, is said to have been piloted by a black.

Blacks were with the explorers Ponce de León and de Soto during their explorations,[2] clearly indicating that blacks were in the New World during the fifteenth century and possibly earlier. Though precise information is scant, it seems likely that these earliest blacks were in some form of bondage, probably indenture, and that accompanying these expeditions was part of their terms of bondage. As we know that persons of color were very much part of the founding of cities in early California (discussed in Chapter 4) it is likely that many of these bonded individuals of African heritage remained in the New World and took their place with other bondsmen on a more or less equal basis. The freedoms offered by the New World applied to them on the same terms as it applied to white bondsmen.

As early as 1493, on Columbus' second voyage, a group of black slaves was brought to a Spanish settlement in the New World. Official sanction for introducing slaves in the Spanish colonies was given by royal ordinance in 1501. Because blacks were considered rebellious, Spain imported white rather than black slaves to Hispaniola (also in 1501). Between 1502 and 1600, nine hundred thousand black slaves were brought to Latin America.[3]

Even before English colonies began the use of slaves and slavery, blacks were part of what was to become the United States. Lucas Vásquez de Ayllón, a Spanish explorer, took black slaves to the Carolinas in 1526 in an attempt to establish a settlement. Those slaves are considered the first blacks to have set foot in what is today the United States. The attempt was unsuccessful. The blacks fled the colony and lived with the Indians. Blacks accompanied Alarcón and Coronado in New Mexico in 1540. Estevanico, a black explorer, went with Narváez on his expedition to Florida and the Mississippi region in 1527. He lived with Cabeza de Vaca among the Indians for several years and traveled with him through Texas and Mexico to the Gulf of California.[4]

The Spanish and Portuguese had entirely different attitudes toward blacks and more benign patterns of relatedness than the English, who soon began to colonize North America and the West Indies. English settlements, which began in 1619 at Jamestown, Virginia, began a new chapter in the history of the Negro in America and a more ominous one.[5] Peter Bergman claims that the juridical and religious systems of Spain and Portugal, which stressed that servitude is due the state and/or church rather than a single master, allowed some tempering of the oppressive conditions of ser-

Under Spanish rule, he adds, baptism and miscegenation further mitigated the brutality of slavery. But the English settlers were from a different tradition, a different culture, and they evolved a quite different system of slavery and servitude that was much crueler and more all encompassing than that in Latin America. As Bergman explains:

> The English settlers, contrary to the Spanish, were hard-working, puritanical, sell-reliant, and influenced by the then upcoming myth of race superiority, a fallacy in which even Martin Luther and Thomas More believed. These church reformers supported the idea that slavery was a necessary social institution and thus even humanitarian-minded and educated Englishmen lost shame and conscience in their views on the Negro.[6]

Yet, in many ways, the early experience of slaves in the English colonies was similar to early settlements of the Portuguese and Spanish.

Black bondage among English colonists is generally considered to have begun with the arrival of twenty blacks in Jamestown in 1619, a year before the Pilgrims landed at Plymouth Rock. It involved a group of captives seized by Dutchmen from a Spanish ship and sold to the labor-short colonists. There were no statutes or traditions at the time on which to base the treatment of the blacks. They were not free, yet there were no special familiar and useful categories in which to fix their standing. Evidence suggests that they had the same status as white servants.[7]

Both blacks and whites in colonial America were in varying degrees unfree, and many persons bore some sort of service obligation from which they later gained their freedom. Evidence suggests that these first blacks to arrive in Jamestown, as well as many of those who followed them in the next few decades, were treated as additions to an already existing status that previously only whites had occupied, that of indentured servant. The point is made by E. Franklin Frazier:

> Contracts of indentured Negro servants indicate that the status of the first Negroes was the same as that of the white servants. Moreover, court records show that Negroes were released originally upon completion of a term of servitude.[8]

The primary labor force during this early colonial period was made up of indentured servants, as the massive influx of slaves had not yet begun. In 1624 there were only 32 blacks in Virginia; in 1649 there were 300 slaves; and by 1671 there was an estimated 2,000 plus slaves. The indentured servant population was clearly larger than the slave population for a number of years in Virginia, as was the case for the entire colonial system.[9] During this time several gains were made that have had enduring value to blacks as a social group. Some of these are the following:

❖ The beginning of a class of free blacks, which Frazier says continued to grow until the Civil War.[10]

❖ The beginning of the Quaker tradition of active protest against black slavery and advocacy of equality. (George Fox and William Edmundson, English Quakers, were early initiators of this tradition in the years 1671 and 1676, respectively.)

❖ Active protest among slaves themselves, who ran away as early as 1672 and began establishment of Maroon communities. (Maroons were runaway slaves who collectively set up independent communities. There is evidence of at least 50 such communities between 1672 and 1864, established mainly in the mountain forests and swamps of the Carolinas, Virginia, Louisiana, Florida, Georgia, Mississippi, and Alabama.)[11]

Although some parcels of land were granted to blacks during this period, this was but a short-lived phase of black history. Even well before 1680, (the end of Phase 1) there were ominous signs of a more oppressive future for black Americans. Slavery was rapidly advancing as an ingrained feature of colonial life. As early as 1629 slavery was introduced in the colony of Connecticut, in Maryland in 1634, and in Delaware in 1636.[12] As indicated earlier, the number of slaves in Virginia Colony increased from 300 in 1649 to an estimated 2,000 twenty years later in 1671. The number was still small, but increasing significantly each year throughout the colonies.

Just 20 years after the end of Phase 1 of black American history, there were 27,817 slaves in the British colonies of North America; 5,206 in the North and 22,611 in the South.[13] In 1708 Virginia itself had an overall black population of about 12,000, with about 1,000 additional blacks imported annually. Already in 1705, Virginia had stopped all office-holding by Negroes, either military, civil, or ecclesiastic.

The latter years of Phase 1 saw conditions for blacks deteriorate from indenture to subhuman chattel whose bondage lasted for life. Unrest among the imported blacks increased as their numbers grew and as their conditions deteriorated. England passed an act regulating blacks on British plantations in 1667. The legislation referred to the blacks as wild, barbarous, and savage, to be controlled severely. Slaves were forbidden to leave the plantation without a pass; they were not allowed to leave on Sunday; they were forbidden to have weapons. In 1670, a Virginia law was enacted declaring that all servants in the colony who were shipped into the colony and not Christian were to be slaves for life. In the same year Virginia abandoned universal suffrage. The intent of this act was to disenfranchise persons recently freed from servitude. In 1772, a Maroon law was passed evidently in response to growing dissatisfaction, unrest, and escape by black slaves. The law urged and rewarded the killing of Ma-

established and maintained colonies out of easy reach of their captors and lived a nomadic life.

The culmination of repressive legislation in Virginia saw enactment of the first major slave codes, dated 1680-82. These codes, according to Leon Higginbotham, would become the model of repression throughout the South for the next 180 years.[14] A 1680 statute (Act X) was enacted to prevent slaves from assembling during feasts and burials, for such meetings were considered dangerous.[15] The process of repressing the dignity and desire for freedom among blacks was intensified in Phase 2, which firmly established the castelike mentality and the slave system as a solid and dominant element of American economic and cultural life.

Phase 2 (1680-1865): Slavery. If, in 1690, the emancipation of Negroes had been legislated throughout North America, as was the case about 183 years later, there probably would be no question today of the retardation of blacks as an ethnic group. The slave experience, by 1680, had not been too deeply ingrained; there was a developing free community among blacks and a growing level of skill and resources. It was the next 180 years of experience in North America, years that constitute Phase 2 of the social process, that so severely crippled blacks as a social group. This period began with a wave of increasingly repressive legislation sweeping throughout colonial America, legislation modeled essentially after the Virginia legislation of 1680-82, only more comprehensive, more repressive, and more dehumanizing.[16] This body of repressive legislation constitutes the bulk of ever more demeaning enactments passed by assemblies throughout colonial America. It has left severe and yet unhealed wounds on the conscience of the United States, and on the lives of its citizens, both black and white.

The various codes passed in colonial America showed some variation in different locations. Some colonies passed this repressive legislation more rapidly than others. Yet, within the span of a few years after 1680, slavery was a well-entrenched institution in the English colonies, and the few freedoms earlier enjoyed by blacks were abolished. The following elements were essential ingredients of the slave codes:

- ❖ Perhaps the most fundamental idea underlying slave holding was the principle of human chattlehood, or of human beings defined in law, and later in customary treatment, as physical objects or things. (One version of this principle is stated in a Louisiana statute of 1806 as follows: "Slaves shall always be reputed and considered real estate; shall, as such, be subjected to be mortgaged, according to the rules prescribed by law, and they shall be seized and sold as real estate."[17] Another Louisiana statute clearly indicates the same condition: "A slave is one who is in the power of a master to whom he belongs. The master may sell him, dispose of his person, his industry and his labor. He can do nothing, possess nothing, nor acquire anything, but what must belong to his master."[18]

- ❖ Slaves, in whom each master had a financial investment, were regarded as mere instruments for the convenience, use, and pleasure of slaveholders. Respectable members of colonial America provide ample public testimony to the effect that "slaves are neither considered nor treated as human beings . . . slave-holders never recognize a human being in a slave.")

- ❖ Slaves were sold, purchased, bartered, mortgaged, and shipped as was the case with any other property.

- ❖ Slaves were seized as property for payment of debts of the owners. (Creditors often seized slaves in payment of debts owed by slave owners. This sometimes was even against the will of the slave owner, and often it indiscriminately severed close and intimate ties among slaves themselves as among parents and children, husbands and wives, close friends, and so on.)

❖ Slaves were transmitted by inheritance or by will and distributed, like other property.

❖ Being property, slaves could own no property. (Their acquisitions were the property of their owners as they themselves were.)

❖ Slaves could not marry nor make other forms of binding contract.

❖ Slaves could not constitute families. (Being property, they had no claim on one another, no security from separation, no family rights, no family governance, nor family protection. The parental relation among slaves was simply not recognized.)

❖ The power of the slave owner was absolute and unlimited, and there was no redress for injuries inflicted by him or his designated representative. (Many cruelties of an outrageous kind were inflicted on slaves, which included torture, mutilation, and even death.)

❖ Slaves were worked at the discretion of the owners, as were his machines, animals, and other chattel.

❖ Slaves were cared for, fed or starved, sheltered or unsheltered, at the convenience of the owner.

❖ Slaves could not demand and receive a change of owner.

❖ Slaves had no right to religious or other education.

Clearly, these proscriptions did not apply with total uniformity and for the total time of Phase 2 throughout North American settlements. There was individual variation among owners in applying them. Yet they effectively separated the two racial groups, not by voluntary decision, but by decree of the existing powers. In addition, they rendered blacks utterly helpless victims of slave owners. This period of black history was the longest and the most characteristic experience of blacks in the United States.

Of course, Phase 2, as with each of the other phases, not being a uniform entity, showed important internal variation. It showed the kind of internal change and progression that ultimately revealed a transition.

The system of slavery and its accompanying dehumanization went virtually unchallenged until the 1760s. There were protests, particularly early ones by Quakers, but they were sporadic and not widely effective. The vested interest in slavery was too great to allow serious moral challenge. Some social changes did occur, however, that transformed isolated protests into a broad and militant social movement against slavery.[19]

One change was the weakening of the vested interests in slavery. By the latter half of the eighteenth century this weakening was well under way in some areas of the world. The various crops grown by slave labor, such as sugar and tobacco readily exhausted the soil. Slavery thus became more profitable in new and fertile areas and less so in areas long under cultivation. Even at the time of the Revolution, according to Duncan Rice, it was difficult to grow tobacco profitably in the tidewater colonies.[20] Three interest groups that were formerly proslavery had become indifferent or apathetic by the late eighteenth century. These were the northern mainland colonies, the tidewater planters, and some of Britain's more powerful support for slavery. Corresponding with this decline of vested interests was another change, a growing religious and intellectual assault on the institution of slavery. The force of these factors operating jointly, Rice contends, accounts for the gradual buildup of effective and eventually triumphant antislavery agitation.

The signal event during this transition to Phase 3 was the colonists' effort to gain independence from England.

Blacks of varying degrees of bondage played an important role in the events of 1776 and, overall, gained a degree of relief from the devastation of slavery and its dehumanization. Much of this change had to do with their role in the military.

In July of 1776 the British army on Staten Island included 800 former slaves who had joined the British on the promise of freedom. In Virginia, slaves were ordered to be moved inland, away from British forces, to prevent their escape and linkup with the British. The same was done in North Carolina. In November of that year an appeal to blacks was made in a Williamsburg, Virginia, newspaper, urging them not to join the British forces, saying that the British would not grant them freedom after the war but sell them in the West Indies. In this same year 140 black soldiers helped cover Washington's retreat in the Battle of Long Island. They were praised for this. Similar rearguard actions involved blacks at Trenton and Princeton, New Jersey.

By 1777 there were 33 blacks in the 2nd Regiment of Pennsylvania who served under Washington at the Battle of Monmouth. A regiment of black troops from Rhode Island was sent to aid Washington at Valley Forge. They also fought at Monmouth and Red Bank, New Jersey. Washington, in this year, asked the Continental Congress to approve reenlistment of blacks in the army, and Congress agreed. In the following year a black battalion of 300 men was formed in Rhode Island; some former slaves received the same compensation as white soldiers and the same rewards after the war for their services.

The military clearly provided one inroad against the long-standing tradition of oppression and dehumanization of blacks. There were other areas in which similar gains were beginning to be made. For example, in 1776, the Continental Congress passed a resolution ending the importation of slaves. Also, in Jefferson's original draft of The Declaration of Independence, there appeared a strong accusation against George III based on his legitimation of the cruel war against human nature itself, meaning slavery. This section was deleted at the request of delegates from South Carolina and Georgia, as well as of some slave-trading New England states. In addition, the Vermont Constitution forbade slavery in 1777, being the first state to do so. Pennsylvania passed an act granting gradual abolition of slavery in 1780. In 1783 Maryland prohibited the sale of slaves, and in the same year the Philadelphia Meeting of Quakers voted to admit a black to the Society of Friends. In 1784 New Jersey law freed all blacks who had taken part in the Revolution. In the next two years New York had banned slavery and New Jersey had forbade the importation of slaves. Additional instances of such events could be cited. They all reflect the beginnings of widespread relief from the dehumanization of North American slavery at the time of the American Revolution.

Around this same time blacks themselves tried to push back the dehumanization of slavery and its effects. By 1777 Massachusetts blacks had twice petitioned the government for freedom citing its troubles with Great Britain as evidence of the unreasonableness of the plight of blacks. In 1779, in Portsmouth, New Hampshire, 20 blacks petitioned the legislature for freedom arguing that freedom is an inherent right of humans. In 1780 five Negroes in Dartmouth, Massachusetts, petitioned the general court for freedom from taxation because they were denied the privilege of citizenship. Significantly, in the same year, Lott Carry was born. As a former slave he founded Liberia.

By the time of the actual signing of the Emancipation Proclamation decreeing freedom for the slaves after more than 150 years of dehumanization, a widespread crystallization and transformation had taken place among blacks. First, the overwhelming majority had made little educational or economic progress during this span of time, resulting in very large numbers of blacks being uneducated and hopelessly poor. The free intelligence and creative entrepreneurship of blacks had not been operative during these years, except in rare instances. The small group of free blacks that existed was an epiphenomenon, invisible by comparison with the overwhelming majority.

Second, physical segregation, caste, and class confinement, had become virtually complete and thoroughgoing. The condition of worthlessness and dehumanization among blacks and a vision of whites as superior (the caste mentality) had taken firm hold in black culture by the end of the Civil War. The many years of bondage, the physical torture, the deprivation that accompanied slavery along with family dismemberment and economic oppression, left black culture psychologically with a fear of whites and with a belief in black worthlessness and inferiority. In other words, with a castelike mentality. Only in recent years has this outlook changed significantly.

It is the many years of slavery to which the current retardation of black Americans is attributable. Even when slavery ended, as subsequent discussion will show, blacks still faced strong hostility from whites and formidable efforts by whites to again suppress blacks. This continues today to be a major dynamic in black-white relations though less formidable than at earlier times. The rigidity of black caste and class confinement in North American society was broken for good with emancipation, which signaled the beginning of Phase 3 of black history, Emancipation and Reconstruction. This is the first phase during which official steps were taken to ensure incorporation of blacks into North American society in a manner consistent with both the wishes of blacks themselves, and with the cultural tradition of equality of opportunity and the several freedoms enunciated in the Constitution.

Phase 3 (1867-77): Emancipation and Reconstruction. Phase

3 begins with the eleven former Confederate states being required to reconstruct their state laws and regulations consistent with the new federal mandates granting citizenship and equal rights to blacks. The beginning of this phase was also marked by federal troops occupying the South to ensure the new rights recently granted by the federal government. During this period, which ended in 1877 with the removal of federal troops, many new and important gains were made by blacks.

An important area of gain was through increased and continued military opportunity and participation. The Emancipation Proclamation that freed the slaves was announced January 1, 1863. The War Department authorized the recruitment of black troops during the early months of that year. By May of 1863 the War Department had ordered control and centralization of black troops as the United States Colored Troops, or USCT. From this point on blacks were mustered directly into the army. A Bureau for Colored Troops was established to administer the affairs of the USCT. By July, 30 black regiments had been federalized and the government was officially supportive of their presence and use. Black troops were often cited for heroism and exceptional courage in combat; they were dealt with harshly by Confederates when captured and they suffered discrimination from racist whites. It should be added that they were enlisted in white regiments and that they engaged white Confederates at many points in battle. Blacks were also in the Confederate army though in smaller numbers. During the war 178,895 blacks served in the Union army, nine to ten percent of the total Union forces. About 3,000 were killed in battle; more than 26,000 died from disease. By 1864 Congress had authorized the same bounty for military services for blacks as for whites. Also, the families of blacks killed in the war were granted pensions (see Adaptation I).

By 1865, the early time of Reconstruction, several gains

in business and property holding could be noted. An estimated 100,000 of 120,000 artisans in the South were black. They were at that time numerically dominant among skilled workers in the South. In Cincinnati blacks owned a half million dollars in taxable property. Blacks in New York had $775,000 invested in new business enterprises. In Brooklyn this figure was $76,000 and in Williamsburg it was $151,000. In this same year 1,800 blacks were settled in confiscated plantations in Mississippi. At year's end their cash balance was $159,200. By the following year freedmen in Florida had secured homesteads that covered 160,000 acres.

By 1872, a black-owned savings and trust company had 70,000 depositors, and in 1873, the Freedman's Bank of Charleston, South Carolina had $350,000 in deposits and 5,500 depositors. In Georgia in 1874, blacks owned more than 350,000 acres of land. Near the end of Phase 2, the African Methodist Church had a membership of 75,000; by 1876 it had 200,000, and the church's property value had increased sevenfold.

Perhaps the most prominent area of gain for blacks during Phase 3 was political. The first northern state to elect blacks (Edward G. Walker and Clarence L. Mitchell) to its legislature was Massachusetts, in 1866. In July 1867 the Republican party was organized at Columbia, South Carolina, and a state committee was formed that included J.H. Rainey, a black. South Carolina's voting records of the same year showed 78,982 black and 46,346 white registrants. Ten counties had a majority of white voters, and twenty-one counties had a majority of black voters. Mississippi voting records for that year listed 60,167 blacks and 46,636 whites. Black voters were in a majority in thirty-three out of sixty-one Mississippi counties. But the numbers of white delegates were far greater than black delegates, at state constitutional conventions (estimates vary): Alabama, seventeen black and eighty-three white; Arkansas, seven black and sixty-eight white;

Florida, seventeen black and twenty-nine white; Georgia thirty-three black and 133 white. Similar patterns of racial representation appeared in other state constitutional conventions. Nevertheless, these were the statewide bodies that provided for universal manhood suffrage, granted equal rights to blacks, established a system of public education, and instituted democratic governmental reforms.

South Carolina was readmitted to the Union in 1868. When the legislature met in July there were twenty-one whites and ten blacks in the state Senate, and forty-six whites and seventy-eight blacks in the House. Francis Cardozo, a black, served as secretary of state until 1872, and from 1872 to 1876 he was state treasurer. A similar scenario was acted out in other former confederate states. By 1870 the racial composition of some state legislatures in the South was the following:

	Blacks	Whites
Alabama	27	73
Arkansas	9	71
Georgia	26	149
Mississippi	30	77
North Carolina	1	101
South Carolina	75	49
Texas	8	82
Virginia	21	116

This is a very different picture of the American South with reference to the position of blacks than had ever existed before. Many tangible, clear, and concrete gains were made in other areas such as education, and the forming of religious and civic institutions within black communities. This was an unprecedented new day for blacks, made possible by the success of the various antislavery forces. This expansion of opportunity facilitated the enactment of pro-black legislation. It was blatantly contrary to the many volumes of anti-black legislation progressively adopted in earlier years. The state (federal government) had become an ally in the cause of equal rights and in ensuring these rights for blacks.

The achievements made during Reconstruction were many, but they were made only with turmoil and struggle as partisans fought out controversies and issues on the local level, sometimes in hand-to-hand combat. Although gains were the predominant feature of this phase, there were also losses. The forces of white supremacy were sullen about their defeat and containment and sought every opportunity to stem the tide of change in their favor.

The importance of the military continues as a factor in black upward mobility. This is underscored by the following Adaptation dealing with black participation in the 1991 conflict between the U.S.-led Allied Forces and Iraq.

Adaptation I

> The following adaptation illustrates the continuing importance of the military in black upward mobility. It is an article from the Wall Street Journal, Thursday, April 18, 1991. Mr. Page is a nationally syndicated columnist for the Chicago Tribune who won the 1989 Pulitzer Prize for commentary.

The Military and Black America

by Clarence Page

Gen. Colin Powell poses an unusual dilemma for many of today's black leaders. As the first black chairman of the Joint Chiefs of Staff, he is too "positive" a role model to be ignored, yet too politically incorrect to be enthusiastically praised. A century after Frederick Douglass pleaded with President Abraham Lincoln to let African-Americans share the Union's military burden, Coretta Scott King, Jesse Jackson, and other pillars of the civil rights establishment are complaining that blacks bear too much of it.

Some call black servicemen and women "economicconscriptees." ("If that war breaks out, our youth will burn first," Mr. Jackson said two days before Operation Desert Storm began.) Others, like Howard University political science Prof. Ron Walters, a former Jackson adviser, say the Pentagon is "skimming the cream off the black middle class" and should "adjust" its qualifying tests so that they will no longer reject poor blacks.

More Opportunities

No one bristles at that suggestion more than black career officers do. "Black leaders should leave those kids alone," says retired Marine Lt.-Gen. Frank Peterson who, as the Marine Corps' first black pilot, battled prejudice at many levels. "The black youngsters who join the military today are well educated, talented and working hard to improve themselves. Black leaders should concentrate on trying to open up more opportunities for these kids when they get out."

The protests of black leaders against the black presence in the military may, however, help explain why black support lagged well below white support for the Persian Gulf War. They may also help to explain why a recent National Opinion Research Center survey of racial attitudes found that most whites think blacks are "less patriotic" than whites.

As a black Vietnam-era draftee who hated that war but loves his country, I think black reservations about the Gulf War resulted less from a lack of patriotism than from a widespread perception of unfairness, a perception that blacks are contributing disproportionately to defend a society that continues to deny too many opportunities to blacks outside the military.

If there is any point on which Gen. Powell and other military officers stand on common ground with civil rights leaders, it is that the question should not be why the military has so many blacks but, rather, why do civilian companies have so few?

America's military in the past two decades has attracted more black talent and created more opportunities for blacks than any other sector of American society. Although blacks are 12% of America's population, they fill 29% of the positions in the army: 32% of its enlisted personnel and 11% of its officers, including 27 of its 374 generals.

Mr. Walters is right that today's high tech military is dipping deeper into the best and brightest of black America. A 1982 Brookings Institute study found that 42% of black youths who met the military's requirements were enlisting, while only 14% of similarly qualified white youths were join-ing up. With Department of Labor projections showing white males to be the slowest-growing sector of the workforce over the next 20 years, the military may have a lot to teach private companies that are looking for the best way to hire and promote minority talent without resorting to quotas.

Charles Moskos, military sociology professor at Northwestern University, suggests that the military's level playing field has itself proved to be particularly attractive to blacks simply by rewarding merit, not race. "Where else," he asks, "does a young black man know that, with a little hard work, he can earn the opportunity to yell orders at young white men?"

Conversely, the lingering racism in the civilian world is exemplified by the relative difficulty black colonels and generals—who have been retiring in record numbers in recent years—have faced in getting the senior executive-level positions major corporations routinely offer to retiring white officers.

Gen. Peterson is one of the growing number of excep-tions. Now director of corporate aviation for Du Pont, he says he was hired along with retired Navy Rear Adm. Wil-liam Powell as a result of a Du Pont effort to eliminate color barriers in executive recruitment. But, he notes, "You still have black retired four-stars out there who have not been welcomed by corporate America." Blacks' success in the military has not come easily. Blacks have fought in every war America has fought, but never before in roles as central as those played by Gen. Powell and Lt. Gen. Calvin Waller, second-in-command to Gen. H. Norman Schwarzkopf. In World War II, segregation and discrimination at first kept blacks out of combat roles. But the National Association for the Advancement of Colored People's "Double-V" slogan (victory against fascism abroad and victory against discrimination at home) won breakthroughs like the "Tuskegee Airmen," the first and only all-black combat flying unit. In 1948, President Harry Truman ordered the military to desegregate.

Even then, blacks felt some ambiguity about this accomplishment. As blacks took a disproportionate share of front line-duty and combat casualties in the Vietnam War's early years (black combat casualties reached 22% of the total in the years 1965-67, according to the Department of Defense), Martin Luther King, Muhammad Ali, Stokely Carmichael and other blacks joined the anti-war coalition. Yet, moderate voices like the NAACP's Roy Wilkins and columnist Carl Rowan held to the "double-V" argument: If blacks refused to fight for their country, they could not rightfully demand fair treatment in it.

During those difficult days, and while support for the Vietnam War unraveled outside the military, a revolution was taking place inside. Racial friction on military bases and Navy ships around the world prompted the Pentagon to take its war against segregation a step further: a vigorous human relations campaign designed to attack racial prejudice itself.

With that, it was no longer enough to say blithely that "The only color that matters is green (or blue or khaki)." Courses in black history and racial dynamics became an integral part of training. More important, the efficiency reports that help determine promotions were revised to include evaluations of race relations skills.

"Ironically I saw Dr. King's dream come alive in Vietnam," says Wallace Terry, a *Time* magazine reporter in Vietnam and author of the best-seller *Bloods*, about black soldiers in Vietnam. "I saw, as King said, 'the sons of former slaves and the sons of former slave owners' sit down together at 'the table of brotherhood.'"

Gen. Peterson concedes that the military's human relations methods have limited applicability to the private sector, whether you're talking about its training methods

("Shave their heads, put them in boot camp and make them all afraid," he quips) or its discipline standards.

Nevertheless, he says, there is much the private sector can learn when it comes to changing traditions of corporate culture that discriminate against talented minorities and women: "Make sure that pay is based on performance and you'll get the kind of results you want."

Good Example

Mr. Terry suggests that white resentment of programs intended to upgrade minority opportunities can be avoided by constructing the programs not as an "advantage" to minorities but as "support" for those whose productivity is held back by deficiencies that can be alleviated. A good example, he says, was the "catch-up program for reading, math, and speaking" devised by Gen. David Jones, then commander of the U.S. Air Force (Europe), for whom Mr. Terry worked as an adviser in 1971. The program was designed "not as a favor to blacks, but as a way to enable them to become more productive."

Of course, the military has not reached racial perfection. Black pilots and senior officers number more than they used to, but still less than their proportion in the general population. Nevertheless, with more blacks in its management ranks than you can find in similar civilian jobs, America's military offers a realization of a hard-fought dream that Dr. King said was "as old as the American Dream." For the captains of private industry, it is a model worthy of praise and imitation in their own never-ending battles against the enemies of justice, equality and profitability.

End of Adaptation

On July 13, 1863, the New York draft riots broke out.

Irish draftees felt they had to fight a war to free blacks who would then flood the city and take their jobs for lower pay. The rioters found blacks and beat them, often to death. A black orphan asylum was burned to the ground. These riots lasted thirteen days and took at least 1,200 lives and caused $2 million in property damage. Paradoxically, the following year New York City cheered its black regiment at a citywide parade that included the USCT.

In 1865 the Ku Klux Klan was formed in Tennessee. In the following year there was a riot in Memphis, Tennessee, in which forty-six blacks and two white liberals were killed. About seventy-five persons were wounded and ninety homes, twelve schools, and four black churches were burned. A riot occurred in the same year in New Orleans that left thirty-five blacks killed and more than 100 wounded. In 1868, a report by the Congressional Committee on Lawlessness and Violence was issued. It stated that between 1866 and 1868, 373 freedmen had been killed by whites, and ten whites by freedmen. The KKK was especially violent in Florida where there were 235 murders from 1868 to 1871. In 1868, anti-black whites gained partial control of the Georgia state government and ejected all black members of the legislature. Their claim was that the right to hold office had not been given to the freedmen. Their congressional representatives were denied seats and the state was again placed under military rule. Georgia was readmitted to the Union in 1870, after complying with federal directives.

Amid this contention, turmoil, and achievement of gain by blacks, a subtle and formidable resistance to these gains re-established itself. Even in the North the formerly militant forces against white supremacy were not so militant, forceful, or successful as before. The major event in stemming the tide of black progress, the event that marks the end of Phase 3, was a betrayal of blacks by their most powerful ally: the federal government. The importance of the federal government in establishing and maintaining the mechanisms for black equality cannot be underestimated. The government, by 1877, had done the following:

❖ Issued the Emancipation Proclamation;
❖ Passed the Thirteenth, Fourteenth, and Fifteenth Amendments to the Constitution ensuring black rights;
❖ Conducted a military occupation of the Confederate states to ensure compliance with federal mandates in behalf of blacks;
❖ Gained compliance by the former Confederate states and reunified the nation, with black rights officially built into a reunified nation;
❖ Mandated black participation in the military on an equal basis with whites;
❖ Established the Freedman's Bureau to help blacks more fully achieve and adapt to their new freedom.

Yet, the forces of resistance eventually gained the upper hand in the South and stopped the rate of progress for blacks. This change is well symbolized by the removal of federal troops from the South, a presence of major importance in ensuring Confederate compliance.

This event, in 1877, marks the beginning of a fourth phase of black history; a phase immediately preceding the current phase. Phase 4 was the phase of Redemption and Jim Crow. It was a time when pro-black forces throughout the country went into decline and lost much of their momentum, thus opening the opportunity for reestablishing white supremacy. From 1877 to about 1954, a different and virulent form of racism established itself in North America. This form of racism has been in decline decisively only a few years.

Phase 4 (1879-1944): Redemption and Jim Crow. The term Redemption refers to the eventual overthrow of the northern Republicans and the return to power in the South of the former Confederates, via the Democratic party shortly after the removal of federal troops from the South in 1877. This withdrawal meant that the federal government had abandoned its guarantee to blacks of their political and civil rights. The matter was left in the hands of local southern whites. Several negative and long-lasting consequences resulted.

Bergman calls the period after Reconstruction the darkest time in the history of blacks in America. Practically all political rights gained during Reconstruction were lost again. This was true not only in the South, but also in the North where blacks faced the wrath of immigrant whites who saw them as threats to their jobs in a new and thriving industrial development. Yet, as we shall see, not all previous gains by blacks were lost, for there had been a gradual buildup among blacks of a modicum of defensive capability not previously there.

The early part of Phase 4, until the formation of the National Association for the Advancement of Colored People and the rise of a cadre of prominent black national spokesmen, was clearly dominated by the forces of white supremacy. These forces swept back into political control of the South, and the North also began to cater increasingly to blatant racist practices.

A very early ominous move toward a return to power by the Confederates in the South was the disenfranchisement of blacks in 1878 in Louisiana and South Carolina just after the removal of federal troops. In the 1878 congressional elections only 62 of the 294 southern counties with black majorities went Republican, whereas 125 had done so in 1876. In fact, in Abbeville County, South Carolina, which then had twice as many blacks as whites, only three Republican ballots were cast in the county. In 1878 Virginia began a practice of reapportionment in order to minimize the black vote. In December of that year an attorney general's report revealed that southern Democrats had stuffed ballot boxes and committed political murder in a number of southern states. A Senate committee appointed to investigate southern elections found, among other things, that in Louisiana alone 40 political murders had been committed. The committee called for renewal of federal protection for blacks. In 1879, at least 40,000 blacks migrated to the Midwest to escape the deteriorating political and economic conditions in the South. By 1880, however, about 75 percent of all U.S. blacks still lived in the former Confederate states. Blacks had large population majorities in several southern counties that constituted the Black Belt, stretching through 25 counties of eight states.

Practices of segregation grew enormously, but not immediately following Redemption. The southern states retained existing segregation practices but showed no inclination to expand them at first. More than a decade went by before the first Jim Crow law appeared in a southern state. It was more than 20 years after Redemption that the older states of Virginia, and North and South Carolina, passed Jim Crow laws. First reports by northern observers on the South after Redemption were favorable, even reports by black observers were favorable. Yet, by 1898, the Jim Crow movement segregating public transportation had taken hold in the South and West. Only three states had adopted Jim Crow waiting room laws for railroad stations before 1899, but in the next ten years nearly all of the southern states had done so. Streetcars had existed in southern states since the 1880s, but only one state, Georgia, had demanded segregation in them before 1900. At that time segregation spread rapidly: to North Carolina and Virginia in 1901; to Louisiana in 1902; to Arkansas, South Carolina, and Tennessee in 1903; to Mississippi and Maryland in 1904; to Florida in 1905; to Oklahoma in 1907. Throughout the South, as Vann Woodward pointed out, there appeared an enormous number of signs of "White Only" once again to separate the races.[21]

The first Jim Crow law segregating railroad coaches was passed in 1881. Railroad car segregation was challenged in the courts in 1890. The Louisiana law authorizing it was challenged by Homer Plessy, a black. He was arrested and convicted, even though the matter was appealed as far as the Supreme Court.

Other rather standard and effective devices were employed by white supremacists to undermine black political gains. The first step was to take away the vote, or disenfranchisement. The first assault was made in Mississippi, which mandated special qualifications for voters that blacks could scarcely meet. Property and literacy requirements were among these, but they also included grandfather clauses and good character clauses, the kinds of demands that surely only whites could meet. Some variations on these arrangements were enforced by South Carolina in 1895, Louisiana in 1898, North Carolina in 1900, Alabama in 1901, Virginia in 1902, Georgia in 1908, and Oklahoma in 1910. For those blacks who miraculously met these qualifications, a further, equally sinister hurdle had to be faced, the white primary. This was a law first adopted by South Carolina Democrats in 1890. It restricted voting in Democratic primary elections to white people only. This meant that blacks had no influence on who was selected within the Democratic party to compete against rival parties. Georgia followed with a similar mandate in 1898.

The effectiveness of these political devices on the black vote is illustrated by the case of Louisiana. This state had 130,334 registered black voters in 1896, yet by 1904 it had only 1,342 registered black voters. Between these two dates literacy, property, and poll tax qualifications had to be met in order to vote. In 1896 black voter registrants were a majority in 26 Louisiana parishes (counties). By 1900 they were a majority in none. Obviously, literacy, property and poll tax qualifications had their desired effect.

In 1882, forty-eight blacks were lynched; fifty-two the following year. Also, in 1883, there came a significant setback for blacks in the Supreme Court declaration that the Civil Rights Act passed in 1875 was unconstitutional. In August 1890, the Mississippi Constitutional Convention met to re-write the 1868 Reconstruction Constitution. Of the 133 delegates only one (Isaiah Montgomery) was black. Yet, at that time, blacks represented 56.9 percent of the population in Mississippi. From 1882 through 1892, a total of fourteen hundred blacks had been lynched. The Republican party platform of 1892 denounced the practice. Yet in the same year, in Georgia, white Democrats murdered fifteen blacks during an election campaign. They also stuffed ballot boxes and intimidated voters in order to achieve their political goals. The yearly lynchings of blacks by this time was well over 100. By 1895 South Carolina revised its Reconstruction constitution, seriously reversing gains formerly made by blacks in that state.

By 1900 many blacks had migrated north still attempting to escape the devastation of southern practices of white supremacy. Northern cities began to develop sizable black populations, though by far the majority of blacks were still rural and southern. In Chicago there were 30,150 blacks; in New York, 60,666; in St.Louis, 35,516; in Philadelphia, 62,613; in Washington, D.C., 86,702; and in Baltimore, 79,258. In many of the southern cities blacks outnumbered whites. The percentage of blacks living in urban metropolitan areas in the United States then was 26.6.

During the first few years of the twentieth century more white primaries were adopted in southern states and more Jim Crow laws separating the races passed. Lynchings continued to be frequent. Yet by 1905 there were defensive capabilities emerging among blacks that went beyond the individual court challenge in separated local communities. That year W.E.B. Du Bois called a conference of black leaders in Niagara Falls. They produced a declaration of principles affirming the belief in black equality and demanding equal economic opportunities, equal education, and a fair administration of justice for blacks.[22] This meeting had been preceded in 1904 by formation of a broad group of black leaders called the Committee of Twelve. It was financed by Andrew Carnegie and called by Booker T. Washington. Initiating a number of activities in the interest of blacks, its most enduring and significant achievement was the formation in 1909 of the National Association for the Advancement of Colored People (NAACP) under the initiative of Du Bois. A permanent committee of forty was established to administer the affairs of the organization.

The increasing numbers of riots in northern cities as well as other violence against blacks became focal points for practical action by the NAACP. The organization held regular conventions and publicized black grievances. It defended blacks in the courts and sought and maintained allies among whites. It came to symbolize progress to the great mass of blacks and gained widespread support among them. By 1918, its magazine, *Crisis*, had a circulation of 100,000. For many years it was edited by Du Bois. Another widely influential black advocacy organization was founded two years after the NAACP. This was the National Urban League, which tried to open new opportunities for blacks in industry and to help them adjust to urban life.

These national organizations, which today are at the forefront of progress and change, were possible due to the cumulative, slow, and all too inadequate gains that blacks had painfully made. A brief review of a few of these gains made by the year 1900 will serve to illustrate the point:

❖ The total value of farm property owned by blacks was $499,943,734.

❖ There was a small group of black professionals: 21,267 teachers and professors; 15,528 preachers; 1,734 doctors; 212 dentists; 310 journalists; 728 lawyers; over 2,000 actors and showmen; and a number of blacks had achieved national recognition in the arts, sciences, and literature.

❖ Approximately 24 percent of blacks owned their own homes.

❖ There were four black banks in the United States.

❖ More than 2,000 blacks had college degrees.

❖ Four states had black colleges.

Blacks were far from parity with whites in any of these areas. Yet, by 1900, they were very far from their slave and indentured beginnings. Enormous gains had been made even while daily atrocities and dehumanizing conditions were faced by the race.

The second part of this fourth phase found blacks still confronted by formidable racism, but at the same time it saw unprecedented new gains made. New, popular, and effective national spokesmen for blacks emerged to help solidify black identity in the cause of equality. The formerly isolated assaults on blacks now became matters of national and international information. Adam Clayton Powell, Jr., Bayard Rustin, A. Philip Randolph, Marcus Garvey, and a number of others helped to create a nationwide consciousness and recognition of racial atrocities and enlisted more and more blacks in their own defense. World Wars I and II were conditions that facilitated the new gains sought by blacks. New jobs and increased income, opportunity, and training were among the many benefits brought by these conflagrations. Throughout the entire period the upper hand was held by white supremacists but amid a growing militancy and defensive capability among blacks.

The fourth phase of black history ended with the United

States Supreme Court striking down the white primary and its white supremacist counterpart: school segregation. On May 17, 1954, the Supreme Court, by a 9-0 decision, ruled that school segregation was unconstitutional because separate educational facilities are inherently unequal. Earlier, in 1944, in the case of *Smith v. Allwight*, the Supreme Court had declared that white primary laws and rules that excluded blacks from taking part in party primaries were unconstitutional. Once again the political tide began to turn in favor of blacks in education and in access to places of public accommodation.

Beginning in 1944, the political process was again open to blacks, as it had been during Reconstruction. From that time to the present the effects of this ruling have been felt. This is also the case with the separate but equal education legislation. From this decision the vast body of legislation mandating racial separation in public places and facilities has been declared illegal. We are still reconstructing in the aftermath of these momentous decisions. Generally, they have opened up the opportunity structure of the society to blacks to an unprecedented extent, making upward mobility possible on a much wider scale than ever before. Has the promise of Phase 5, the New Reconstruction, been fulfilled? Is the unilinearity of gains for blacks continuing as claimed above?

In characterizing Phase 5, I shall present data in two distinct forms. The first, in Chapters 4 and 5, provides a narrative close-up account of developments in California. The second, in Chapters 6, 7, and 8, draws on the census and other pools of aggregate data. Thus, data presentation is the primary task of the following five chapters. Adaptations from recent research are utilized to provide a current assessment.

Questions for Review and Further Study

1. In what ways is black American history the same as and different from the history of white ethnic groups?

2. How would you explain the lack of proportional class representation?

3. What are the suggested phases of black American history and crucial turning points for each phase?

4. What phase was the most long lasting and has had the greatest impact?

5. Cite five of the most debilitating features of U.S. slavery.

6. It has been argued that much of the prosperity enjoyed in U.S. society was produced by black Americans. In what way would you support this view?

7. In what concrete ways did Emancipation lead to gains by black Americans?

8. What were the techniques used to usher Confederates back into power in the South during Redemption?

Notes

1. Leon A. Higginbotham, Jr., *In the Matter of Color* (New York: Oxford University Press, 1978), p. 39.

2. Lulamae Clemons, Erwin Hollitz and Gordon Gardner, *The American Negro* (St. Louis: McGraw-Hill, 1965).

3. Much of the data utilized in the discussion of the several phases of black history come from Peter M. Bergman, *The Chronological History of the Negro in America* (New York: Harper & Row, 1969). Other data used are indicated by appropriate references.

4. Ibid., Ch. 1.

5. Ibid., p. 10.

6. Ibid.

7. Here I follow the discussion of Higginbotham, p. 21.

8. E. Franklin Frazier, *The Free Negro Family* (Nashville, Tenn.: Fisk University Press, 1932), p. 1; see also John H. Russell, *The Free Negro in Virginia* (Baltimore: Johns Hopkins Press, 1913), p. 29; and Ulrich B. Phillips, *American Negro Slavery* (New York: Appleton, 1969).

9. See Abbot Emerson Smith, *White Servitude and Convict Labor in America 1607-1776* (Gloucester, Mass.: University of North Carolina Press, 1947), pp. 307-37. Exact and sufficient data on the number of slaves and indentured servants in colonial America are not available. Smith, in the above study of white servitude in the colonies from 1607 to 1776, supports the argument presented here of a diverse work force with large numbers of white indentured servants working under the same official circumstances as many blacks. In addition to those servants there were increasing numbers of black slaves in the labor force of colonial America. In his appendix, Smith cites Virginia census data from 1624 to 1625. The total population of the colony was 1,227, with 487 servants and twenty-three blacks. By the year 1671 he suggests a servant population of 6,000 in a total population of 40,000, with 2,000 black slaves. Excluding the Puritan migrations of the 1630s Smith argues that not less than one-half nor more than two-thirds of all white immigrants to the colonies were indentured servants or redemptioners. During the 1670s there were maintained between 12,000 and 15,000 (white) servants laboring in the plantation, of whom about 6,000 were in Virginia. About one in every ten white persons was under indenture. After the 1670s the proportion of servants to the total white population declined until 1750.

10. Frazier, p. 2.

11. Bergman, p. 18.

12. Ibid., pp. 11-12.

13. Ibid., p. 25.

14. Higginbotham, p. 39.

15. Ibid., p. 30.

16. Ibid., p. 39.

17. William Goodell, *The American Slave Code* (New York: Arno Press, 1969), p. 24. Slave codes in early America are discussed in a number of scholarly works. This discussion draws on Goodell.

18. Ibid., p. 23.

19. C. Duncan Rice, *The Rise and Fall of Black Slavery* (New York: Harper & Row, 1975), ch. 5.

20. Ibid., p. 156.

21. C. Vann Woodward,*The Strange Career of Jim Crow* (New York: Oxford University Press, 1966), ch. III.

22. Also during this year the National League for the Protection of Colored Women was formed in New York City, aiming at equality in economic and social conditions for blacks. See Bergman.

4

TRANSITION IN CALIFORNIA I

There are fewer blacks in the West than in other regions of the United States. In 1980, 52.7 percent of the South was black, but only 8.2 percent of the West. Yet, the recent pattern of political, economic, and educational achievement for blacks has been similar throughout the country. A view of the process in California reflects in a general way what happened elsewhere in the United States.

The focus here is on Los Angeles, San Francisco, and Oakland. These cities mirror in many ways what happened in Atlanta, Birmingham, Cleveland, and Newark. These are all major metropolitan areas with substantial concentrations of blacks. Each of these cities has been involved in the evolving prosperity achieved by black Americans over the past twenty-five years.

Persons of African ancestry have a history in California that goes back to the early Spanish expeditions to the New World. In fact, California was won for the Spanish by troops of mixed origin.[1] Such persons participated in most or all of the sea expeditions along the Pacific coast, and they later came to form a substantial part of the population of California and Baja California. Jack Forbes reports that in 1794, of 1,469 Spanish-speaking persons in these areas combined, 23.2 percent were de color quebrada, or part African; and 29.3 percent were mestizos.[2] Thus, 52.5 percent of the Hispanos were recorded as of mixed origin. Individual communities in California reflected this pattern.

In 1781 the total population of Los Angeles was 46 persons, 26 of whom were African or part African,[3] a surprising 56.5 percent of the population. By 1790 the Los Angeles population had increased to 141. Forbes estimates 22.7 percent of these to have been persons of some degree of African ancestry. This element of the Los Angeles population was recorded as 38.5 percent by 1792. Early census figures for Santa Barbara show 19.3 percent of its 191 persons to have been part-black, while over half were classed as non-Spanish. In 1790, 24.3 percent of all the settlers in San Jose were part black, and more than half (59.5 percent) were classed non-Spanish. A similar pattern held for Monterey. The 1782 census for San Francisco recorded an adult male population that included several Afro-Americans. Half the families in San Francisco in 1790 were of hybrid lineage. Of the total population, at least 14.7 percent were of black ancestry.

Forbes summarizes the overall racial picture for California in 1790 as follows:

> It can be seen that persons of part-Negro ancestry constituted at least 17.7 percent of the population, and in addition, the Castas group, or 13.1 percent, undoubtedly included many Afro-Americans. . . . Conservatively, we can estimate that at least 20 percent of the Hispano-Californians were part Negro in 1790, while probably 25 percent of the Hispano-Baja Californians possessed African ancestry.[4]

The population classifications used in Hispano-California were essentially the same as those employed throughout the Spanish colonies. In order of highest to lowest prestige, they were Españoles, mestizos and coyotes, mulattoes, Indians, pardos, and castas.[5] An important feature of this classification system was its comparative flexibility. Although it was essentially based on ancestry, an ascribed characteristic, one could at times purchase a different classification if financially able. In 1790, 24.3 percent of San Jose's settlers were part black, whereas four years later the part-Negro proportion had been reclassified to form only 12.2 percent . . . thus indicating that some pardos and mulattoes had become mestizos. Further,

> The upper-class Hispano-Americans were a color-conscious people, and they were very interested in keeping track of racial ancestry. Otherwise, they would not have invented so many different terms to refer to various kinds of mixtures. However, this race consciousness was greatly modified in practice. Necessity may have forced a Spaniard to marry a mixed-blood, Negro, or Indian in cases where eligible girls were rare or absent. In addition, the crown encouraged such mixture by allowing wealthy non-Spaniards to purchase 'purity of blood' certificates; for example a pardo could become a Spaniard in 1795 for 500 reales.[6]

The surprising proportions of the Hispano-Americans that were black or nonwhite (non-Español) seems strange from today's standpoint. Patterns of race relations in California today are strangely different from those of 1790. In spite of the larger proportions of blacks and other nonwhites, violent racial conflict between the two groups appears to have been infrequent. Also, patterns of racial discrimination as we know them today were apparently nonexistent. In other words, nonwhites in California under Hispanic rule were more extensively integrated into the culture than are nonwhite (especially black) Americans today.

Comparing Anglo (white) attitudes (from the eastern United States) toward various racial groups and Hispanic attitudes (from California) during the same period, George Frakes and Curtis Solberg conclude the following:

In general, the Spaniards and Mexicans were more tolerant than the English colonists and the Americans during this period. Hispanic customs and law permitted intermarriage and encouraged assimilation of Indians and blacks into society. This unbiased attitude toward racial differences was particularly noticeable in California because many of the Spaniards themselves and the Mexican pioneers after 1821 were persons of mixed racial background.[7]

This is not to say that social and economic equality existed among the various racial groups. As Frakes and Solberg go on to point out,

Greater tolerance and acceptance of non-Hispanic people in California did not mean, however, that minorities were necessarily the social and economic equals of Spaniards. . . . There was, however, opportunity for upward social mobility, because in the Spanish colonies a wealthy person of Indian or black ancestry could legally delete his true origins and gain Spanish status. Indeed, scholars of early California history believe that many of the most distinguished early Spanish families could also trace their family roots to Indian and African sources.[8]

Black and other nonwhite groups under Hispanic rule were involved in a social process of assimilation into Hispanic society, a process that ranged as broadly as the geographic boundaries of Spanish rule itself. The basis for this process was laid down in sixteenth-century Spain during which a great debate was waged over the proper conditions of conquest.[9]

Spanish rule in California was ordered by the king of Spain, in 1769, more than 200 years after its discovery.[10] Settlements were ordered for San Diego and Monterey. Gaspar de Portolá, who became the Hispanic governor of California, set out from Mexico with Father Junípero Serra in that year and established a mission at San Diego. The next year one was established at Monterey. By 1834 the Franciscans had established a number of missions along the coast from San Diego to Sonoma. A number of military outposts, or presidios, had grown up around them as protection accompanied by a number of pueblos.

By the eighteenth century there is evidence that blacks were in many cities and towns throughout the Spanish Empire, playing a major role in the early settlement and exploration of California. During the Spanish period, a few blacks did rise to some degree of social and political prominence. As Royce Delmatier et al. explain,

> Francisco Rey, a mulatto rancher, served as mayor of Los Angeles from 1793 to 1795; Jose Bartolomé Tapia, a mulatto who owned the scenic Rancho Malibu, served as majordomo (a supervisory position) of San Luis Obispo Mission as did Miguel Pico at Ventura Mission from 1819 through 1821.[11]

The Mexican government declared its independence from Spain in 1821 and then acquired California. During the Mexican period, a mulatto, William Alexander Leidesdorff, became one of San Francisco's most prominent businessmen. He was also a member of the council and of the school committee and was active in city politics.[12] In 1844, Leidesdorff became a Mexican citizen and later became the U.S. vice-consul, serving under Thomas Larkin.[13]

During the period of Mexican rule a number of Anglo settlers entered California. They were explorers, fur traders, business entrepreneurs and so forth, and some of them settled there. By the time of the outbreak of hostilities between Mexico and the United States, in 1846, many Americans were well settled in the area. At that time, however, the population was predominantly non-Anglo and the customs and life ways predominantly Hispanic. This changed within a few years as Mexico ceded California to the United States in the Treaty of Guadalupe Hidalgo (1848). This move fatefully altered the relationship between nonwhites and whites. The discovery of gold in California in the same year accelerated the change. California was admitted to the Union as the thirty-first state in 1850. Two years earlier there were 15,000 residents in the state; by 1850 there were 92,000 and ten years later nearly 380,000.[14] By 1850 the period of Hispanic rule in California was over and drastic changes in the relationship between the white (Anglo) population and the nonwhite minorities were in process.

With the large influx of people from traditionally Anglo-ruled states in the United States came an influx of American blacks. Hardy Frye states that before 1841 there were few Negroes in California.[15] News of the discovery of gold, however, inspired many American blacks to pull up stakes and head for California.

> It was no uncommon sight to see individual Negroes or even entire families of free colored people travelling to California . . . free Mulattoes (150,000 in 1850) excited by dreams of wealth had sold out small businesses in the east, and had invested their capital in covered wagons, supplies and mining equipment. Many of the Negroes walking beside the wagons of the Oregon trail or travelling on the coastal steamers to San Francisco, were being brought to the coast as slaves . . . they were referred to as "indentured servants."[16]

Blacks settled early in California cities. By 1860 San Francisco and Sacramento had become major areas of settlement. Churches, newspapers, and private schools were first established by blacks in these cities. Initially, there was little overt discrimination against blacks in these and other California cities. Hispanic-Mexican mores and customs were yet operative. Eventually, the rivalry for gold led to frequent and intensely hostile episodes.

The pattern of social relations that eventually emerged between Anglo-whites and nonwhites was fundamentally different from that between the Hispanic-whites and the nonwhites. The emergent pattern can be described as relentlessly oppressive, exploitative, and separatist toward nonwhites, a pattern of racist oppression that has endured to the present day. White Anglo-Californians brought with them more intense images of racial superiority to nonwhite peoples than already existed in Hispanic culture and began to institutionalize these patterns in all areas of social life. Rampant prejudice and discrimination against blacks that became endemic to California's social institutions had their origin in this cultural transition. At this point institutional racism began and prospered in California.

Racism was rampant in the first California constitutional convention held in Monterey in 1849. Though this convention adopted a free state platform strenuous efforts were made to adopt amendments that excluded all free persons of color from the state. The first Anglo governor of California, Peter H. Burnett, introduced a bill (earlier as an Oregon legislator) intended to rid the state of free Negroes and mulattoes by flogging those who did not leave.[17] Many of the Anglo migrants to California were pro-slavery southerners who attempted to establish in California a way of life consistent with that in the South. Although they were unsuccessful in having California declare itself a slave state, they did initiate a formidable and enduring pattern of racist oppression. In 1852 the pro-slavery southerners in the legislature passed a fugitive slave law that provided that any owner or agent could recover a fugitive slave, and that blacks could not give testimony in their own behalf.[18]

In 1850 California passed a law that prohibited blacks, mulattoes, and Indians, from giving evidence in a court of law against a white.[19] This meant that nonwhites were unprotected by law in either their lives, their liberty, or property. Any grave injustice suffered at the hands of whites could not be brought to court and adjudicated. By wording of the law itself (it applied only to free white persons) nonwhites were not allowed homestead rights. This combined with the inability to give testimony in court, essentially deprived nonwhites of the opportunity to acquire land. Only after modification of the restriction on the right to give testimony could nonwhites purchase property securely.

The oppressive prohibitions and restrictions erected by Anglo-Californians were not new racist devices. They were essentially patterns of racism that already existed in many areas of the United States. Even though certain rights were won eventually, the pattern of relations between whites and nonwhites became essentially hostile, oppressive, and segregated. The idea that nonwhites were inferior beings was never seriously questioned by Anglos, even by those who were against slavery and other of the more brutal forms of racist oppression. Nonwhites were forced into a pattern of subordination that came to be deeply rooted in the folkways and mores of California. The acceptance that nonwhites had achieved and enjoyed under Hispanic rule gradually faded as a rigid and lingering pattern of racism gripped the entire state.

It should be pointed out that nonwhites waged a constant battle to gain and retain freedoms and civil rights in California. From the beginning of U.S. rule to 1862, the pro-Southern faction (the main source of numerous anti-black legislative enactments) maintained an influential position in the California legislature. Blacks organized and attempted to resist these encroachments. For example, in 1855 the first Convention of Colored Citizens of the state was organized, a group that lasted until World War I. They fought for equal legal protection, fair housing, and education. In 1862 the Franchise League was organized by blacks in San Francisco to secure the right to vote. According to Delmatier et al.,

The efforts of these groups . . . were ineffective, for it was not until the Republican party assumed control over California politics that the barriers of discrimination and segregation began to break down. In 1863 blacks obtained the right to testify in cases where whites were defendants, and in 1870 the first black jury was convened in Sacramento. Although not ratified by California, the Fifteenth Amendment gave blacks the right to vote which they began to do in the 1870's. It was not until 1874, when the legislature decided that non-white children could go to a white school if no colored school existed, that the statewide segregated school system, which was formally established in 1870, began to change its posture. Continuous boycotts, lawsuits, resolutions by the Colored Citizens Convention and editorials in *The Mirror of the Times* ended the dual school system of education after 1875.[20]

Emerging Black Politics

From the mid-1870s to 1940 black population growth in California slowed. Between 1850 and 1860 California blacks increased from approximately 1,000 to 4,000, making up roughly 1 percent of the state population. From 1860 to 1910 the number of blacks grew to 21,645, but due to more rapid influx of whites this figure was less than 1 percent of the state's population. It was when the mass exodus of blacks from the South started that their numbers in California showed significant increase. Between 1920 and 1940 the black population in California jumped from 21,645 to 124,306. More than half of this population settled in the Los Angeles area. It is not surprising, therefore, that during this time California blacks began to realize some small increments of prosperity.

Frederick M. Roberts, a black, was elected to the state assembly from Los Angeles in 1918. Roberts held this seat for sixteen years, eventually being unseated by Augustus F. Hawkins, another black who later became a respected congressman from California. Hawkins defeated Roberts in 1934 and maintained his seat until 1962, when he became the first black from California elected to the U.S. House of Representatives. He retired from this position in 1990.

Hawkins began the serious battle in the California legislature for the rights of blacks. In 1961 he introduced a bill that was designed to prohibit discrimination in the sale, lease, or rental of all private housing (except for owners of single-unit residences occupied by owners as residences). This bill passed in the assembly but failed in the senate. However, the matter was later taken up by another black legislator, William Byron Rumford, a Democrat from Berkeley.

Rumford first was elected to the California Assembly in 1948. The year that Hawkins went to Congress, 1963, Rumford proposed new fair housing legislation. This legislation (A.B. 1240) banned discrimination in the sale or rental of all publicly assisted housing and all privately financed housing other than dwellings with four or fewer units. This legislation passed both houses of the state legislature. Final passage took place in the last hour of the last day of the 1963 legislative session. California became the twelfth state to enact a fair housing law. An effort to repeal this legislation failed. Yet, by February 1964, the California Real Estate Association had successfully mounted a campaign that required the issue to be submitted to the voters as Proposition 14. It was overwhelmingly approved by the voters, but Proposition 14 was ultimately declared unconstitutional by the U.S. Supreme Court.

These were the early beginnings of black political prosperity in California, the first serious and continuous gains since the transition in California from Hispanic to Anglo rule. Chapter 5 provides a more detailed and recent account of this progressive effort.

Questions for Review and Further Study

1. What were the differences in Hispanic rule in California versus Anglo rule as concerns black/white relations?
2. Who were some of the early black legislators in Anglo-California?
3. What are the names of two black mayors of the city of Los Angeles?
4. What has been the role of persons of African ancestry in the early settlement of Los Angeles?

Notes

1. George E. Frakes and Curtis B. Solberg (eds.) *Minorities in California History* (New York: Random House, 1971), p. 23.
2. Jack D. Forbes, "Black Pioneers: The Spanish-Speaking Afro-Americans of the Southwest," in Frakes and Solberg, pp. 20-33.
3. Ibid., p. 24.
4. Ibid., p. 29.
5. Magnus Morner, *Race Mixture* (Boston: Little Brown, 1967).
6. Forbes, p. 30.
7. Frakes and Solberg, p. 3.
8. Ibid., p. 23.
9. Lewis Hanke, *The Spanish Struggle for Justice in the Conquest of America* (Boston: Little Brown, 1949). See discussion in Chapter 1.
10. Henry A. Turner and John A. Vieg, *The Government and Politics of California*, 3rd ed. (New York: McGraw-Hill, 1967), especially Chapter 1.
11. Royce D. Delmatier, Clarence F. McIntosh and Earl G.

Walters (eds.) *The Rumble of California Politics* (New York: Wiley, 1970).

12. Hubert Howe Bancroft, *History of California* (San Francisco: History Co., 1866, 1890), V, pp. 455, 648, 652-56.

13. Ibid., p. 6, Delmatier, McIntosh, and Walters.

14. Ibid., p. 6, Turner and Vieg.

15. Hardy Frye, "Negroes in California from 1841 to 1875," vol. 3, no. 1, San Francisco Negro Historical and Cultural Society (April 1968).

16. James W. Pilton, "Negro Settlement in British Columbia," vol. 2, no. 1, monograph, San Francisco Negro Historical and Cultural Society (September 1967), p. 4.

17. Ibid., p. 6.

18. Ibid., p. 7.

19. Ibid., p. 8.

20. See Delmatier, McIntosh, and Walters, p. 7.

5

TRANSITION IN CALIFORNIA II

The ebb and flow of blacks in public office has been charted over the past few years in the National Roster of Black Elected Officials, *published by the Joint Center for Political Studies.[1] The trend in electing blacks to public office has been one of progressive increase in their numbers in recent years.[2] Note should be taken that the rate of increase, however, has varied. It declined in 1972. It picked up again in 1975 only to further decline over the next four years, through 1979. Then in 1980 the rate again increased from 2.3 percent in 1979 to 6.3 percent in 1980. From these data it is clear that increasing access to public elective office is available to blacks. However, in spite of continuing increases, proportional representation of blacks holding elective public office is far from achieved. What is certain and important is that as of 1988 progress in reaching this level of representation was still underway. By that year there were 6,793 black elected officials throughout the nation, nearly double the number in 1980. Brief description of aspects of the process in three California cities provides a closer acquaintance with this transformation.*

California was no exception to the national trend of electing unprecedented numbers of blacks to political office during the past few years. The number of black elected officeholders in California prior to 1960 was minuscule. By 1988, there were 286 black elected officials in the state. The majority of them assumed office after 1960. This was a national trend which is still operative though, as we will see, not with its earlier intensity.

Los Angeles

The first blacks to be elected to the Los Angeles City Council—Thomas Bradley, Gilbert Lindsay, and Billy Mills—assumed office in 1963. In 1963 they became the first blacks on the fifteen-member city council. (In fact, Bradley is currently mayor [1991], having been reelected several times.) For a few years this represented the highest percentage of blacks in city government in the state. Black representation on this official body then became proportionate to the number of blacks in the city's population, estimated to be 17.9 percent.[3] In Los Angeles, the councilmanic representation of blacks remains proportionate to their representation in the city population. This achievement was made early in the 1960s and has been maintained over time. It was the successful outcome of strategy and struggle.

Heightened political awareness among blacks during the early 1960s took a specific form in Los Angeles. In every election, going back to the 1950s, Los Angeles's blacks had unsuccessfully run candidates for district representation in the heavily black districts.[4] The Tenth District was the location of continual attempts. Only in 1961 did there appear an important change and the prospect of success. In that year, Charles Navarro, the longtime incumbent in the Tenth District, was elected to the position of city comptroller, leaving the council seat vacant. Even before this event, blacks had made known to the city council their wish to have a black appointed to replace Navarro in case of a vacancy. Several members of a group called the Committee for Representative Government, formed in 1961 to further the election of blacks to public office, met. The city council replaced Navarro with a white, Joe Hollingsworth, although a black, George Thomas, was placed in nomination with him.

This move had a disquieting effect on blacks in the Tenth district. A small group of citizens met the next day to decide on a strategy to counteract this appointment.[5] The group initiated a recall drive against Hollingsworth, which failed due to the city clerk's decision to invalidate a sufficient number of signatures collected by the petitioners. However, events involving the drive against Hollingsworth left the black community highly irritated and in a mood to seek revenge. No blacks were elected in the Los Angeles municipal election of 1961 but in 1963 the picture changed. That year there were three contests in which blacks competed for council seats—those in the eighth, ninth, and tenth council districts and each candidate was successful.

Blacks in 1988 still maintain one-fifth of the seats on city council, three of fifteen: Robert Farrell, Gilbert Lindsay, and Nate Holden, for the eighth, ninth, and tenth districts respectively. There was speculation that Mayor Bradley, a black, would run for governor of California. Bradley, however, chose to remain mayor of Los Angeles. Since first election of blacks to the Los Angeles City Council, two Chicanos (Richard Allatore and Gloria Molina), an Asian (Michael Woo), and four women have been elected. In 1988 the Los Angeles City Council was much closer to proportional representation of the voting population than ever before.

The School Board. The first black to join the Los Angeles School Board did so in 1938. Fay Allen was appointed that year and was later elected to a four-year term, serving five consecutive years to 1943. The next black became a board member in 1965, more than 20 years later. This was Reverend James E. Jones, who served through 1969. Jones was board president during his last year on the board. Diane Watson was the next black to appear. She was elected in 1975 and served until her election to the state assembly in 1978. Rita Walters, another black, replaced Watson in 1979. Walters is today the one black on the seven-member school board. This board now includes three minorities and five women.

The Judiciary. Blacks are more numerous in the judicial branch of Los Angeles government than elsewhere in the state. In 1973 there were nineteen blacks serving in the Los Angeles judiciary: three were commissioners who have judicial functions; fifteen were municipal and superior court judges; and one was on the appellate court. As of May 1981 there were thirty-three black judges, excluding commissioners, and by 1988 there were forty-eight. Many of these judges were appointees of either former Governor Pat Brown or former Governor Ronald Reagan. As of 1974, no black incumbent judge had been defeated in a bid for reelection, although Judge Tom Griffith, Jr. retired in 1972. Once a judge achieves the status of incumbent, reelection is virtually assured.

The State Legislature. The Los Angeles area has elected several blacks to the state legislature. The distinguished Senator Mervyn Dymally was the first black in recent times elected to the state legislature from Los Angeles. He was first elected assemblyman in 1961 and served until 1966. He then was elected state senator. Dymally is well known throughout California as an outstanding legislator and able politician. In 1974 he was elected lieutenant governor, the highest state office ever held by a black in California. Defeated in his bid for reelection in 1979 by a white candidate, Mike Curb, Dymally sought and won a congressional seat from District Thirty-one in 1980. He continues to serve (1991) as congressman from that district.

In 1963, three additional blacks were elected to state office from Los Angeles: Yvonne Brathwaite from the Sixty-Third District, Bill Greene from the Fifty-Third District, and Leon Ralph from the Fifty-Fifth District. In 1972, Brathwaite (now Mrs. Burke) was the first black woman elected to Congress from California. Ralph and Greene were elected to state office from heavily black state assembly districts in Los Angeles, whereas Burke was elected from a state assembly district with a majority of white constituents. Julian Dixon was elected state assemblyman in 1972 from the Forty-Ninth District, and in 1974 two additional blacks were elected: Assemblymen Curtis Tucker, from the Fiftieth District and Holden from the Thirtieth District. The court-ordered redistricting in 1974 created the Thirtieth District, which was won by Holden, who defeated Frank Holoman in the primary.

Of the six state assembly districts in the Los Angeles area held by blacks in 1974 (sixty-third, fifty-fifth, fifty-third, fiftieth, forty-ninth, and thirtieth), only two were held by black incumbents by 1981. Three came to be held by whites and one by a Mexican-American. Black representation in the state senate increased from one in 1974 to four in 1981, and by 1988 had decreased to two members. These were Senators Greene and Watson. The number of blacks in the California state legislature in 1991 was seven, one more than in 1974. These legislators were Assemblymen Willie Brown, Teresa Hughes, Gwen Moore, Willard Murray, and Curtis Tucker, Jr., and Senators Watson and Greene.

In addition to having more blacks in elected office, Los Angeles has had blacks in elected office longer than any other California city. Black representation since the beginning of Anglo control in Los Angeles goes back to 1918 when

Frederick Roberts was elected to the state legislature. He was replaced by Augustus Hawkins in 1934. Hawkins remained a state assemblyman until 1961, when he was elected to Congress. He has held public office longer than any other black in the state and has pursued a successful and outstanding career as a public official for more than 40 years.

Oakland

Oakland had a population of 361,561 in 1970, of which 213,512 were white, 124,710 black, and 23,339 listed as other. Blacks constituted about 35 percent of Oakland's population. Ten years later the population had decreased to 339,337, of which 129,692 were white and 159,281 were black. Also listed were 32,492 persons of Hispanic origin. This reveals a large exodus of whites from Oakland. The black percentage of the population thereby became roughly 50 percent, with another 10 percent also nonwhite.

City Council. Unlike Los Angeles, where city councilmen have elaborate offices and extensive staff support, Oakland's council is part-time; members share a single office in city hall. The city manager is a central figure in government operations. The first black elected to the Oakland City Council was Joshua Rose in 1965. He was continually reelected until his retirement, June 30, 1977.

For some years Rose was the only black on the eight-member Oakland City Council (the mayor was a ninth but ex-officio member). Although blacks were a much larger proportion of the Oakland population than they were of Los Angeles, they were slower to reach proportional representation on the council than blacks in Los Angeles. For a number of years, in spite of extensive effort, their gains were few. However, there have been dramatic gains for blacks in Oakland in recent years.

The retirement of Rose in June 1977 resulted in District Four going to a white. Soon thereafter, however, two blacks, Wilson Riles, Jr. and Carter Gilmore, were elected to represent Districts Five and Six respectively. By 1981 blacks held two of eight seats on the Oakland City Council, plus the office of mayor. By 1989 there were five black (including one woman) members of the council including the mayor. In addition, there were three female members of the council plus an Asian councilman. Clearly, Oakland has compensated for past deficits in councilmanic representation. Proportional representation on this influential body has been achieved.

The most well-known recent gain in black representation in Oakland has been the office of mayor. In 1977 former Judge Lionel Wilson, a black, retired from the bench and successfully sought this office, easily overcoming a broad field of aspirants to the post of retiring Mayor John Reading. Wilson made a broad appeal to all groups in the city and offered an appealing option to Oakland voters. Since his first election, he was continually reelected until his defeat in 1991 by Elihu Harris, also black. This eight-member council now consists of four blacks, one other minority, and three women. The black group includes the mayor, who is also a councilmember.

The Judiciary. In 1961 Judge Wilson became the first and only black member of the Municipal Court. He was an appointee of Governor Edmund Brown. By 1974 Wilson was joined on the Oakland bench by another black: Justice Allan Broussard. Wilson was replaced by Broussard in 1964 and elevated to the superior court. Including Supreme Court Justice Gordon Baranco, there were nine blacks on the bench in Oakland in 1988, a very different picture from that of the early 1960s.

The number of blacks in the judiciary has remained constant since 1980. The Oakland Municipal Court in 1980 consisted of fourteen judges, of whom Baranco, Benjamin Travis, and James S. White were black. By 1988 Judith Ford, Horace Wheatley, and James Stanford White were the three black municipal court justices in Oakland. As of 1980 the Oakland Superior Court had thirty justices, five of whom were black: Broussard, Richard Bancroft, Donald P. McCullum, Henry Ramsay, Jr., and Wilmot Sweeney. By 1988 there were also five black superior court judges: Richard Bancroft, Jr., McCullum, Henry Ramsay Jr., Wilmot Sweeney, and Travis.

The School Board. For some years, blacks in Oakland have had representation on the seven-member school board. The first black elected to that body was Barney Hilburn, in 1958. Hilburn was continually reelected for several terms. Another black, attorney Thomas Berkeley, was elected to the school board in 1966. He resigned a few months later and was replaced by another black, Charles Goady, who served as school board president. Oakland's school board in 1980 had three blacks among its seven members: Jane Norwood, Hilburn, and J. Alfred Smith. In 1988 blacks continued to hold three seats on this body.

The State Legislature. Oakland, or the larger metropolitan environment of which it is a part, elected its first black to the state legislature in 1949, Assemblyman William Byron Rumford. A second black, John Miller, was sent to the state legislature from the Oakland-Berkeley area in 1968. Although Los Angeles sent its first black to Congress in 1962 (Hawkins), this did not happen in Oakland (Alameda County) until years later. Ronald Dellums was elected to Congress in 1970.

San Francisco

A number of blacks in San Francisco, mainly middle-class professionals, had pressed for political representation at least as far back as the 1950s. Many of these early advocates for a voice in government for blacks came to hold important elective and appointive office.

The Board of Supervisors. The 1970 black population of this city was roughly 13.4 percent, or 96,078 persons of a total of 715,674. This proportion has remained about the same through the 1980s, though there is now a Hispanic population of about 12 percent in San Francisco. The first representation of blacks on the eleven-member city-county board of supervisors came in 1963, when Mayor John Shelley appointed a black attorney, Terry Francois, to fill an unexpired term. Francois successfully maintained incumbency in that prestigious office until 1977, refusing to run again in the new district elections that were initiated that year.

Increased black representation on the board of supervisors within the next few years may have had to do with a change in the selection method. In 1977, San Francisco voters adopted a district method of electing board members, an important departure from the long-standing practice of electing them on a citywide basis. It might be noted that a very ardent opponent of the change from the citywide to the district election process was the then only black supervisor, Francois. The district plan was voted in. Immediately, plans were made by the opposition to resubmit the matter to the electorate. This was done in November, 1980, and the district plan was defeated. Nevertheless, black representation increased from one to two members. Ella Hutch, a black was elected. She was replaced by another black, Willie Kennedy. Doris Ward was elected in 1976, making a total of two blacks on this eleven-member body. This is beyond proportional representation.

The Judiciary. By 1974 there were two black superior court judges in San Francisco: the Honorable Joseph Kennedy and the Honorable Raymond Reynolds. Judge Reynolds, who first assumed office in 1969 and has since retired, is the only black justice to claim affiliation with the Republican party. Judge Kennedy, who assumed office in 1963, was an incumbent until his death in 1979. Another, Judge John Dearman, was first appointed, then elected, to a six-year term in 1980, thus maintaining black underrepresentation in this elective body. It then consisted of twenty-seven members. The Municipal Court of San Francisco had seventeen members in 1980, one of whom, Justice Perker Meeks, Jr., was black. He was appointed by Governor Jerry Brown.

As of 1988 there remained three black members of the San Francisco bench: John E. Dearman, superior court justice, Charles J. James and Perker L. Meeks, Jr. both municipal court justices.

The School Board. Although the seven-member school board became an elected body in 1972, black representation on it goes back to 1963, when James Stratton was appointed. He was succeeded in 1968 by Zuretti Goosby. The election of Charlie Mae Haynes in June 1972 represents a continuation of black representation on this influential body. The Board of Education of San Francisco maintains its earlier level of black representation, one of seven members. A black representative, Julie C. Anderson, was appointed in 1978 and later elected to a four-year term. By 1988 the numerical representation of blacks had not changed, although the incumbent then was Sedonia M. Wilson. She has served as president of that body.

The State Legislature. Perhaps the most widely known elected official to emerge from San Francisco is State Assemblyman Willie Brown. First elected in 1964, he has been in the public eye on a number of issues and is considered a potential contender for higher elected office. He has been chairman of the legislature's powerful Ways and Means Committee. He is now speaker of the house and widely popular among the San Francisco electorate and is a regent of the University of California.

This brief survey of blacks who hold elective office serves to demonstrate the rapid acceleration of blacks into public office since 1960. It further indicates that the momentum of this movement appears to be yet fully underway. To indicate the social history of the group and its orientation, attention is given to interviews by the author in 1980 with black public officials in California.

Social Background Characteristics

An overwhelming majority of the black elected officials in California are not native Californians. With the exception of two who were born in California and one born in Trinidad, the group is drawn from immigrants to California from the American South. Virginia, Texas, Louisiana, and Mississippi are typical states of origin. The frequently elected mayor of Los Angeles, Thomas Bradley, was born in Texas and came to California at an early age. This is a typical pattern. Yet most have lived in California more than 25 years. Thus, most of the black elected officials are migrants to California. Their childhood was spent largely in the South and in the former Confederate states.

The level of academic achievement of the group is high. Only one in this group had not earned a law degree or a bachelor's degree. There are four doctors of jurisprudence among them and three holders of master's degrees. The age range of the group is from 39 years to 67 years. The judges as a group are older than the other officials. Also, they have a higher average number of years of service as elected officials.

California's black elected officials are an upwardly mobile group, reflected in the contrast between their educational and occupational achievements compared with those of their fathers. The level of educational achievement of their fathers, with minor exception, is below that of the officeholders themselves. This also holds true for levels of occupational achievement. There are only thirteen high school graduates among their fathers, whereas all of the elected officials are high school graduates. There are three college graduates among the fathers, whereas each of the elected officials is a college graduate except one. Occupations of the fathers of this group tend to cluster in the semiskilled and unskilled classifications. On the other hand, the occupational classifications for the elected officials themselves cluster at higher levels.

Finally, the predominant political affiliation of the group is with the Democratic party. Though there has been some recent indication that blacks are no longer as fully committed to the Democratic party as they once were, the change is not reflected in this group of officeholders. Most of them did claim, however, that their party of official affiliation was of little or no help in their election. They generally ran their own campaigns, or had personal friends and acquaintances do so. Financing was mainly a matter of contributions from friends and well-wishers, plus their personal funds. The fact that local elections are nonpartisan accounts for the lack of official party involvement in supervisorial contests and contests for the judiciary. State and national elections, however, are another matter. Lack of official party support at this level can be accounted for by the reluctance of current party agents to accept and assist the rise of blacks to proportional levels of power. It is the voice of the voters themselves and the entrepreneurial skill of black aspirants to public office that force recognition of the official party machinery. The party is apparently a reluctant recipient of this new political reality to which it must adjust.

In summary, black elected officials are a relatively recent and highly qualified breed on the political scene in California. They bring to public office a limited history of political involvement and a level of educational achievement far above the ordinary. They are the first wave of blacks to represent in California the nationwide gains to nonwhites that were realized by the civil rights efforts of the 1960s and 1970s.

With this brief social profile in mind, it is appropriate to consider some of the activities of these officials since they were elected to office. This is because there appear to be significant differences between black elected officials and their white counterparts. I shall later refer again to this difference because I believe it is central to the process by which broader social change in society is likely to appear.

Responses to Selected Questions

It is important to get some idea of what the new prosperity for blacks means in terms of the outlook of these prominent persons on issues bearing on racism. Do they, as is often claimed, now see the world in white middle-class terms? Have they become critical and disdainful of blacks and of the need for racial equality? Selected responses by California black politicians to the following questions testify to their continued concern about racial equality and the nature of that concern. These responses were recorded during interviews conducted in 1980.

Are things getting better or worse in general for black Americans?

❖ There is probably no objective evidence or indication that will convince all blacks that things are better or worse. Ultimately, we must refer to impressions and feelings. It is my feeling that the overall lot of blacks is slowly improving. I hasten to add that I am not nearly satisfied with the pace of progress. There are several areas where one might attempt to document the improvement. Income, education, life expectancy, politics, athletics, entertainment, etc. In all of these areas, the statistics will show that we are improving both in absolute terms and vis-à-vis the white population in this country. But we can never lose sight of the fact that we continue to be second-class citizens in all respects. The only way that we can continue to progress is by continual vigilance and aggressiveness and efforts to challenge each and every effort to frustrate our progress.

❖ Without an exhaustive study it is difficult to say whether they are, truly. Certainly, from the standpoint of general services hotels, motels, restaurants, stores—things once denied them . . . they are open wider than ever. Job opportunities in certain categories seem more existent. More blacks than ever before are in high salaried positions and holding down executive positions. A demand appears for more. The increase in blacks in elected and appointed positions has increased most significantly (and with greater unity more will succeed). The black entrepreneur is emerging. Development and renewal, in spite of the criticism of black removal, has provided better housing opportunities for blacks, albeit not enough. School integration is lifting the achievement level of Negro

students. And sports offer unusual and lucrative occupations for the black athlete.
❖ On the negative side, too many black ideologies and
solutions to the black problem exist. Some are obviously designed to confuse and to exploit and to keep
things in turmoil. The impression is that masses of
blacks are an integral and permanent part of an in-
centive-deadening welfare and relief system, which
has and is destroying their will to develop and care
for themselves, for the most part.
❖ In spite of improvements in housing, health facilities,
schools, and the like, black communities are crime-
ridden and rapidly decaying, particularly in the cases
of once flourishing business districts. Blacks are too
much a part of the drug scene. Entirely too many
blacks are in the penal institutions and involved in
the justice system processes; the economic cost and
burden stagger the imagination. More positive aspects are opportunities provided blacks by affirmative action programs across the nation and
opportunities for equity investment.

*What meaning does the idea of black advancement have for
you?*
❖ Black advancement, of course, means that we continue to close the gaps existing between our prerogatives and the prerogatives of whites. But more than
mere catch-up, black advancement means that black
people continue to explore and develop their own
consciousness and appreciation of who they are. Advancement is a better understanding of self and confi-
dence in self. Black advancement is an increasing
respect for other blacks.
❖ For blacks to come together themselves. No respect
until you can bring power and strength. It is not by

gift of government or morality but by numbers and collective solidarity that gains are made. Politically sophisticated, too, blacks. Until this happens, no good gains! Black past can help but can't go too far. Must now educate blacks to what the game is all about. Nationally!

❖ Black advancement must mean that the mean standard of living for all blacks will be three good meals daily, adequate health care when sick, safe and healthy housing, an education that is truly that (a tenth-grade black being able to function at that level or above), and no more cops killing and beating our folks.

What is the importance of black studies departments, programs, and courses in colleges and universities to black advancement/equality?

❖ Black studies programs can be important in the search for black survival and equality. If these programs are vigorous in the pursuit of knowledge by, about, and for black people, they can prepare blacks for the struggle against well-equipped whites in the real world. These programs can provide an environment that will encourage excellence in black scholarship in a wide variety of disciplines. Black studies will be important if they can encourage black youngsters to master science, technology, medicine, engineering, computers, accounting, law, oceanography, biology, etc. If, in the guise of blackness, they allow black youngsters to wallow in mediocre aspirations and achievement, they should be dismantled now!

❖ Black studies and programs have a tendency to eliminate the idea that only that which is Caucasian or white is important in American life. Race pride is important. Black studies and departments will result in black students having racial pride. Also, it will result in the majority race having greater respect for blacks by virtue of their having greater knowledge of Negro Americans and their heritage.

❖ The study (ethnic and black) can be very important in providing improved self-images of blacks to one another and to the larger community. They had never heard of a "nigger" being on city council before 1963. Until I see this or hear of it I won't think I can. These programs should provide this self-assurance to black students. I feel strongly that these departments should not be closed to others or run only by blacks. This is dangerous. Whites need it even more. They should flourish and integrate.

❖ Provides the black student with a sense of identity, self-respect, and dignity. He can take pride in his own worth and the worth of his predecessors. He can gain a better understanding of his own heritage, reasons for the conditions that affect the lives of his contemporaries, what improvements are needed, and how to accomplish them. He can understand better his role in the white world in which he ultimately must live and earn a living. He can enlighten the white world and become a source, a fountain of inspiration against continued racism and oppression. He has to be careful, in my opinion, to keep the benefits of black studies in their proper perspective.

Is capitalism a useful direction for black people in this country?

❖ Black capitalism is an important direction for black people because, like it or not, this country is a capitalistic country. If black people are to make economic progress, such progress will necessarily take place in a capitalist environment. A major handicap for us is that we do not have capital. We must therefore find ways to get capital.

❖ I can't conceive of black or white capitalism! Even in the South of yesteryear Negroes successfully operated insurance companies, coal yards, barbershops (for whites), undertaking establishments, farms, and other businesses. Many became wealthy. Black capitalism is a new name for something not at all new!

❖ This is a Nixon gimmick. Yet we live in a capitalist system. If blacks are to be equal in it, they must also be capitalists, meaning ownership, producing, etc., the entire range of resources. Not just working for somebody else, however. It can be a meaningful concept.

❖ Yes. But black capitalists must be prepared to perform in a highly competitive atmosphere. To succeed in this atmosphere they must be in the nature of supermen or willing to sacrifice short gains for longtime advantages. Also, it is questionable that black capitalism will make much of a dent in the black community on economic needs like jobs and wages. A limited number of black capitalists will succeed but not enough, I am afraid, to affect the overall problem of black unemployment.

What is your view of black radicals and their importance to black equality?

❖ Black and radical may well be redundant depending on how one defines either black or radical. But in the usual or commonly understood meaning, black radicals are an integral and not exclusive part of the struggle for black liberation and advancement. Black radicals can function as a continuing check on the integrity and consistency of our struggle for progress. They should always raise questions about how much progress we have really made and why. Black radicals should constantly remind us that our occasional victories may not have won the war. Black radicals should not presume to have all the answers. Even radicals can differ.

❖ The shouting of black radicals has been embarrassing to too many black Americans at times, particularly the more mature ones, but there can be no question but that their efforts have brought results. There were, and probably are at this time, many, many white Americans who had no conception of the true condition of Negroes. Most of them thought Negroes were happy and satisfied. The demands of the black radicals have resulted in the door of opportunity being partially opened by the majority. Inasmuch as the majority might be pushed just so far, how far no one knows, it might be well that the radical activity has somewhat subsided. We might suffer from repression.

❖ Black radicals (except for the so-called lunatic fringe) are a shock value. They tend to jolt, which is often necessary. Many have jolted and shocked with no apparent benefit to themselves but with doors opening in many cases that would not have opened otherwise. Many blacks owe their advancement to the action of radicals.

❖ The black radicals on a whole have been very important in the program for black equality. One significant accomplishment is helping open the doors for the advancement of the cause by the more responsible blacks. However, whites have played up black radicals in a manner and to an extent that makes for repression.

❖ They served a purpose initially: shock value and dramatizing the extent of black discontent. However, the subsequent violence and threats of violence have seriously damaged the cause of black equality and caused us to lose our forward momentum.

Is the fact that a number of blacks now hold elective office important to the general welfare of black people as a group?
❖ I, of course, feel that black elected officials are important to the general welfare of black people. Government is increasingly involved in more and more facets of all of our lives, from welfare for mothers, to government contracts for businesses, to the setting of economic policies, to the laws that might protect our rights. We are all more involved with political decisions. Blacks need to be a part of these decision-making processes.
❖ Very important. It gives status to the blacks who point to black representatives with pride. Further, it results in the majority having greater respect for blacks. To participate in government from the inside tends to open doors to jobs, to business, to public service in many fields for blacks.

What has been your major concern and effort as an elected official in the interest of racial advancement/equality?
❖ I have authored approximately eighty-five legislative proposals in this area. About fourteen are now state law.
❖ I assisted in the organization of a county human relations commission and was instrumental in securing funding for it from city council. It has become an effective force in the field of civil and human rights and in the creation of similar services in the county. My earlier efforts on open housing legislation failed but have since had the beneficial weight of state and federal legislation.

In your view, what are the major obstacles to election of blacks to public office?

❖ Probably the greatest difficulty facing black elected officials is the raising of money for campaign financing. For the same reason that blacks do not have surplus capital, blacks are not in a position to contribute to campaigns. Also, black officials who attempt to work for the benefit of the black community run into the strength of various vested interests. If a legislative program is proposed that would deliver benefits to blacks, there is the belief that somebody else's benefits would be reduced. The white economic structure is a major difficulty for us.

❖ Prejudice, lack of financial means to compete in campaigning, lack of political know-how.

❖ Entrenched interests, fragmented black community organization, and unity. Black indifference leading to failure to register, vote, and support qualified candidates. Inability of black elected officials to deliver in the first stages of the exercise of power. Black impatience with the system. Polarization of the conservative white vote out of fear of radical changes. The tendency on the part of the black community to produce too many candidates and thus divide the vote, already meager.

End of Interviewee Comments

It has been argued, especially by radical spokesmen, that the cause of racial equality is helped very little by blacks who hold public office because they invariably fail to reflect the interests of black people. They become, it is said, part of the problem rather than part of the solution, to borrow an overworked comment from Eldridge Cleaver's repertoire. The responses of black officials to the issues cited above reveal them to be heavily aware of persisting racism and of the persistent need to mobilize against it. In other words, the data contradict this cliche.

Black Officeholders and the Legislative Process

Alvin Sokolow did a comparative study of black and white legislators in California, focusing on the year 1969.[4] At that time there were six black members of the state legislature. The following were major points made in the Sokolow study: (1) the black members of the California legislature sponsored more bills, on average, than any of the selected groups of white assemblymen; (2) the black members came last in the ratio of bills proposed to bills passed; (3) the legislation sponsored by blacks was more people-oriented than the legislation of their white colleagues.

Although the present study did not replicate Sokolow's study, some of the findings do confirm his. This is especially true regarding the third item. Eight black legislators were asked to list and describe the three most important legislative proposals made by them since their terms as elected officeholders. Some of their responses are listed below. The respondents included local and state officials and U.S. congressional officials.

❖ State-operated lottery (ACA 18 of 1973) to allow the legislature to authorize a state-operated lottery through a ballot proposition. Currently before the Committee on Constitutional Amendments.

❖ Replacement Housing Act (AB 1072 Chapter 953 of 1968) to authorize the department of public works to provide relocation assistance to low-income families who are displaced as a result of freeway or highway construction. Adopted and enacted on August 1, 1968.

❖ Urban Community Schools Act (as proposed in AB 781 and 782 of 1970) to provide special attention to educational priorities for schools in economically disadvantaged areas to upgrade the quality of education through demonstration projects and to allow parental participation in educational policy decision-making for alternative programs. Vetoed by the governor in 1970.

❖ Human Relations Ordinance to establish a human relations commission/bureau for Los Angeles to assist in resolving potentially explosive community conflicts, including areas of housing, health and welfare, police-community relations, employment, education, and youth. Adopted and enacted.

❖ Employee Relations Ordinance to establish policies and procedures for administration of employee relations in city government including recognition of employee organizations and resolution of disputes. Adopted and enacted.

❖ Contract Compliance Ordinance to set forth certain provisions pertaining to nondiscrimination in employment and recruitment of minorities in the performance of certain city construction contracts. Adopted and enacted.

❖ Central City Plan to completely revise plans for the development of the central city. Adopted and enacted.

❖ Street Lighting Assessment to light up all of the streets in the southern part of Ninth District. Adopted and enacted.

❖ Salary Adjustment for Low-Paid Employees to adjust the salaries for low-paid employees along with an adjustment for those in the upper bracket. Adopted and enacted.

❖ Establishment of Citizens Committee to review police

practices. Adopted by the city council following the killing of a black youth by a city policeman in December 1972. Resolution authorized mayor to appoint a twenty-five-member citizens committee to investigate police practices throughout the city. There is contention in black and brown segments of the community that there are differences in police activities and protection for these sections from the community at large. Committee still meeting to develop its report. Delayed. Not yet enacted.

It is clear from the foregoing legislative proposals that what Sokolow referred to as a people orientation is predominant. Notably, this sample of black legislative efforts is not restricted to the state legislature. It applies as well to local government. By far the majority of the legislative proposals cited by these officials seek to meet the needs of the nonaffluent, inarticulate elements of the population. Black legislators show a wide departure as a group from their white legislative colleagues. Some of these proposals have already initiated significant change throughout the state. These data also show continued awareness of and resistance to racism by these elected black officials and are at variance with the opinion of black politicians held by Haynes Walton, Jr.[6] Walton argues, essentially, that their efforts may be insufficient to meet the growing dissatisfaction of the black community. It would appear that this group is moving significantly in the direction of making significant change. Black legislative efforts attempt to address themselves to people programs. This fact bears a direct relationship to the importance of this group for social change, which I shall address in a subsequent chapter.

Questions for Review and Further Study

1. What is the social background of black officeholders in California?

2. What is their view of black studies departments, black radicals, and capitalism?

3. In what metropolitan area has black influence been most highly developed in California? How and when did this influence and development come about?

4. What are some of the legislative enactments proposed by black legislators in California?

5. How do black legislative proposals differ from those of white legislators according to Sokolow?

6. Assuming this difference to be fact, how would you account for it?

Notes

1. See the *National Roster of Black Elected Officials* (Joint Center for Political Studies, Washington, D.C., 1970). Several volumes of this publication were used as data sources for this chapter. Table 5.1 was made possible by data presented in volumes 8 and 10 of this publication series.

2. See *Black Americans, A Chartbook* (Washington, D.C.: U.S. Department of Labor, 1970).

3. See 1970 U.S. Census Advance Report on Los Angeles, California, city and county populations.

4. Alvin Sokolow, "Black Member White Legislature," *The Black Politician* (Fall 1971), pp. 23-29.

5. Beeman C. Patterson, "Political Action and Negroes in Los Angeles," *Phylon* (Summer 1969), pp. 170-83.

6. Haynes Walton, Jr., *Black Politics* (New York: Lippincott, 1972), p. 218.

6

POLITICAL GAINS

In 1944 one of the devastating, malicious, and crippling racist realities was legally struck down. This was the all-white primary, which had essentially barred blacks from public office-holding since its inception during the late nineteenth century. Shortly after 1944 there began a slow increase in registration and voting by blacks. Twenty years passed, however, before significant registration and voting changes took place. This was but a few years ago.

Gradual increments in political participation by blacks over time are reflected in data on Virginia. The following table on voter eligibility from 1941 through 1947 shows top limits of possible registration and voting. These are the numbers of blacks who had met existing poll tax requirements designed specifically to discourage them.[1]

Poll Tax Requirement

1941	25,411
1942	28,845
1943	32,504
1944	41,579
1945	44,051
1946	48,448
1947	57,796

The pattern for Virginia during these years was rather typical for the South. Some small increases are noted in political participation by 1947. Yet, even then, the highest proportion of the adult black population in the South qualified to vote was one-fourth of its potential. This, as the next table shows, was in Tennessee.[2]

These estimates are in glaring contrast to more recent data on registration and voting by southern blacks. Two papers issued by the Voter Registration Project show this contrast. In a series of elections in the South in 1970 blacks gained considerably. More than 110 black candidates, out of 370 persons seeking public office, were elected in the South in November. This brought the total number of black elected officials in the South to 665.[3] Voter registration in the region increased by 212,000 from 1968 to 1970.

Qualified Black Voting Population

Alabama	6,000	1.2 (%)
Arkansas	47,000	17.3
Florida	49,000	15.4
Georgia	125,000	18.8
Louisiana	10,000	2.6
Mississippi	5,000	0.9
North Carolina	75,000	15.2
South Carolina	50,000	13.0
Tennessee	80,000	25.8

There were an estimated five million voting-age blacks in the South, only 30 percent of whom were registered in 1962, the year the Voter Education Project began. From 1962 through 1964 black registration in the South increased by 700,000. With enactment of the Voting Rights Act of 1965 more rapid progress was made. For example, in 1962 less than one-tenth of the black voting-age population was registered to vote in Mississippi. There were at that time less than

50 black elected officials in the South. Within a year of the act's enactment, percentages of black voter registration in some states rose 50 to 60 percent.[4] In Mississippi, black voters increased from 28,000 to over 175,000. By 1971 there were over 700 black elected officials in the South, several of whom were elected in Mississippi.

The full potential for black political strength in the South has not been realized even today. More than two and one-half million voting-age blacks remain unregistered. Also, the voting participation record of those registered is often less than it could be. Yet, John Lewis, a former executive director of the Voter Registration Project and now a congressman, is optimistic regarding the political power of blacks:

> The problems facing blacks in this country are enormous, but through the political arena black people can continue to struggle for the power necessary to participate in the decisions that affect their lives. The choice is clear. Blacks, standing on the verge of wielding tremendous regional, national, and international power, can see their mission realized and their dreams fulfilled only if there is immediate and substantial support for continual voter registration, organized efforts toward citizenship and voter education, and increased assistance to black elected officials.[5]

Adaptation II[6]

> *Adaptation II, which follows, is from a study by the American Council on Education. It was published in 1988 with the official title One-Third of a Nation. I have selected portions of this study that deal with political participation and that bear on the major hypothesis of this book.*

One Third of a Nation

Political Participation. Until the l960s, black political activity was primarily directed toward the attainment of basic democratic rights. Exclusion of black Americans from voting and office-holding meant that blacks had to seek political and civil rights through protest and litigation. The civil rights movement arose out of long-standing grievances and aspirations. It was based on strong networks of local organizations and given a clear focus and direction by articulate leadership. Because most blacks were unable to vote, move freely, or buy and sell property as they wished, their efforts were directed to the objective of attaining these basic rights of citizenship. During the civil rights movement, civic equality and political liberty came to be viewed by increasing percentages of Americans as basic human rights that blacks should enjoy. By the 1960s, the federal executive branch and a congressional coalition backed by a sufficient public opinion was finally able to legislate black civil equality.

Active participation by blacks in American political life has had a major impact on their role in the society. The number of black elected officials has risen from a few dozen in 1940 to over 6,800 in 1988. However, blacks constitute only about 1.5 percent of all elected officials. The election of black officials does result in public sector jobs and more senior positions for blacks in appropriate public office.

The black proportion of federal, state, and local public administrators rose from less than 1 percent in 1940 to 8 percent in 1980; even so, it was less than blacks' 13 percent proportion of the U.S. population. As measured by the proportion of delegates to the national party conventions, black participation in the political party organizations has increased dramatically among Democrats since 1940, although black participation in Republican party affairs, after declining during the 1960s and 1970s, has returned to be about the same level as in 1940.

Blacks' desires for political rights were not merely based on abstract principles of equality, but also on the practical fruits of political participation. Blacks sought democratic rights because they believed that direct access to political institutions through voting, lobbying, and office-holding would lead to greater material equality between themselves and the rest of society. However, changes in blacks' socioeconomic status, although complex, have not attained levels commensurate to black-white equality with respect to civil rights. But black influence in the political sector has been an important factor in determining many of the important gains that have occurred.

In particular, the extensive development of equal opportunity law has improved the status of blacks (as well as that of women and other minorities) in the areas of education, occupation, health care, criminal justice, and business enterprise.

Blacks have also benefited from increased public-sector provision of job training, health care, social security, and other cash and in-kind benefit programs.

Although political participation has not been the only important determinant of changes in black opportunities, resulting alterations in American politics have had influence in many areas of life. A review of blacks' status shows that increased civil rights have been important in all areas of society.

Conclusion. After our intensive review, the committee has a concluding reflection on the wider implications of the finding. We believe it is consistent with the research data and the best available historical understandings of how American society functions.

To survive, every society has to adapt to its environment and maintain its resources over time. It must cope with the basic economic problem—"the efficient allocation of scarce resources"—as well as with its external relations with other societies. Every society must also develop practical arrangements for the internal distribution of power, economic goods, and social prestige and respect. Finally, societies over the long term must safeguard their own legitimacy and historical meaning. These latter tasks of social integration and cultural maintenance tend to be discounted and neglected in a task-oriented society that focuses attention on short-term payoffs.

In the United States of the coming decades, any agenda for these basic needs will have to give high priority to dealing with the fissures that have been created by the history of relations among black and white Americans.

Our review leads us to believe that now is an appropriate time for serious national effort to grasp the means at hand to accomplish this vital assignment.

End of Adaptation

The next adaptation presents some empirical evidence of political gains over the past few years. As the data show, gains made have progressively increased each year although the rate of gain has varied.

Adaptation III[7]

Adaptation III presents some recent empirical specifics as of 1988 regarding black elected officials. This includes state, federal, and local politics; men and women; and geographic areas of the country. These data come from the annual review of black politics conducted by the Joint Center for Political Studies, Washington, D.C.

Black Elected Officials

An Overview. The Joint Center for Political Studies (JCPS) first began compiling data on the number of black elected officials (BEOs) in the United States in 1970. Since then, the number of blacks elected to public office has grown steadily each year. This volume shows that last year was no exception. Between January 1987 and January 1988, the number of black elected officials rose from 6,681 to 6,829 (an increase of 148, or 2.2 percent. Increases occurred in seventeen states and the Virgin Islands, and decreases occurred in sixteen states and the District of Columbia. No change took place in seventeen states.

Fifty-four blacks were elected to positions that blacks had never won before. Forty-four (81 percent) of these ground-breaking elections took place in the South, five (9.3 percent) in the North Central region, and five (9.3 percent) in the Northeast.

Despite these overall gains and the increasing visibility of black elected officials, less than 1.5 percent of all elective offices in the United States are held by black Americans, who constitute 11 percent of the nation's voting-age population. Moreover, the growth rate of black elected officials was lower last year than in 1987. Thus, although the number of blacks in public office in 1988 is higher than ever before, much progress remains to be made.

Geographic Distribution. The geographic distribution of black elected officials clearly parallels the general distribution of the black population throughout the United States. The South contains 52.8 percent of the country's black population and 65.5 percent of all black elected officeholders. The second largest concentration of BEOs, 18.9 percent, is found in the North Central region, where 19.8 percent of the black population lives. The Northeast, with 18.5 percent of the total black population, has 10.2 percent of the BEOs.

State by state comparisons show a similar correlation between the black voting-age population and the number of black elected officials. Mississippi, which has the largest number of BEOs, is the state with the highest proportion of voting-age blacks (30.8 percent of the total electorate). In the District of Columbia, where blacks constitute 66.6 percent of the voting-age population, 65.9 percent of all elected officials are black. Conversely, there still are no black elected officials in Idaho, Montana, and North Dakota, where blacks constitute less than 0.5 percent of the total population in each state.

The ten states with the largest contingents of black elected officials are Mississippi (578), Louisiana (524), Georgia (456), Illinois (443), Alabama (442), North Carolina (428), South Carolina (352), Arkansas (326), Michigan (316), and Texas (300). These states all share two characteristics: (1) blacks constitute at least 11 percent of the state's voting age population, and (2) women make up more than 12 percent of the state's BEO.

Female Black Elected Officials. JCPS first began compiling data about female black elected officials in 1975. Since then, their number has more than tripled, growing from 530 to 1,625 by 1987. The growth rate of these female officials has been higher than the rate for all BEOs in each year since 1975.

The distribution of black female officeholders is similar to that of BEOs as a whole. More than half of these female officials serve in the District of Columbia (105) and nine states: Illinois (122), Mississippi (103), California (94), Michigan (93), Alabama (88), New York (88), Georgia (84), South Carolina (80), and Louisiana (73).

Since 1975, the gap between male and female BEOs has narrowed. In 1975, there were 5.7 times more men than women among black elected officials. By 1988 there were 3.2 times more men than women. Among both men and women, the largest number hold offices in the municipal category followed by offices in education. However, the third largest number of female BEOs are in judicial offices, whereas the third largest number of male BEOs are in county offices.

Twelve women, already in elective office, were elected to higher positions last year. One notable example is Yvonne B. Miller of Norfolk, Virginia. Miller became the first black woman elected to the Virginia State House in 1984, and became Virginia's first black female state senator in 1987.

Federal. Blacks hold twenty-three seats in the House of Representatives. (District of Columbia Del. Walter Fauntroy, who is included in this number, is among the four nonvoting members of the House.)

The geographic distribution of black congresspersons is unlike that of the majority of all other black officeholders, who are primarily from the South. Only six (26.1 percent) of them are from the South, although eight (34.8 percent) are from the North Central states of Illinois, Michigan, Missouri, and Ohio. Five are from the Northeast, and four are from the West.

Fourteen members (61 percent) of the Congressional Black Caucus (CBC) were elected from majority-black districts. Only two (Ronald Dellums of California and Alan Wheat of Missouri) are from districts where whites constitute the vast majority of the voting-age population. The remaining seven members of the CBC are from districts that have large concentrations of both blacks and Hispanics.

State. The number of black state legislators increased slightly, from 410 in January 1987, to 413 in January 1988, and the number of black statewide executives remained the same. At the statewide level there are still seven blacks in office: James Lewis, state treasurer of New Mexico; Francisco Borges, state treasurer of Connecticut; Roland Burris, comptroller of Illinois; Richard Austin, secretary of state of Michigan; L. Douglas Wilder, lieutenant governor of Virginia; and Alexander Farrelly and Derek Hodge, governor and lieutenant governor, respectively, of the Virgin Islands.

Substate Regional. Five regional transit and hospital board officials in California, along with sixteen education officials in the Virgin Islands and one conservation district official in North Carolina, make up the total of twenty-two black holders of elective positions in substate regional government. Generally, the responsibilities of these officials include administering the activities of at least two counties or municipalities and overseeing the provision of services such as transportation, park maintenance, fire protection, education, and recreation.

County. Eighteen blacks (a 2.5 percent increase) were newly elected to county offices bringing the total to 742. Eighty-three percent of all county-level BEOs are in the South, and of these, ten were elected to offices that blacks had not previously held.

Municipal. Of all black elected officials, 4 to 9 percent hold municipal positions. As of January 1988, 3,341 had been sworn into office, up from 3,219 the year before. The largest municipal subgroup is councilmembers (2,621), followed by mayors (301).

The number of blacks who serve as mayors in cities with populations over 50,000 decreased, from 34 to 28. The six who left office are: Harvey Gant of Charlotte, N.C.; James A. Sharp, Jr. of Flint, Mich.; Jack McLean of Tallahassee, Fla.; Lawrence D. Crawford of Saginaw, Mich.; Samuel A. Thomas of West Palm Beach, Fla.; and James W. Holley III of Portsmouth, Va. Holley was recalled, the other five lost re-election bids and all were replaced by white officials.

In these cities with populations of 50,000 or more, four black mayors were elected (three by popular vote, one through a special city council election) to offices previously held by blacks. They are: Kurt Schmoke of Baltimore, Md.; Thomas Barnes of Gary, Ind.; Carrie S. Perry of Hartford, Conn.; and Eugene Sawyer, who was chosen to succeed the late Mayor Harold Washington in a special Chicago City Council election.

Judicial and Law Enforcement. There are 738 (up from 728) black elected officials in this category: 689 in judicial offices and forty-nine in law enforcement offices. Black judges in eight states (Alabama, California, Florida, Maryland, Michigan, Mississippi, North Carolina, and Pennsylvania) preside over state courts of last resort.

Education. Between February 1987 and January 1988, the number of blacks elected to education offices increased by three (less than 1 percent). The largest subgroup in this category is local school board members, who constitute 95 percent (1,476) of all BEOs in education offices and over 20 percent of the total number of BEOs. Forty-five BEOs hold offices on university and college boards.

There are fourteen black elected school superintendents, all of them in the South. Mississippi, Alabama, Florida, and Georgia each have two.

Conclusion. Although blacks continued to make progress in winning public office between January 1987 and January 1988, the annual growth rate continued its decline since the mid-1970s. The growth rate was only about half that of the previous year. This declining growth rate may be attributed to a number of factors, including at-large elections and impediments to voter registration. The quest for increased black voter participation, and, in turn, increased black representation, led to several important judicial actions and decisions in 1987. In Danville, Illinois, blacks won a voting rights suit challenging at-large elections. This led to the election of two blacks to Danville's city council. This was the first time a black was elected to that body since the 1920s. In Hamilton County, Ohio, a suit to ensure the election of blacks by changing judicial elections from an at-large to a district system was brought by Ohio State Rep. William Mallory (D-Cincinnati) and others. As a result, a black woman was elected county judge. In Louisiana, the U.S. Fifth Circuit Court of Appeals, in *Chisholm v. Edwards* broke down invidious barriers to the selection of black judges when it ruled that the Voting Rights Act may be used to ensure that minority voting strength is not diluted in judicial elections. And in Mississippi, the first district court, in *Operation PUSH v. Allain* struck down discriminatory dual-location voter registration statutes and practices that had allowed county clerks to limit the times when registration can take place.

To a considerable extent, future increases in the numbers of black elected officials will depend upon the success of continuing efforts to eliminate all devices and tactics that seek to disenfranchise minorities or to dilute their votes.

Questions for Review and Further Study

1. What was the "all-white primary" and how did it affect race relations in the United States?

2. How effective is black use of the ballot in national and city elections?

3. What are the trends in elections of blacks to public office from predominantly black election districts? From predominantly white election districts?

4. How far from proportional is the number of black elected officials nationally?

5. What is the current trend in election of blacks to public office?

Notes

1. V. O. Key, *Southern Politics in State and Nation* (New York: Knopf, 1949).

2. Ibid., Ch. 24.

3. *What Happened in the South*, 1970, publication of the Voter Education Project, Atlanta, Ga.

4. *Voter Registration in the South*, 1965, publication of the Voter Education Project, Atlanta, Ga.

5. *What Happened in the South, 1970.*

6. For the complete study see National Research Council *A Common Destiny: Blacks and American Society* (Washington, D.C.: National Academy Press, 1989).

7. For the complete study see *Black Elected Officials: A National Roster* (Washington D.C.: Joint Center for Political Studies, 1988).

7

WAGE AND EMPLOYMENT GAINS

In the areas of employment and income there have been gains in recent years though they do not reflect statistical parity with whites.

The percentage of nonwhites employed as professional, technical, and kindred workers rose from 11.1 percent in 1960 to 17.9 percent in 1970. The comparable figure for whites was 23.9 percent in 1960 and 29.5 percent in 1970.[1] The rate of gain was slightly higher for nonwhites than for whites.

There was also a large percentage increase in the number of nonwhites who are clerical and kindred workers. In 1960 nonwhites were 13.4 percent of this group, whereas by 1970 they were 26.6 percent. Whites in the same category increased from 39.2 percent in 1960 to 42.0 percent in 1970. There was also a slight increase in rate of gain by nonwhites over whites in the crucial category of craftsmen, foremen, and kindred workers. Notable also is a decline in the proportion of nonwhites in the traditionally low-paying and low-prestige occupational categories. Nonwhites as laborers declined from 21.0 percent in 1960 to 14.2 percent in 1970. The percentage of whites in the same category remained roughly stable. As a percentage of private household work-

141

ers, nonwhites declined from 34.9 percent in 1960 to 14.5 percent in 1970.

In 1960 black families nationwide earned about 54 percent as much as white families, whereas by 1970 it was 61 percent.[2] The income level of black husband-wife families in the decade 1960-70 went from 57 percent of average white family income to 72 percent. More dramatic income gain was made by young northern two-parent black families. The 532,000 northern two-parent black families under age 35 averaged 91 percent of the income of their white counterparts. In 1960 this group averaged only 62 percent of the income of their white counterparts.

It has been reported that at the 1940 to 1960 rate of gain, black males as professional, technical, and kindred workers will not reach equality with whites for 530 years.[3] The general occupational gap is said to be so wide and closing so slowly that it is not likely to disappear within the next century unless the rate of gain for blacks sharply increases. Some acceleration did take place in the 1960s.

I do not argue that the increments of gain just described are themselves sufficient to bring about racial equality in the United States. They are, rather, necessary means that further strengthen the process by which, ultimately, racial equality can be achieved. Certainly there is now the beginning of a higher level of technical, professional, and managerial competence among blacks than ever before. The point is that these are beginnings. These beginnings should be extensively expanded during the few remaining years of this century, based largely on numerical increases of nonwhites and on the increase in the number of those who get into and through the rigors of higher education.

By the end of the century, the strength, here defined as competitive capability, of black Americans should be enormously greater than it is currently. Such competitive capability is a necessary precondition for the next and most crucial decades during which nonwhites are likely to become full members of this society. That is, the transition to full class status, now in its very beginning, will then be far along. The transition will mark a major break in the traditional oscillation of black history between gain and loss. It will also mark the complete decline of caste-based status and identity as competence and achievement predominate in black communities and in the allocation of jobs and income.

A more complete discussion of income, jobs, and labor force participation by blacks is provided in a recent study by Smith and Welch.[4] Portions of this study make up Adaptation IV, which now follows.

Adaptation IV

> *This adaptation comes from a 1986 study by two researchers of the Rand Corporation: James P. Smith and Finis R. Welch. It is entitled Closing the Gap: Forty Years of Economic Progress for Blacks.*

Closing the Gap

Summary. Forty years ago Gunnar Myrdal published his masterwork on race relations in America, *An American Dilemma.* He began his chapter on the economic situation of blacks with the following summary:

> The economic situation of the Negroes in America is pathological. Except for a small minority enjoying upper or middle class status, the masses of American Negroes, in the rural South and in the segregated slum quarters in Southern cities, are destitute. They own little property; even their household goods are mostly inadequate and dilapidated. Their incomes are not only low but irregular. They thus live from day to day and have scant security for the future. Their entire culture and their individual interests and strivings are narrow.

In the forty years since Myrdal's bleak assessment, this country has gone through a series of dramatic and far-reaching changes. The economy shifted from its traditional agricultural and manufacturing base to one that is service and technology oriented. As a part of this shift, during the 1950s a major technological advance eliminated the system of black sharecropping in cotton, the primary economic activity of Southern blacks since the Civil War. As a result, large numbers of southern rural blacks accelerated the move to the inner cities of the North, eventually transforming the black population from predominately rural to largely urban. During the 1970s, the American economic structure suffered additional shocks. Because of increased international competition, the older industrialized sectors of the Northeast and North Central states, where blacks had made hard-won advances, were particularly hard hit.

Racial tensions have persisted throughout this forty-year period. The civil rights movement achieved stunning judicial and legislative successes in the 1950s and 1960s, partly by appealing to the moral conscience of the nation. The Civil Rights Act of 1964 and subsequent executive orders prohibited employment discrimination on the basis of race. Today, many believe that the civil rights movement has lost its way as it has attempted to move beyond guaranteed civil and political rights to strive toward economic equity. Others charge that it has also lost the moral high ground because of repeated accusations that it has defended reverse discrimination. Controversy also besets affirmative action, the legislative program for employment antidiscrimination and enforcement. Many scholars now question whether affirmative action has even achieved its primary aim of improving wages and empoyment for minorities.

Postwar progress in race relations has been marred by race riots in American cities. In reaction to these riots, twenty years after Myrdal wrote An American Dilemma, a presidential commission issued the Kerner Report. Its portrait of black America was as bleak as that of Myrdal two decades earlier. Its pessimism about the economic status of blacks was compounded by its sense of hopelessness about the prospects for the future.

That pessimism and the pervasiveness of black poverty prodded government to devise an elaborate system of publicly financed assistance that in some way now touches a majority of blacks. The primary aim was to provide a safety net, protecting black families from the worst ravages of poverty; but critics have charged that the safety net evolved into a web, trapping blacks into a self-perpetuating culture of poverty.

This research project was based on a conviction that a reassessment is made possible by the recent 1980 census micro data file as well as the newly released micro data files for the 1940 and 1950 censuses. These data allowed us to conduct the most comprehensive examination of the economic status of black America since Myrdal. In doing so, we have found a partial American resolution to his American Dilemma.

We took up several issues in this report. Our most basic concern was whether the economic lot of black men has improved significantly since Myrdal's day. We went beyond that issue by also examining whether economic progress has touched all parts of the black community. We dealt also with the thorny problem of isolating the underlying causes of black economic progress. We sought to determine, for example, the extent to which education and its quality, migration to the North, and affirmative action have affected the economic progress of blacks. Finally, we looked to the future and made an assessment about the likelihood of further racial economic progress.

Signs of Progress. Several salient trends in the size of the racial wage gap between 1940 and 1980 were identified in this report. Most important, this forty-year record clearly points to a significant and quantitatively large improvement in the relative economic status of black men. In 1940, the typical black male earned around $4,500 (in 1984 dollars); a similarly employed black male earned almost $19,000 by 1980. Between 1940 and 1980, black male wages increased 52 percent faster than white. The typical black male worker in 1940 earned only 43 percent as much as his white counterpart; by 1980, the figure was 73 percent.

The extent of the improvement in the relative economic

status of blacks over the last forty years is obviously impressive. This improvement is largely an untold story, belying the widely held view that the relative economic position of blacks in America has been stagnant. However, one must remember that even in 1980, black male incomes still significantly lagged behind those of whites.

We also investigated the notion that the wage gains achieved by black men would disappear over their work careers. Some observers have expressed concern that significant parts of these wage gains would eventually be lost as competition between the races intensifies over job careers. However, the reality is that, if anything, black men actually improved their status relative to whites as their respective careers unfolded. Among every cohort of workers between 1940 and 1980, black men narrowed the gap between their incomes and those of their white contemporaries as their careers evolved.

The Distribution of Black Economic Progress. As part of our project, we examined the distribution of these wage gains within the black male population. Our concern was that these average labor market gains were heavily skewed, with some blacks receiving the bulk of the benefits, leaving large numbers of black men behind. The evidence does not support this view.

Whether we distinguish among low- or middle-income blacks, between the old and the young, or the more and less educated, the incomes of black men have risen relative to comparable whites. The only group of working black males whose relative wage gains could accurately be characterized as small were those within the bottom 10 percent of the black income distribution. Although all blacks participated in this economic progress, some groups did gain more than others. For example, younger blacks gained more relative to whites than did more experienced black workers. And when we separated our samples by education class, we found that col-lege-educated blacks enjoyed the largest wage improvement.

Our study of income distributions yielded a number of important findings. If income is the measuring rod, black and white men were indeed divided into two separate and unequal societies in 1940. In that year, only one in twelve black men earned incomes larger than that of the average white. While by no means identical, these two income distri-butions have converged sharply across these forty years. By 1980, 29 percent of working black men had incomes above that of the median white.

Our research simultaneously illustrates the persistence of black poverty, the growth of the black middle class, and the emergence of a noneligible black upper class. In 1940, three-quarters of black men were destitute, with little hope that their lot or even that of their children would soon im-prove. The black middle class in 1940 was correspondingly small, counting among its members only one in five black men. At the other extreme, the black economic elite resem-bled an exclusive white club.

The changes over the last forty years were dramatic. Fully 20 percent of working black men in 1980 were still part of the poor black underclass, a reminder that many blacks remained left out and left behind. But placed in historical perspective, such figures still represent enormous progress toward eradicating black poverty. Political rhetoric on the race issue must eventually balance two compelling truths. America has made considerable strides in reducing black poverty; but by the standards of a just society, black poverty remains at unacceptably high levels.

However, the real story of the last forty years has been the emergence of the black middle class, whose income gains have been real and substantial. The growth in the size of the black middle class was so spectacular that as a group it outnumbers the black poor. Finally, for the first time in

American history, a sizable number of black men are economically better off than white middle-class America. During the last twenty years alone, the odds of a black man penetrating the ranks of the economic elite increased tenfold.

Causes of the Narrowing Wage Gap. In this report, we tried to quantify how much of the closing of the racial gap was due to black gains in education and its quality, and how much should be attributed to migration and the resurgence of the southern economy. First, we explored schooling's role in promoting black economic mobility and in explaining the closing of the racial wage gap. Many observers have disputed the historical importance of schools as a vehicle for achieving pay equity. Their claim is based largely on two beliefs. First, they point to a series of historical studies showing that black income benefits from schooling were negligible. They also argue that long-term advances in black education did not produce any closing of the racial income gap, at least until the mid-1960s. In this report, we demonstrate that black schools have played a far more fundamental role in shaping the economic history of blacks than these claims would suggest.

Our evidence began with a description of some prominent patterns associated with racial wage ratios across schooling classes. Racial wage disparities within education levels have historically been quite large. Evaluated at the same amount of schooling, black male wages averaged 50 to 55 percent of those of white men. By 1980, comparably educated black men earned 75 to 82 percent as much as white men. These wage ratios were ten percentage points higher than the aggregate ratio across all schooling groups in those years. That contrast informs us that education does play a significant role in explaining part of the racial wage gap. However, it also warns us that simply equalizing the number of years of schooling alone would leave a sizable racial wage gap left unexplained.

Across the full forty-year period, the two dimensions of education that closed the racial wage gap in a quantitatively significant way were the narrowing of education disparities between the races and the improving economic return to black schooling.

Agriculture. Forty years ago, the traditional system of share-cropping in southern cotton still dominated the economic activities of blacks. By 1940, one-third of all black men were still employed in agriculture. But the changes after 1940, and particularly between 1940 and 1960, were swift. As a percent of the total work force, black agricultural employment fell by 70 percent between 1940 and 1960. By 1960, only one in ten black workers worked on the farm, with rates even lower among young black workers. And in 1970, black farm employment, particularly among young workers, was a thing of the past. We can now safely describe for the first time in American history the economic role of blacks with no mention of agriculture.

There were long-term trends already in place in 1940 that were shifting the black labor force out of agriculture, but this process accelerated markedly during the 1950s. Since the Civil War, cotton cultivation had remained a labor-intensive process.

The technological change that would revolutionize black agriculture was the introduction of the mechanical cotton picker. In 1950, over 90 percent of all cotton produced in the United States was picked by hand. Twelve years later, in 1962, over 70 percent was picked by machine.

These changes in the methods of cultivation reduced the demand for black labor in southern agriculture and also ended the system of tenant sharecropping. One of the consequences of ending the system of tenant farming is that there was a switch from tenants to hired wage labor. As a result of the use of the cotton picker, output per man rose by 238 percent between 1950 and 1970 in a period during which total farm output increased by 36 percent.

As a consequence, during the 1950s, there was a sharp decline in the demand for a largely southern black labor force in cotton. This gave additional impetus to the migration of young southern blacks to the North. There were negative short-run consequences, but positive long-run effects. In the short run, this reduction in demand for black workers temporarily reduced black incomes. In our view, this is the primary reason why the 1950s were a temporary departure from the long-run trend toward improving economic status of blacks. However, the long-run effects were quite different. Blacks were able to end their dependence on low-wage southern agriculture and become more integrated into a wider scope of American economic activity.

Labor Market Participation. In spite of the improvement in their labor market opportunities, an increasing number of black men have dropped out of the labor force in the middle of their careers. For both races, the fraction of men who worked at least one year has remained basically stable from 1940 to 1970. However, these participation rates declined sharply after 1970 and did so at a much more rapid rate among black men. For example, black labor-force participation rates fell by almost six percentage points among men 36 to 45 years old, four times the decline observed among whites. The drop is even steeper among those 46 to 54 years old, where black labor-force participation rates fell by ten percentage points. Once again, the fraction of black men who left the labor force far exceeds that of white men. Within each race, the sharpest declines in labor market work occurred among the less educated.

Most economic research has indicated that the increased

generosity of the Social Security Disability Program was the primary cause of this decline in market participation among mature men. The concentration of these falling participation rates among blacks and among the less educated suggests that the men who dropped out of the labor force had lower incomes than those who remained. Because of this correlation with income, these declining participation rates could distort observed trends in black-white wages during the 1970-80 period. In particular, some have argued that these supply-side reductions in the relative number of working black men was an important cause of the post-1965 rise in the relative income of blacks, at least among older workers. In a nutshell, the argument is that many low-income blacks left the labor market between 1970 and 1980. As a result, the wages of the black work force (which now excludes those low-wage blacks) would artificially rise.

Our research attempted to test this hypothesis. Black-white male wage ratios in 1980 were adjusted for the more rapid declines in labor force participation among blacks and among the less educated. We also adjusted for the fact that, within education groups, wages of dropouts are less than the wages of those who remained in the labor force. These adjustments explain a very minor part of the observed increase in black-white male wages between 1970 and 1980 among older men.

The increasing tendency of many middle-aged black men to drop out of the labor force is an important and neglected social problem. By severing their connection with the labor force, they are forfeiting opportunities for economic self-reliance and advancement. However, our research indicates that this problem, although important for other reasons, did not significantly affect trends in the racial wage gap.

Affirmative Action. Affirmative action still dominates the political debate concerning governmental labor market policy regarding race. This debate began with the passage of the 1964 Civil Rights Act, which was aimed at eliminating employment discrimination against protected minority groups. American blacks, who had endured centuries of blatant and intense discrimination, were the principal group that this legislation was meant to protect. Since the Civil Rights Act prohibited discrimination on the basis of race and sex on all major terms of employment such as pay, promotion, hiring, training, and termination, the protection was quite broad.

Two governmental agencies have been given the primary responsibilty to enforce affirmative action. The Equal Employment Opportunity Commission (EEOC) was set up to monitor compliance with the provisions of the 1964 Civil Rights Act. All private sector firms with 100 or more employees were required to report to EEOC on the numbers of minorities employed and the types of jobs they held. The second major federal enforcement agency was the Office of Federal Contract Compliance Program (OFCCP). This agency was established by a 1965 Executive Order (No. 11246) and was given the primary responsibility of monitoring discrimination and enforcing penalties among government contractors.

Our research highlighted two possible labor market effects of affirmative action. The first question we asked was whether affirmative action significantly altered the firms where black men worked and the jobs they were able to obtain. The second question dealt with the wage side of work. Put simply, How has affirmative action affected the incomes of black men?

Because only establishments with 100 or more employees must report to EEOC, affirmative action reporting coverage varies widely across industries. For example, coverage is almost universal in the large-scale durable manufacturing goods sector. On the other hand, less than 10 percent of workers are covered in the retail trade, personnel services, and construction industries, where small establishments are common. As a result, firms can be divided into three sectors: (1) federal contractors, (2) other EEOC reporting firms, and (3) those firms not covered by EEOC or OFCCP.

It may be surprising to learn that only about half of the nongovernment, noneducation workforce is directly covered by affirmative action. In the same vein, federal contractors employed 35 percent of all nongovernment, noneducation institution workers in 1980 and 70 percent of all EEOC-covered workers.

Employment Effects of Affirmative Action. We tested for employment effects by measuring whether affirmative action has altered the location of black employment among these three sectors. If affirmative action is effective and is adequately enforced, minority representation should expand more among firms that are required to report to EEOC than among firms that are not. In addition, because federal contractors have more to lose, the greatest relative gains in employment and wages should occur among those EEOC-reporting firms that are federal contractors.

Although such relocation of black workers should occur in total employment, the largest minority gains should be detected within professional and managerial jobs for firms that are reporting to EEOC. Once again, these changes should be even larger among those firms that are federal contractors.

Our statistical evidence strongly supports these hypotheses. Black men were 10 percent less likely to work in covered firms in 1966. By 1980, however, black men were 25 percent more likely to work in EEOC reporting firms. To put these changes in another way, less than half (48 percent) of black male workers were employed in EEOC-covered firms in 1966; the figure rose to 60 percent by 1980.

The largest employment changes occurred between 1966 and 1970 (the first four years of reporting). Between those years, there was a 20 percent increase in the number of blacks working in covered firms. The trend continued at a diminished pace until 1974 and then apparently stabilized. After 1974, there was little further change in the location of black employment by EEOC coverage. Within the covered sector, black jobs shifted toward firms with contracts from the federal government. Between 1970 and 1980, black employment in nonfederal contractor firms that report to EEOC grew by 5 percent. Among federal contractors, total black employment expanded by more than 15 percent.

As large as those increases in total employment seem, they pale next to changes within the managerial and professional jobs. Black managers and professionals were half as likely as white managers and professionals to work in covered firms in 1966. By 1980, black managers and professionals were equally likely to be found in covered firms. Some of this improvement is exaggerated. In our research, we found evidence that firms have been reclassifying jobs held by blacks into the professional and managerial categories in order to inflate overall minority representation. But many of the gains in the covered sector were real. The number of black managers and professionals who work in covered employment is far larger as a result of affirmative action. Once again, this growth in black representation in managerial and professional jobs was concentrated in firms with federal contracts, and most of the change was completed by 1974.

In summary, affirmative action resulted in a radical reshuffling of black jobs in the labor force. It shifted black male employment towards EEOC-covered firms and industries and particularly into firms with federal contracts. Reshuffling is the right term because the mirror image is that black employment in the noncovered sector plummeted. Affirmative action also increased the representation of black male workers in the managerial and professional jobs in covered firms.

Wage Effects of Affirmative Action. Unfortunately, affirmative action's ability to raise the incomes of black men has proven to be far more difficult to achieve. We reached three conclusions regarding the effect on minority incomes. First, affirmative action apparently had no significant long-run impact, either positive or negative, on the male racial wage gap. The general pattern is that the narrowing of the racial wage gap was as rapid in the twenty years prior to 1960 (and before affirmative action) as during the twenty years afterwards. This suggests that the slowly evolving historical forces we have emphasized in this report that enhance the labor market skills of blacks "education and migration" were the primary determinants of long-term black economic improvement. At best, affirmative action has marginally altered black wage gains about this long-term trend.

Second, affirmative action did have a significant positive effect on wages of younger black workers, an effect that was unfortunately short lived. In the early stages of affirmative action, covered firms were desperately attempting to increase the number of black workers they employed. To achieve this aim, they bid up the wages of young black workers, the age group where most of the new hiring was taking place. Wages of young black workers increased dramatically from 1967 to 1972, but these wage gains were eroded by 1977.

For example, among new college graduates, black men earned 75 percent as much as whites in 1966; by 1972 there was complete racial wage parity. Similarly, the racial wage gap for new high school graduates narrowed from 80 percent to 90 percent over the same years. However, after covered firms reached their target number of black workers, these wage gains evaporated. In the five years after 1972, young black male wages fell by almost 10 percent relative to whites.

The final wage impact of affirmative action was a pro-skill bias. The essential purpose of affirmative action is to increase employment of blacks in jobs where they had previously been scarce. Because there is an abundance of blacks in low-skill jobs, the main pressures will be concentrated in the higher-skill jobs where blacks had previously been scarce. The main plot of affirmative action's impact must be one of nonneutrality with respect to education, with strong positive effects for college graduates and less strong, not necessarily positive effects at lower education levels. Young college-educated blacks were the main beneficiaries of affirmative action.

Glimpses of the Future. These last forty years have seen a partial American resolution to Myrdal's American Dilemma. But what of the future? Will black progress continue at the pace of the last forty years or have we entered instead an era of black stagnation or even retrogression? This report helps to provide a more informed answer to these questions.

The lessons history teaches provide us with both optimistic and pessimistic glimpses of black America's future. The most fundamental reason for optimism is the emerging and growing size of the black middle class and particularly the black elite. There are real questions about continued racial progress, especially among the black poor. But the continued growth of the black elite is a safe bet. There are good reasons for our optimism here. Until recently, black college graduates were previously employed almost exclusively in government jobs. Now they are moving in droves to the private sector. The real prizes in our economic race are won in the private sector, and the black elite have now joined the game.

Second, there is now substantial evidence that salary increases and promotions for the new black elite will be at least as rapid as for their white competitors. A new black leadership, fully one-fifth of black men, is being created that will be far different from the past reliance on the clergy and the civil rights organizations. Finally, the new black middle class and elite will be able to perpetuate their achievements across future generations. For the first time, many blacks now have the financial ability to secure the American dream for their children.

Unfortunately, there are also reasons for concern about the future, especially for the still large black underclass. There was nothing magical about the long-run black progress we document in this report. It reflected hard-won underlying achievements that enhanced black market skills in the context of a forty-year period of rapid American economic growth. Take away those underlying achievements and lose that growth, and black progress will stop.

One of the underlying causes, migration, has already lost its clout. With the end of the substantial black wage disparities between the South and the North, the potential for further sizable black wage gains from migration is minute. There are good reasons as well to be concerned about continued progress in the quality of black inner-city northern schools.

During the last decade, there were four other disquieting signs that temper our optimism: 1) the deterioration of the black family; 2) the decline in American economic growth; 3) rising black unemployment; and 4) a confused and unfocused public policy debate on race. These four events have started to blunt the translation of the still-improving black labor skills into a higher standard of living for black America. These events raise questions mainly about the future of the underclass. During the 1970s, there was continued progress in narrowing the racial wage gap among working men. For example, black working men earned 73 percent as much as whites in 1980 compared with 64 percent in 1970. But these four events dissipated some of the continuing black economic progress during the 1970s.

Economic Growth. The sustained and rapid growth of the post-1940 American economy carried with it impressive benefits in material well-being that benefited blacks and whites alike. How much of the long-term reduction in black poverty reflects the improving relative skills of blacks and how much is due to post-1940 economic growth? Had there been no growth, 46 percent of black working men would be poor today instead of the actual rate of 24 percent. Put another way, 45 percent of the reduction in black poverty since 1940 was due to economic growth and the remaining 55 percent to blacks' expanded labor market skills (relative to whites). Economic growth and improving black labor market skills, principally through education and job training, go hand in hand as the key weapons that history identifies as eradicating black poverty.

The importance of economic growth has had a negative side lately. Between 1970 and 1980, real earnings grew by less than 3 percent, one-tenth of the growth achieved during the previous decade. The virtual absence of real income growth during the 1970s carried a terrible price in limiting reductions in the ranks of the black poor. The disappointing American economic performance during the 1970s had many sorry consequences; one of the cruelest was that the ranks of black poor was 25 percent larger than it would have been had economic growth continued unabated at the pace of the 1960s.

What has happened to the relative economic status of blacks since 1980 and the Reagan years? A fair assessment is that it is too early to tell. Real incomes of black men who worked full-time were only 1 percent higher in 1984 than in 1980. Although this compares favorably with the 5 percent decline during the Carter years, it falls short of the standards set in the 1960s. It also falls well short of what is necessary for a significant reduction in the numbers of the black poor. The key to the ultimate evaluation of the Reagan years is whether the rest of the decade will be typical of 1980 to 1982 when real black incomes fell by 1.2 percent, or by 1982 to 1984 when black real incomes rose by 2.3 percent. If the latter, inflation-adjusted black incomes during the 1980s will rise by 8 percent and economic growth will again diminish the ranks of black poor. If, on the other hand, another recession of the 1980 to 1982 type occurs, there will be little likelihood of further reductions in black poverty during this decade.

End of Adaptation

Questions for Review and Further Study

1. What have been recent trends in wages and employment for blacks?

2. What was *An American Dilemma* and what were its findings?

3. What was the "safety net protecting black families from the ravages of poverty" and what has been its relevance to race relations?

4. Has the "economic lot of black men" improved since Myrdal's day? Explain.

5. What has been the effect of affirmative action and northern migration on the economic progress of blacks?

6. What happened in the class structure among black men from 1940 to 1980 that was fateful to their economic progress?

7. What is the size of the upper, middle, and lower classes among blacks? Among whites?

8. What are the future prospects for the several classes among blacks?

9. What are the future prospects of the three classes among blacks?

10. What has been the effect of affirmative action on wages and employment among blacks?

Notes

1. U.S. Department of Commerce, Bureau of the Census, *General Social and Economic Characteristics of the Population of 1970*, United States Summary, 1-375, Table 81. Nonwhite groups are of varying sizes. Blacks are by far the largest, being more than 90 percent of nonwhites. Mexican-Americans are the next largest, being about 0.5 percent of the total U.S. population. The move to fully developed ethnic status by these groups and the effective use of ethnicity for upward mobility is more recent than with Japanese- and Chinese-Americans. Yet, only as these two groups also achieve a firm and prosperous ethnic status can the full force for the needed class-based changes be realized.

2. Data on black family income were taken from U.S. Department of Commerce, Bureau of the Census, *The Social and Economic Status of the Black Population in the U.S., Special Studies, Current Population Reports, 1970*, No. 42.

3. Leonard Broom and Norvell Glen, *Transformation of the American Negro* (New York: Harper and Row, 1965), p. 84.

4. James P. Smith and Finis R. Welch, *Closing the Gap: Forty Years of Economic Progress for Blacks* (Santa Monica: The Rand Corporation, 1986). Prepared for the U.S. Department of Labor.

8

EDUCATIONAL GAINS

Gains for blacks have probably been more continuous in education than in politics, income, or occupation, since Emancipation. The illiteracy level among blacks has declined sharply. Today it is nearly the same in both black and white populations. High school, college, and graduate education show large increases among blacks since Emancipation. Accelerated gain in education in recent years is correlated with the general increase in gain across a broad spectrum.

The vast body of legislation mandating racial separation in educational facilities has been declared illegal. The country is still reconstructing in the aftermath of this momentous decision. In further characterizing Phase 5, I shall now consider educational gains.

For many years it was illegal for blacks to become educated. Smatterings of formal education were achieved by free blacks early on, but for most blacks education was a rare commodity. The great masses of blacks languished for many years bound by white supremacist law to ignorance and illiteracy. More than 200 years passed after the first arrival of blacks in the United States before there were the beginnings of a thriving tradition of formal education among them. Most of what has been achieved to date was within a span of a little more than 100 years, and these years have been fraught with formidable resistance by white supremacists, essentially unsympathetic to black education.

From a slave background and essentially African culture in the sixteenth century to 1865, about one in every twenty blacks had learned to read and write. This proportion had become one in every two by 1900. Much of this change was possible through the efforts of various religious groups. For example, in 1865 the Baptist Home Mission helped found Virginia Union University in Petersburg, Virginia, and Shaw University in Raleigh, North Carolina. In the same year the American Missionary Association founded the prestigious Atlanta University in Atlanta, Georgia. In the following year the Methodist Episcopal Church founded the Centenary Biblical Institute of Baltimore, Maryland, the predecessor of today's Morgan State University, another predominantly black center of higher education. The American Missionary Association founded Trinity College at Athens, Alabama, and Gregory College at Wilmington, North Carolina, as well as the now famous Fisk University at Nashville, Tennessee, all in 1866.

The following year Howard University in Washington, D.C., was chartered by the federal government. That same year the American Missionary Association founded four additional colleges: Emerson College at Mobile, Alabama; Storrs College at Atlanta; Beach College at Savannah, Georgia; and Talladega College in the Alabama city of the same name. The Presbyterians in that year added Biddle University to one they founded some years earlier called Lincoln University. The famous Morehouse College in Atlanta was founded during that year. Originally called the Augusta Institute, it was located in Augusta, Georgia, and supported by the American Baptist Home Mission Society. Other educational establishments founded during the following few years were Hampton Institute, where Booker T. Washington was educated; Knox College in Athens, Georgia; Burwell College in Selma, Alabama; Straight University in New Orleans, Louisiana; Le Moyne College in Memphis, Tennessee; and Tougaloo College in Mississippi.

By 1870, the literacy rate among blacks was 18.6 percent. By 1880 it had risen to 30 percent, and by 1890 to 42.9 percent. Most of this rise in literacy was the result of the efforts made by various religious groups to promote the cause of education among blacks. These various groups have been a major force in the educational history of American blacks, especially during slavery and Reconstruction. The federal government, too, particularly in later years, came prominently into the picture, as it did in education for the entire society.

Just after the beginning of Phase 3, Jim Crow, there were 6,580,793 blacks in the United States, 13.1 percent of the total population. They had achieved a literacy level of 30 percent. This was by the year 1880. Just ten years earlier it had been 18.6 percent. The percentage of blacks in southern schools by that date was 13.07, up from 3.07 ten years earlier. For whites the comparable figures were 18.3 percent, up from 13.5 percent in 1870.

By the end of the nineteenth century, the illiteracy level among blacks was continuing to decline and some additional educational gains were beginning to appear. By 1900, more than 2,000 blacks had college degrees. Between 1900 and 1910, four doctorates were awarded to blacks, two from all-black institutions and two from integrated institutions.

A number of additional indicators also show educational gains made by 1900. For example, the number of illiterate blacks continued to decline. In 1910 it was down to 30.4 percent; by 1930 it was down to 16.3 percent; and by 1960 it had reached a low of 7.5 percent. The median years of school completed by nonwhites 25 years and older rose from 5.8 in 1940 to 6.9 in 1950, to 8.2 in 1960. The college dropout rate in the 25 through 29 age group in 1960 was about the same for black and white females. However, black males had a considerably higher drop-out rate than white males (this applies to the population that completed one but less than four years of college).[1]

In a report issued in 1976 by the National Board of Graduate Education,[2] it appeared that, although gains were substantial at the elementary and high school levels and considerable at the college level, they had been least at the level of graduate education. This report issued a series of recommendations to the federal government designed to accelerate graduate education among minorities, and to close the remaining gap between black and white achievement levels.

Accelerated enrollment in college by blacks continues, and recent growth of black enrollment in higher education has been rapid.[3] In 1916 only 2,641 blacks were reported in college, whereas by 1926 there were 12,000. Fred Crossland provided the following data showing the range of reasonable expectation for blacks in college from 1900 to 1970 at ten-year intervals.[4]

Black Enrollment Increase

1900	700-800
1910	3,000-4,000
1920	6,000-8,000
1930	20,000-25,000
1940	45,000-50,000
1950	95,000-105,000
1960	195,000-205,000
1970	470,000

The rate of increase in college attendance among blacks has outstripped the growth rate , for the total population, for the total black population, and for the percentage total enrollment in higher education. At the beginning of the twentieth century blacks constituted less than 2 percent of all college students. By 1970, they were nearly 6 percent.

Crossland made the following assessment of nonwhites in higher education in 1970:

Estimated Nonwhite Enrollment in Higher Education, U.S., 1970

Black Americans	470,000	0.5%
Mexican-Americans	50,000	0.6%
Puerto Ricans	20,000	0.3%
American Indians	4,000	0.1%
Subtotal	544,000	6.8%
All others	7,506,000	93.2%
	8,050,000	100.0%

In 1970 there was underrepresentation of approximately 779,000 nonwhites in higher education. At the same time there had occured enormous change. There should have been 1,323,000 nonwhite students in college in 1970 rather than the actual 544,000. For black Americans, statistical parity would have meant 1,013,000 persons enrolled in 1970 rather than the 470,000 actually enrolled. In other words, parity would have required a 116 percent increase.[5]

During the next three decades of this century the number of black Americans enrolled in higher education will continue to increase as a proportion of the total black population. Given this impetus, along with a similar trend for other nonwhite groups, a major qualitative change in self-conception and sensitivity to remaining race-related restraints on achievement and reward is likely. Sufficient exposure to, and involvement in, higher education will generate new and more positive self-definitions among blacks and in the wider society. This means accelerated preparation for technical, professional, and managerial functions in the society. In addition, higher levels of education among blacks mean an increase in their capability to make maximum use of political potential. The skills of political organization and office-holding are still not currently widespread among black Americans but are growing rapidly, as discussed in Chapter 6.

A recent study of minority education provides a useful current view of education with reference to underrepresented groups. Selections from the findings of this study are presented in Adaptation V, which follows.

ADAPTATION V

> Apparently America is moving backward, not forward, in its efforts to achieve the full participation of minority citizens in the life and prosperity of the nation.[6] This is the message of the study, One-Third of a Nation, sponsored by the American Council on Education and The Education Commission of the States, May 1988.

Education for One-Third of a Nation

In education, employment, income, health, longevity, and other basic measures of individual and social well-being, gaps persist and in some cases are widening between members of minority groups and the majority population. If we allow these disparities to continue, the United States inevitably will suffer a compromised standard of living. Social conflict will intensify. Our ability to compete in world markets will decline, our domestic economy will falter, our national security will be endangered. In brief, we will find ourselves unable to fulfill the promise of the American dream.

As a nation, we must attack this problem now, with new energy and in new ways. The progress of the past cannot be cause for complacency about the future.

The goal we suggest is simple but essential: That in 20 years, a similar examination will reveal that America's minority population has attained a quality of life as high as that of the white majority. No less a goal is acceptable. For if we fail, all Americans, not just minorities, will be the victims. But if we succeed, all Americans will reap the benefits.

In 1988, we are seeing the emergence of another one-third of a nation: the Blacks, Hispanics, American Indians, and Asian Americans who constitute our minority population, many of whom are afflicted by the ills of poverty and deprivation. The visibility of these groups in the American tapestry is growing rapidly.

❖ Today, 14 percent of all adults in the United States and 20 percent of children under seventeen are members of these groups. By the year 2000, one-third of all school-age children will fall into this category.
❖ Already, in 25 of our largest cities and metropolitan areas, half or more than half of the public school students come from minority groups. By the year 2000, almost 42 percent of all public school students will be minority children or other children in poverty.
❖ Minority group members are far less likely to have a college education. In 1986, 20.1 percent of whites over twenty-five had completed four years of college or more. The rate for blacks was 10.9 percent, and for Hispanics only 8.4 percent.
❖ Between 1985 and 2000, minority workers will make up one-third of the net additions to the U.S. labor force. By the turn of the century, 21.8 million of the 140.4 million people in the labor force will be non-white.

Those figures are testimony to the nation's increasing diversity, cultural as well as demographic. At the same time, they confront us with a distinct challenge, for these same groups suffer disproportionately from unemployment, inadequate education, ill health, and other social and economic handicaps.

It should be noted that levels of educational attainment and income for Asian Americans are comparable to those for whites, and sometimes exceed them. In fact, the experiences of this group may offer valuable lessons as the nation seeks ways to promote minority advancement. Nevertheless, some segments of the Asian American population experience problems similar to those of other minority groups. This report concentrates on blacks, Hispanics, and American Indians. Together they comprise over 90 percent of the minority population. Their impact on the total society is thereby greater, and data on them are more readily available.

Rapid progress in eliminating these disparities may prove more difficult for the disadvantaged among the new one-third of a nation than for many of whom President Roosevelt spoke. Minority Americans are burdened not by a sudden, universal, yet temporary economic calamity, but by a long history of oppression and discrimination. They remain largely segregated in minority neighborhoods and minority schools. For many, full participation in the dominant culture imposes a painful choice: to dilute or abandon a rich and distinctive heritage. Above all, they are marked by the color of their skin as different, and therefore more vulnerable.

Yet, minority citizens are not separate. They are, in a real sense, the new America. In a few years they will comprise one-third of the nation's children; soon afterward they will be one-third of the nation's adults.

They are not other; they are us. How well and under what conditions minority groups are integrated into American life and the extent to which they participate in and contribute to our educational system and the economy, will determine the continuing strength and vitality of the nation as a whole.

The United States has made significant progress toward disadvantaged groups. Understandably they are eager to focus the attention of their fellow citizens on unfinished business. They often ignore or minimize the very markers of improvement that might inspire new energy for their cause. Those who question the efficacy of government programs or court mandates also have been eager to cite examples of regression, and to render verdicts of failure.

This unwitting alliance has had at least one unhappy result: because so many successes have gone unnoticed and unremarked, a sense of weariness and discouragement has come to characterize the national debate over the pace and process of minority advancement.

Yet the progress is there—on the record, revealed in census figures and the lives of real people. We must recognize and underscore that progress. It is impressive proof of what we can achieve together, and of what disadvantaged citizens can achieve for themselves. It is a tribute to the perseverance and frequent heroism of minority citizens in demanding their rights. And it is a tribute to the capacity of our democratic, system to respond and change.

Celebrating progress should not engender complacency. Nor do we want to paint a false picture: Successive waves of inflation and recession in the 1970s and early 1980s, accompanied by dramatic changes in our economic structure, eroded much of the improvement cited above, and the sustained growth of recent years has not made up the difference. Also, such averages must not obscure the fact that young people bear the greatest burden of deprivation.

Lost Ground. The lesson that progress is possible, given the right economic conditions and a strong national commitment, is especially relevant now. In the past ten years, not only have we lost the momentum of earlier minority progress, we have suffered actual reversals in the drive to achieve full equality for minority citizens.

In higher education, for example, the picture of stalled progress is dramatically clear. During the same period when the pool of minority high school graduates was becoming bigger and better than ever, minority college attendance rates initially fell, and have remained disproportionately low.

These figures illustrate the dimensions of the problem:

❖ Between 1970 and 1975, the percentage of black high school graduates 24 years old or younger who were enrolled in or had completed one or more years of college rose from 39 percent to 48 percent; over the same period, the corresponding rate for whites remained steady at 53 percent. However, between 1975 and 1985, while the college participation rate for white youths climbed to 55 percent, the rate for blacks dropped to 44 percent. Recently released figures indicate that in 1986, the rate for blacks rose to 47 percent, still slightly below 1975.

❖ The rate of college attendance for Hispanic youths remained stagnant between 1975 and 1985. Available evidence indicates a slight decline, from 51 percent to 47 percent.

❖ For American Indians, high school graduation and college attendance rates remain the lowest for any minority group. A report by the Cherokee Nation found that only 55 percent of American Indians graduate from high school, and of these only 17 percent go on to college.

These figures become even more disturbing when we look beyond college enrollment to college graduation. Minority students continue to complete their undergraduate degrees at rates far lower than their white counterparts. Also, a much smaller percentage go on to graduate and professional schools.

For example, although blacks made up 9 percent of all undergraduate students in 1984-85, they received 8 percent of the associate degrees and 6 percent of the baccalaurate degrees conferred that year. Hispanics made up 4 percent of enrollees, but received only 3 percent of the baccalaurate degrees. Hispanics did better at the community college level, receiving 4.5 percent of the associate's degrees. By contrast,

80 percent of the undergraduate students in 1984-85 were white, but they received 85 percent of the baccalaurate degrees.

At the graduate level, the falloff for blacks is dramatic. Between 1976 and 1985, the number of blacks earning master's degrees declined by 32 percent. Although Hispanics and American Indians registered slight increases, their share of master's degrees remains a disproportionately low 2.4 percent and 0.4 percent, respectively.

The number of blacks earning doctorates dropped by 5 percent in the same period; for black men it declined 27 percent. The number earned by Hispanics and American Indians increased significantly, from 396 to 677 for Hispanics and from 93 to 119 for American Indians, but at the doctoral level, too, their share is a low 2.1 percent and 0.4 percent, respectively.

In certain critical fields of study, the minority presence is nearly nonexistent. For example, in computer science, only one black received a doctorate out of 350 awarded in 1986. In mathematics, blacks received only six of the 730 doctorates awarded in that year.

Current statistics also indicate that fewer minority students are preparing for teaching careers. In the nation's historically black colleges and universities, which traditionally have produced more than half the black teachers, the percentage of first-year students intending to major in education dropped from 13.4 in 1977 to 8.7 in 1986. This suggests that in the future, not only minority students but all students will see fewer minority teachers over the course of their schooling. Such an outcome is a particular problem for minority students, for whom such teachers serve as important role models. But it also is a loss for majority students, who otherwise only rarely may be exposed directly to minority citizens in professional roles.

We stress these trends in higher education because of its

special importance in the life of our country. For more than a generation, a college education has been a key part of the American dream and, for many individuals and families, a good measurement of progress toward its fulfillment. Statistics on incomes and living standards support the belief that college is the passport to greater opportunity and achievement.

Participation in higher education also is an important barometer of well-being for the nation as a whole. We rely on our colleges and universities to impart to young people, and increasingly to older students as well, the knowledge and skills that will prepare them for leadership in business , the professions, and government. A decline in educational attainment by any substantial population group is cause for deep concern, especially at a time when technological advances and global competition put a premium on trained intelligence, advanced skills, and a high degree of adaptability.

The aptitude for higher education and the ability to succeed in college and graduate school do not materialize suddenly at age 18; they are developed in childhood. Currently, we lose disproportionate numbers of minority students at each level of schooling, culminating in low participation rates in higher education. Only through intense, coordinated efforts at every stage, beginning with adequate prenatal care, improved nutrition, and quality child care and extending through programs to increase minority retention and improve student performance at the elementary and secondary levels, can we hope to reverse these dismal trends. Too few children benefit from such efforts. Although preschool programs increase school success and reduce later expenditures for special and compensatory education, fewer than one in five eligible children is enrolled in Head Start. The Chapter I Compensatory Education Program, which reduces the probability that a child will have to repeat a grade, now serves only half of those who need its services.

Beyond those for higher education, other statistics also suggest a reversal of progress toward full minority participation in American life. Such statistics should be a cause for concern to all citizens, and a spur to national action.

With progress in key areas having come to a halt or even moving into reverse, the American people are at a critical point.

End of Adaptation

Questions for Review and Further Study

1. What are current trends in educational gains for black Americans?

2. What has been the value of Head Start programs to minority education?

3. At what level of education do minorities suffer the greatest underrepresentation, and what minority groups are most severely underrepresented?

4. What legislative enactment toppled segregated school systems for blacks and whites in the United States and in what year?

5. What is your view of the merit of a segregated versus an integrated educational system in this country, assuming that expenditure per pupil in both systems is the same? Explain your view?

Notes

1. Leonard Broom and Norvell Glen, *Transformation of the American Negro* (NewYork: Harper & Row, 1965).

2. National Board of Graduate Education, *Minority*

Group Participation in Graduate Education, Report no. 5 (Washington, D.C.: National Academy of Sciences, 1976).

3. Fred Crossland, *Minority Access to College* (New York: Schocken, 1971).

4. Ibid., p. 29.

5. Ibid., p. 13.

6. This adaptation comes from a report, *One-Third of a Nation* (Commission on Minority Participation in Education and American Life, 1988). The report was sponsored by the American Council on Education and the Education Commission of the States.

9

BLACK PRIDE AND THE DECLINE OF COLONIALISM

Having described black American history as an oscillating movement between gain and loss, and having considered a wide range of data showing the process of gain and loss, a very reasonable and appropriate next question is why, at this point in history, gain is expected to become more cumulative and loss diminished. Why should history not repeat itself and within a few years reverse the gains now being made by blacks and destroy large portions of the gains recently achieved?

Serious and continued struggle is a fact that I have constantly emphasized as vital in achieving and maintaining black gains. There is nothing automatic about the process. It requires human direction and dedication by blacks and their allies. That is, by the same forces that so successfully defeated slavery and the slave trade, as well as Jim Crow. Without this continued militant, humanistic effort, in all probability significant retrogression in gains achieved will occur. Assuming, however, a continuous effort by the anti-white-supremacy forces in the country and world, there are two important reasons to believe that further unprecedented success will be achieved.[1]

The first reason is that today American blacks are a very

different people from the people they were during slavery, or during the Jim Crow era, or even during the early years of this century. Blacks are no longer the weary victims of lynch mobs or the passive and helpless objects of racist violence and intimidation. There has been a change in consciousness among blacks about themselves, and about the world, that has released a new assertiveness, a new intelligence, about the world and self. This has made possible an increased ability to survive in dignity. In other words, a new perspective has emerged that is correlated with the transition from caste, to ethnicity, to class (discussed in Chapter 3).

The second reason that history is not likely to repeat itself is connected with a major change in the more fundamental structures generating and sustaining conditions of racial inequality, namely, a decline of colonialism throughout the world. The basic conditions for profiteering through blatant dehumanization, as was the case with the slave trade and slavery, have long since disappeared in the world. Also, for the most part, the associated political, legal, and cultural control over nonwhite countries by white peoples no longer exists. Third World countries are enjoying a new freedom that has changed the terms of relatedness between white and nonwhite peoples throughout the world.

Both factors present a new opportunity for anti-white-supremacy forces in the United States. A brief description of these two conditions follows, beginning with the change in perspective among blacks that has emerged along with the transition from castelike to class status. Linked to this change is a discussion of the recent rise to autonomy and internal control, or decolonialization, by Third World countries and the meaning of this for the forces of racial equality in the United States (see Appendix B).

Employment, education, income, and political gains described earlier are major aspects of an ongoing change process. There is also a correlated process of change taking place regarding self concepts about race within black culture. Taking advantage of the new opportunities for upward mobility requires an internal change in outlook among blacks as well as change in the outside conditions of the struggle. Great creativity, ingenuity, and entrepreneurship must be used by blacks to ensure that maximum advantage is gained from unfolding national and international developments. It is only as care is taken to anticipate these developments and maximize the advantages afforded by them that the sure demise of racism will come about. The ability of the group to utilize unfolding national and international events to advantage requires a fund of knowledge and entrepreneurial effort that allows permanent transition across the historical confines of racial segregation. Needless to say, the social forces in opposition to nonwhite prosperity remain formidable. Nevertheless, I believe, the point of accelerated, sustained growth and prosperity has now been reached and will continue. In discussing this change, the concept of perspectives as organized, symbolic entities is central. What, then, is a perspective and why is the concept of value?

A perspective is an ordered view of one's world.[2] Each person has some sense of order and stability with reference to the surrounding environment. Certain things about the world are taken for granted and are known as fact. We have deep-seated beliefs about propriety and impropriety in concrete social situations. We have distinctive kinds of ideas about others, and about ourselves with reference to them, that are commonly held assumptions underlying our everyday behavior. The knowledge, assumptions, and beliefs we hold are not randomly selected but are assembled into patterns that derive from, and bear a resemblance to, the society and culture in which we live. Perspectives are made up of the symbolic elements of culture that we acquire through socialization. Because of this, perspectives can be seen as shared by a wide range of persons who undergo common group experience. The symbolic elements of culture are a common heritage of a society, and of various subgroups within it. As new generations acquire group membership they adopt commonly shared ways of looking at and thinking about the world. Each person, of course, puts it all together in a unique way, yet internalizes a common store of understandings sufficient to permit meaningful interchange with others. Perspectives, seen as part of the culture of a society, endow us with a rich set of common understandings that are products of the distinctive history of the group and society. We draw on such perspectives to understand others and to be understood by them.

The definition of the situation adopted by acting persons is a creative, individualized formulation that selectively utilizes aspects of our internalized perspectives. The orderliness and meaningfulness of our everyday behavior are possible because we project definitions onto the external world—definitions shared and understood by others, which thus regulate our behavior in situations of social exchange. We do this, as W. I. Thomas emphasized some years ago, by formulating a definition of the situation that guides behavior along understandable and somewhat predictable lines.[3] The storehouses of imagery and past experiences from which our definitions derive are aspects of our perspectives. They are a variegated storehouse of information, of experience, of imagery, and of feelings and emotions that are common to a group with a history of shared experience. They reflect ways of thinking about the world, ways of behaving in it, as well as attitudes and feelings regarding it in everyday experience.

By this reasoning, then, it is not accidental that within black American culture there are to be found typical ways of thinking about and of being with reference to white Americans. The intrusive and life-threatening force of slavery and other forms of involuntary servitude to which blacks have been subjected make this an understandable, indeed an inevitable , development. Yet, as the material conditions of black life have changed, perspectives among blacks also have changed.

Historically, at least three dominant perspectives have emerged among blacks and have been employed in thinking about being among white Americans. I have labeled these the caste, the ethnic, and the class perspectives, suggesting them to be component aspects of a transition process. These perspectives are not mutually exclusive. At any one historical time each is likely to be in evidence. However, they flourish in association with distinctly different external conditions. As the external, or material, conditions change there is evidence of changes in the nature of dominant perspectives among blacks about the racial aspect of their lives. My claim is that a transition in thinking, or in perspectives, is now underway within black culture. The castelike perspective is now a thing of the past; the ethnic perspective is now fully dominant and a class perspective is emerging among blacks. Some indication of a fully developed caste system and of the difficulty of change within it is indicated in the following adaptation, which tells of the Indian caste system. Following this, attention will shift to a more detailed consideration of each of the perspectives in more detail.

Adaptation VI

> *The deaths of young lovers from different classes raise questions of law, justice, and power in a nation where tradition and progress contend. The depth and tenacity of caste, and the difficulties of change in it, are apparent in this adaptation, which tells of the brutality of caste in modern day India. It was written by Mark Fineman, a Los Angeles Times staff writer, and appeared 4/12/91.*

Lynchings Over Caste Stir India

MEHRANA, India.

It was at the entrance to this little village of mud and brick, beside an ancient shrine to Lord Shiva the destroyer, that Mehrana's starcrossed young lovers recently ended their lives side by side. From a sturdy limb of Mehrana's holy banyan tree, Roshni, 16, and Bijendra, 20, were hanged just after 8 a.m. for all the village to see, a symbol of order, the elders had said, of tradition and of the village's *izzat*—chastity and honor.

The young woman, Roshni, was a high-caste Hindu, after all, one of the Jats who own the land, the village and power over the likes of Bijendra and his fellow Jatavs. Bijendra, with whom Roshni had eloped three days before, was from a backward caste, traditionally so impure and inferior that they became known as Hinduism's Untouchables.

So separate are the Jats and Jatavs, not unlike Shakespeare's Montagues and Capulets, only centuries older and with a feud far more stubborn that each has its own well in Mehrana. The Jats live on one side in houses of stone and tile, the Jatavs on the other in huts of mud and straw. Their separate realities intersect only when the Jats need a Jatav to pick a crop, build a house or mend a shoe.

For both sides, Roshni's and Bijendra's was a love impure. They had to die. With that, even Roshni's father, Ganga Ram, agreed.

"For me," the Jat elder had said at the nightlong meeting in the village square that condemned the couple to hang March 27, "the girl is dead already."

And so he helped string up his daughter, her lover and the couple's best friend from the centuries-old banyan tree. But even after three strong tugs on the rope, Roshni and Bijendra refused to die. So the Jats gathered a heap of dry wood, then dragged the young couple, writhing in pain, to the makeshift funeral pyre they had built nearby. And in a final ritual of ancient village justice, the elders burned them to death, Jat and Jatav together, so that none would forget this day.

A single Jatav escaped the village, dodging armed Jat sentries posted all around Mehrana. It was Amichand, the uncle of Bijendra's best friend, who reported every detail to the nearest police station, 10 miles away.

Now Mehrana's modern-day Romeo and Juliet have become a symbol of a far different sort for India, a grisly illustration of the magnitude of the forces defying its march into the modern age forces increasingly outstripping logic and the rule of law as the divisions in its society grow ever deeper.

Decades after India's caste system was constitutionally banned, the lynching of the lovers in Mehrana triggered an outcry from Indian liberals and intellectuals in the nation's capital. The newspaper *Indian Express* condemned it as savagery at its appalling worst in an editorial headlined "Monstrous!"

"What has the modern Indian state done to prevent these monstrous triumphs of kangaroo justice?" the newspaper asked, concluding, "What is necessary is not more speeches and promises, but arrest and punishment of the guilty."

Under unprecedented popular pressure, the politicians and police ordered the arrest of 37 Jat elders who approved and carried out the lynching; 21 of them are now in jail.

But in deeply polarized India poised on the brink of yet another bloody national election, in which the ancient caste system already is a prominent issue, the Mehrana village elders who ordered the hangings have drawn an unprecedented number of defenders as well.

One state government minister paying a condolence visit to the village, for example, lavished his greatest gift not on the Jatavs, but on the Jat mother of Roshni pledging to free her husband from jail within days so he can supervise the spring harvest.

And in a politically paralyzed country where three national governments have come and gone in 18 months and where the institutions of government and its bureaucracy have all but ceased to function at the grass-roots in many regions, defenders of the elders of Mehrana say they are to be commended for keeping a semblance of order in a village that seems centuries removed from the ideal of a modern Indian state.

In reality, Mehrana is just 70 miles south of the capital, New Delhi. It is three hours away, a drive that peels back time and ends in a bumpy ride through rocks, dust and wheat fields.

The Jatavs were out for the harvest this week, plucking the golden sheaves by hand for their Jat masters, even after most had been jailed or had fled to distant villages to escape arrest.

Inside the divided village of 3,000 or so, accounts of the tragic saga of Roshni and Bijendra varied. (Most villagers denied having watched the lynching, although police say nearly everyone did.)

Detectives say that behind the ritual killings was a disbelief in both communities that what occured between Roshni and her lover could ever have happened between members of two groups who refuse to even touch each other.

"My girl was kidnapped by those Jatavs," Bishan Devi, the mother, shouted angrily to visitors. "Everything was forced. First, the Jatavs took away my daughter, fed her liquor and took her in a hay loft. And then the Jats found her there, locked her in our house, threatening to break our bones if we let her out, and finally took her away and killed her."

"I would never have married her to the Jatav boy," she said. "She was a good girl. Four months ago, she was engaged to Ramesh, a boy from another village. On April 8, she was to marry."

Asked whether Ramesh is a Jat or Jatav, a look of horror washed over her face. She was furious. "What are you saying?" she screamed. "Of course he is a Jat. How could you even ask such a thing of me. Now leave this house!"

On the Jatav side of the village, a similar wave of shock swept across the face of Sarawati, the mother of Bijendra. After several minutes of wailing, "My son! My child! My little boy!" she wiped her tears. And as she sat cross-legged in the mud wearing shreds of a shirt held together by a single safety pin and loose stitches, she explained that a love affair between her boy and that Jat girl was, well, simply impossible.

"It was another boy, a Jat boy named Shyam, who had eloped with Roshni," she explained. Indeed, the police confirmed that Roshni had eloped with a Jat boy named Shyam but that it took place nearly 2 years ago.

"She is a whore," Sarawati said of her son's lover. "Never could this have happened."

But several yards away, at the house of Bijendra's best friend, Ram Kishan, relatives told another story. Ram Kishan's mother confirmed that Bijendra and Roshni were lovers, who were aided in their elopement by her son.

It was the village's most powerful elder, a wealthy Jat named Mangtu, who convened the village Panchayat (traditional council) at the request of Roshni's family. Papu, a brother of Roshni, insisted that these people should be hanged, otherwise he was going to hang himself, the mother said.

It is from the official statement of Amichand, Ram Kishan's uncle who escaped within minutes of the hanging, that police say they have gotten the most detailed account of what happened after the young couple returned from a three-day absence from the village and announced their desire to marry.

At the insistence of village elder Mangtu, the Panchayat convened in a 25-foot-square dirt meeting place in the village at 9 p.m. on March 26. There were 37 of them, all Jats.

"The whole night, the Panchayat was on," he recalled. And throughout the night, Mangtu and the others beat Bijendra and Ram Kishan by turns. Then, they were hanged upside down by their feet. They soaked their private parts in kerosene and burned them.

At 5 a.m., the Jatavs were called to the Panchayat, and they were asked about their opinion [of hanging the accused]. They were all scared, so they accepted the decision by consensus. At that time, Mangtu and the others formally accused Ram Kishan and Bijendra of eloping with this girl, and they decided to hang the two boys and the girl.

They were brought to the banyan tree, and then the fathers were summoned, and the Jats demanded that the fathers hang their own children. When they protested, they beat them up. At that point, the mothers were summoned, and they also were beaten.

After that, the fathers of the children were forced to hang them. Then, they were taken down. They only appeared to be dead. They were dragged to the cremation ground, where they were forcibly cremated.

To stop the Jatavs from leaving to report the crime, the Jats surrounded the village. But Amichand told police: " I sneaked out to give you this report. Please take action on it."

The police did act swiftly. Vijay Kumar Gupta, the police superintendent for the district who is based in Mathura, 40 miles away, boasted that he personally arrived on the scene at 12:30 p.m., just four hours after the lynchings.

Although Gupta now insists that the crime was not committed purely because of caste, calling it a multi-causal phenomenon, his own police report blames caste for the killings. Most analysts insist that the police were aggressive in publicizing the case and acting on it because of the Indian national elections, now scheduled for late May.

Among the key issues in the campaign is a controversial quota system, which reserves university slots and government jobs for low-caste Hindus like the Jatavs. High-cast leaders such as the Jats have condemned the new system as reverse discrimination.

When the new law was first proposed eight months ago, it triggered a nationwide wave of teenage suicides by protesting high-caste youths.

Ever since, Mehrana's state of Uttar Pradesh, a populous and vote-rich area where most of the villages remain physically and socially divided along caste lines, has become a flash point for the caste dispute. So it was little wonder that the state's powerful chief minister, Mulayam Singh Yadav, dispatched his minister of religion and sports to Mehrana recently as a gesture to maintain support of both Jats and Jatavs.

But as the minister, Sardar Singh, worked his way through the village's narrow lanes, it was clear that he was more attentive to Jats than to Jatavs. Although Singh is a high-caste Hindu, it was only in the Jatavs' mud enclave that a deeper reason became clear.

When asked how their village's love-and-murder drama is likely to affect their vote next month, Jatavs gathered outside Bijendra's tiny hovel, fell silent, and looked blankly at one another.

Finally, Bijendra's sister, Kesar, spoke. Shaking her head beneath a soiled green scarf, she said quietly: "The vote? Well, we are always forced to vote. Whoever forces us, that is who we vote for. And it has always been the Jats who force us. So that is how we will vote."

_____

End of Adaptation
_____

The first (roughly) 300 years of experience in this country for black Americans was, as earlier indicated, a coercive, inhumane, and brutal reality. This was a condition within which assertions of dignity and self-worth in interaction with whites meant further pain and brutality. Self assertion among whites by blacks often meant flogging, mutilation, or even death itself. It should not be surprising, then, that for a long time a central perspective on race among black Americans was essentially a reflection of the dehumanizing and degrading viewpoint held by slave traders, slave owners, and ordinary white Confederate southerners. The basic characteristic of this perspective, or gestalt, was that blacks are inferior to whites. The alleged inferiority was thought to be particularly apparent in terms of intellectual ability, physical features, as well as qualities of industry and enterprise. In each of these areas (among others) volumes have been written to substantiate, to uphold, and to propagate this perspective.

This caste, or castelike, perspective among blacks is a view of self and world that is essentially an internalization of the subhuman, demeaning definitions generated by those malevolent whites (and their allies) who constructed and enforced the system of slavery and slave trading.

Cognitive or intellectual articulation of the vision goes back at least to Joseph Gobineau, whose *Inequality of the Human Races* was widely read and has been influential on Western thought about race.[4] In this malicious volume, the three racial groups are viewed hierarchically: Caucasians at the top, Mongoloids in the middle, Negroids at the bottom. Caucasians are depicted as those best qualified by nature to carry on civilization. Indeed, Gobineau suggested that it was their duty to do so, and that this involves maintaining their racial purity. For Gobineau, intermixing with the mongrel groups meant the decline of civilization. This view of the three racial groups has been maintained relatively intact, though less widely adhered to, since Gobineau first articulated it. The point here is to recognize that it was a general vision or perspective adopted by white Americans and forcefully imposed upon black people in the New World for many years.

Thus, whites in the West held a vision of themselves as more intelligent than blacks, as more physically beautiful than blacks, and as more industrious and enterprising than blacks. The very beginning and continuity of black experience in the New World was within this coercive framework that enforced its imperatives, by physical brutality. The adaptation that follows reminds us that the threat of increased oppression by a small but growing lunatic fringe is an ever-present reality in American society.

Adaptation VII

This adaptation is from the KLAN WATCH PRO-
JECT of the Southern Poverty Law Center. It is an excerpt
from a letter to the author in April 1991, reflecting the
continuing potential for violence from the racist forces of
the radical right in the United States.

Klanwatch

Montgomery, Alabama

Dear Center Supporter:

The potential for white supremacist violence against the
Center and its staff has never been higher.

Last month nearly 200 Klan members came to Montgomery from around the nation. Part of their known activity
included a march past the Center and the Civil Rights Memorial to show their hatred of the Center and all it represents.

For the past five years we've asked Center supporters
each July to make a special contribution to our Security
Fund. But I'm writing to ask for your help now.

I'm Chief of Security for the Center's Klanwatch Project.
The Klan march showed me that the white supremacists are
more determined than ever to stop the work of the Center.

Members of nearly every major white supremacist
group in the country marched—Klansmen, neo-Nazis, Skinheads, members of the Identity Church. They're furious
about the $12.5 million verdict we won against Tom and
John Metzger, their White Aryan Resistance, and two Portland Skinheads who murdered a black man. The chance of

violence was so high that most of the Center staff was told to stay home and our building was closed.

Without the highly visible presence of hundreds of law enforcement people—from seven different law enforcement agencies—I'm convinced the Center would have been vandalized, and the Civil Rights Memorial would have been damaged.

Georgia white supremacist Ed Fields called the Civil Rights Memorial that sits in front of the Center "a sacrilegious monument to the enemies of the South. We won't be satisfied until that disgraceful monument is removed once and for all."

Klan leader Dave Holland said something with a disturbing note of truth to it: "Morris Dees [co-founder and Executive Director of the Center] has done one good thing— he's driven the weak-kneed cowards out of our movement."

The hard core of the white supremacist movement has now seen the Center. Some may have taken the opportunity to track down and case the homes of Center employees. I can assure you we have no intention of quitting. We have no other moral choice but to continue our efforts to collect all of Tom Metzger's assets for the nine-year-old son of the man who was murdered by Portland Skinheads.

We must continue developing quality educational materials, such as our coming documentary about the civil rights movement, to steer young minds away from the dangers of racism.

We've got to carry on our investigative work so we can inform law enforcement about possible violent white supremacist activity. But none of this work will be accomplished unless the Center and its staff can work in safety.

I've enclosed a memo I sent to Klanwatch Director Danny. It shows why we have good cause to worry. If you had seen the images of the marching white supremacists reflected in the Civil Rights Memorial's waterfall, I know you would have shared my thoughts—how forty people honored by the monument gave their lives for freedom, yet we have so far to go.

The Klan's anger is a measure of our success. As long as you are willing to stick with us, we plan to keep on making them mad, no matter how bold, belligerent or threatening they get.

Please send as generous a special gift as you can today. Help our Security Fund so we can carry on our work in safety.

Sincerely,
Klanwatch Project

P. S. I recently received a message from a law enforcement agency warning of an imminent threat to the Center and its staff. I am not at liberty to give you any details. I can only urge you to continue to support our efforts.

End of Adaptation

What has been the cumulative import of this constantly threatening reality for black Americans, a reality that had its beginnings with the introduction of slavery several hundred years ago? It has meant the buildup of a very long-standing tradition within black culture of self-denigration and a sense of inferiority to white people, as the racist articulation of this viewpoint itself suggested. This is a tradition wherein oppression has become a significant element of cultural life and of the individual psychic life of the oppressed. This is what I refer to as the caste, or castelike, perspective. It is a viewpoint of very long duration among blacks, at first coerced, later becoming more autonomous, and today remaining somewhat influential in the cultural life of black communities in America.

It is well to bear in mind that what is referred to here is a perspective. Historically, it has influenced and guided the thinking and behavior of black and white Americans about one another. It has been profoundly influential in self-definitions among generations of black Americans. Such a perspective has supported a white American view of themselves as being more intelligent, more physically attractive, more industrious, more favored by life simply because of their racial characteristics.

We know, as discussed earlier, that perspectives tend to endure, even when the original conditions that gave rise to them have ceased to exist. Although slavery and the slave trade have long since disappeared, there linger on in U.S. society remnants of this caste perspective, as well as fitful efforts among small enclaves of white racists to revive it again. In recent years this viewpoint has undergone a rapid decline throughout society, but as the foregoing adaptation indicates it is not extinct.

In the transition from caste to class, blacks have now reached an intermediate stage to which I refer as ethnic status. By this I mean that the former castelike perspective is now the exception rather than the rule in black culture; that interaction patterns and process deriving from the oppressive dominance of the vision of white superiority are practically extinct among blacks. Blacks have now achieved a resource—ethnicity—that for most other ethnic groups in America has been available for a much longer time. (Some social conditions associated with this new development among blacks were discussed in Chapter 3.)

Slavery and slave trading throughout the New World were completely abolished by the latter half of the nineteenth century. The social forces in the Western world opposed to these inhumane social practices gained ground and ultimate victory. For black Americans these changes were profound for they released black cultural development from the dehumanizing coercion of the slave trade, slave auctions, and slavery and their associated indignities. This meant a new freedom and thus important new elements in cultural development. These events represent points in historical time when fateful assaults were made on the structural base supporting the caste perspective.

The same perspective however, was supported by Jim Crow patterns of social organization that eventually replaced the slave trade and slavery as forms of oppression. Yet, before the dominance of the oppressive Jim Crow pattern, blacks had lived through an important period of freedom involving widespread participation in the social system as equals. From this great time in American history, Reconstruction, the ingenuity, strength, and intelligence of blacks and of their white allies operated to firmly plant the vision of full equality.[5] Blacks participated freely in the Reconstruction process of the Confederate states and served as politicians in local, state, and federal government. Though this was a short-lived period, it was sufficient as a starting point for a new and different vision among blacks, one diametrically opposed to the imperatives of the caste mentality.

This vision was in large part the heritage of the imperatives of that great period of Western history known as the Enlightenment (discussed in Chapter 2). The tradition of liberty, fraternity, equality, and freedom from oppression dramatized in France in 1789 facilitated the zeal for justice and for basic human rights among black slaves and others held in involuntary servitude. Popular and conventional sentiment were also more readily forthcoming in support of Emancipation due to the previous struggle for freedom from the English Crown, culminating in victory in 1776, just slightly more than seventy-five years before the Emancipation Proclamation.[6]

Emancipation, the first formal, incorporation of black Americans into American society, was the beginning of the development of black ethnic culture; a development that, I contend, has been more or less fully achieved only in recent years. The Emancipation period represents a time when major black national spokespersons began to emerge as advocates for blacks; when a more rapid acquisition of political, organizational, and other survival skills was achieved by blacks; when whites for the first time in American history participated with blacks in roles as social equals and superiors. Small, but important increments of gain were made by blacks in education, in property ownership, and in the crucial experience of learning how to effectively, and successfully, operate the system.

A small circle of educated, professional blacks dedicated themselves to increasing the well-being of others. They formed national organizations such as the NAACP and later the Urban League, both highly influential resources today. They urged other blacks to become educated and promoted educational and cultural achievement in black communities. Booker T. Washington and W.E.B. Du Bois arose as prominent leaders among blacks with national and international appeal and influence. A. Philip Randolph, Adam Clayton Powell, Jr., Marcus Garvey, and others also rose to national importance. These leaders symbolized the increasing emergence of black racial and ethnic pride and promoted a gradual and steady infusion of blacks into patterns of participation in the wider society. It also meant the steady recognition by subsequent generations of whites of a growing capability, power, and influence by blacks. This was, in essence, a decline of the castelike mentality and imperatives that had dominated black-white relations for so long.

Black Americans are now, for the most part, convinced of their intellectual equality with whites. They no longer doubt their physical beauty and attractiveness due to negative judgment by whites. It has also become clear to blacks that industry and enterprise are not restricted to the white race. A general period of good feeling has emerged among blacks typified by ethnic pride and greater solidarity and by aspirations and expectations that are for the most part the same as those of other ethnic groups in America.

The achievement of full ethnic status by blacks also created the condition by which an additional and unanticipated change has begun to occur. Ethnic status, and the gains being brought with it, has initiated a movement toward full class status by black Americans. This means a movement, now well underway, toward proportional representation in the class structure of society. The reality of proportional representation carries with it a perspective far different from the caste perspective. It is also different from the perspective of full ethnic status.

The achievement of proportional class representation brings with it a perspective of diminished racial concern, a viewpoint that is fairly new and not very widespread among black Americans. It is most prevalent among middle and upper-class blacks, those who have the highest incomes and who have attained highest educational achievements. Generally, the upward mobility that has been achieved and maintained by this group has in important ways been made possible by contact and close involvement with whites, usually on the job. Blacks that adopt this perspective are the most articulate, the most successful, and the most acculturated. They associate among whites with ease and often have several close associates and friends who are of other ethnic groups. Frequently they intermarry.

Identity formation for this group is less centered around race than around work, profession, or employment. The great preoccupation with achieving, maintaining, and expanding their advantages and opportunities renders racial concern a secondary, though not necessarily an insignificant matter. Importance and recognition are given to their competitive advantages in the class hierarchy, and racial matters, neither anti-white attitudes nor pro-black effervescence, will be allowed to impede their progress. This group has learned to work the system to its advantage and is in fact doing so. This group is primarily white collar, business, professional, and technical in job characterization. It is the group most effectively competing with whites and represents an expanding segment of the black population as educational, employment, and political opportunities are increasingly available and effectively utilized.

As the number of black Americans reaches parity with whites in the areas of income, jobs, and education, we can expect this perspective to be increasingly dominant among blacks. That is to say, one can expect class interests and identity to supersede distinctively racial or ethnic interests and identity in importance.[7]

The second element facilitating upward mobility by blacks is the recent and momentous decline of colonialism. In addition to the new sense of advocacy and positive sense of self being more widespread than ever in black culture, the decline of white social and cultural control of nonwhite societies and peoples around the world is also a powerful new ingredient in current progress for blacks.

Following the decline of the slave trade and slavery, a long span of extremely profitable and enriching years had come to an end for white Europeans. The monumental profit-making and consequent buildup of European society had greatly benefited from their inhumane, barbaric treatment and use of Africa and African peoples.[8] This was primarily by transport, sale, and exploitative use of Africans as labor in selected areas of the New World. When slave trading and slavery were outlawed, European entrepreneurial interests shifted from the transport, sale, and totally brutal use of Africans elsewhere to more direct involvement in African societies and cultures.

The Industrial Revolution had put Europe in need of

raw materials to produce a range of marketable goods by the mid-nineteenth century. European businessmen and political leaders began to realize that these new societies were fertile soil for trade, for raw materials, and for profits. But this was true only if stable and sympathetic governments were in power. Investment groups began to form in Europe, and the various European powers began to eye one another with suspicion regarding selected interests in Africa.

In 1884-85, European countries held a conference in Berlin that was intended to establish rules by which they might lay claim to and possess areas of interest on the African continent. Thus, Great Britain, France, Portugal, and other European countries began to establish their presence in selected areas of Africa. By the end of 1955 there were only two independent black-ruled countries left in black Africa: Ethiopia and Liberia. Each of the other African societies had been taken over by European governments and was being used as sources of raw materials, cheap labor, and areas of trade and profitability. They had become, in other words, objects of Western European imperialism.[9]

One of the important outcomes of World War I, according to Rupert Emerson, was the final reversal of a centuries-old tide that had swept the peoples of Europe into domination over most of the rest of the globe. The nonwhite peoples of the earth had declared, in terms that none could refute, that they were no longer prepared to accept the position of inferiority that lay at the heart of the imperialist system.[10]

Self-determination among nations thereafter became a dogma supported as a principle for all countries, including those under imperial rule. The door then opened for the development and flourishing of native, or indigenous self-rule within the formerly white-ruled countries long burdened by imperialist domination. Clearly, there were some benefits gained by societies that hosted the imperialists, such as the fruits of modern science and technology, and some increases in material well-being. Yet the trade-off has been a devastating one for nonwhites, as suggested by one of the most vociferous critics of European hegemony, Aime Cesaire:

> Between colonizer and colonized there is room only for forced labor, intimidation, pressure, the police, taxation, theft, rape, compulsory crops, contempt, mistrust, arrogance, self-complacency, swinishness, brainless elites, degraded masses. No human contact, but relations of domination and submission which turn the colonizing man into a classroom monitor, an army sergeant, a prison guard, a slave driver, and the indigenous man into an instrument of production.[11]

The point here is that the damage wrought by colonialism and imperialism has been enormous. It has falsely elevated skin color and race to levels of importance in human affairs far in excess of their true value. It has arbitrarily provided a false security and dignity to white men and a false insecurity and inferiority to nonwhites, a circumstance now being militantly challenged around the world. This resistance now requires new accommodation between the former imperial powers and their former subjects. As Rudolph Van Albertini has pointed out in his volume on decolonialization, if one considers colonialism as a system of domination and superimposition, then decolonization does not mean just the withdrawal of colonial powers, but the establishment of new relations between the colonial power and the former colony on the basis of equal status and self-determination.[12]

To conclude, then, on the factor of the demise of colonialism, after about three hundred years of slavery, resistance to it became so formidable that the practice was halted by appropriate legislation. But halting the importation of African slaves to the Western world did not halt the process of capital accumulation, profit-making, and exploitation of which this inhuman use of black people had become a part.

This more general capitalistic process simply took another form, which was the staking out of claims by European powers to territory on the African continent. Colonial rule was established by the European powers throughout Africa in the nineteenth century. Laws and judicial procedures were set up that ensured Europeans of superior social status within these countries and that ensured them access to whatever native goods and services they deemed to be in their interest. The gradual extraction of the wealth and resources of Africa by Europeans went on practically unabated for more than 100 years.

The end of colonial domination of Africa came about largely in the 1960s, and the process remains incomplete. The enduring oppression of nonwhite peoples in the Western countries, and the skewing of world aggregate income and other resources in favor of whites, must be viewed in terms of the rapacious, predatory, and exploitative social systems of capitalism that developed in the West. The inhumane motives, dispositions, and practices that these systems nurtured were especially pernicious to nonwhites, who were coerced to serve the interests and promote the welfare of white Europeans.

With a few important exceptions, colonial rule in the world is now over. Formerly colonized areas of the world are now rapidly achieving national autonomy and independence. This means that the rampant exploitation of these countries in the interest of white capitalist countries will gradually cease completely. The Western white world can no longer force its will on the rest of mankind with abandon. Non-Western and nonwhite peoples throughout the world are now aflame over the indignities of white rule and over the exploitation of their resources, both social and human, by white Europeans. Their demands are no less than autonomy from white domination. Such demands have a fundamental meaning for status change now underway among black Americans.

The demise of colonialism has drastically enhanced the importance of nonwhites to the American system. This is because there are certain tasks now facing the United States that render nonwhites strategic participants and distinctive assets. They are strategic in assisting the United States to adjust to the new realities of national independence by formerly oppressed colonies. This adjustment requires rapid destruction of the white superiority myth and its replacement with a conception and practice of racial equality. The U.S. nonwhite equality movement already takes these developments as major goals. This movement can and must develop ties of mutual assistance with the peoples of Asia and Africa, such that any thwarting of the goals of nonwhite equality in America becomes an issue of international importance. Such bonds of friendship, based on recognition of a common background of racist oppression, can aid the cause of development in developing areas. It can also aid the cause of equality here for oppressed nonwhites, and consequently the cause of a better adjustment between this country and the Third World powers.[13]

To a limited extent the kinds of ties and mutual support suggested between the developing Third World countries and U.S. blacks have already begun.

A young, talented black with an MBA from Harvard University, Leonard Fuller, joined the Hughes Helicopter Company of Culver City, California, in a distinctive capacity. He had the task of marketing Hughes' non-military helicopters in 46 countries south of the Sahara, excluding South Africa. This man had done research on Africa, and has spent some time in Africa with a private organization for international community development. He learned to appreciate African customs and to understand African folkways. His employers at Hughes were reportedly impressed with him and his distinctive experience and abilities.[14]

A more extensive connection between black Americans and the Third World was initiated by the black mayor of Los Angeles, Thomas Bradley. As a result of his visits to several African countries, an alliance has been formed between these countries (Nigeria, Tanzania, Kenya, Zambia, and the Ivory Coast) and a black-led African task force formed at the University of California, Los Angeles, headed by Dr. Charles Z. Wilson, then a black vice-chancellor on that campus. The group aimed to do the following: (1) bring more small- and medium-sized businesses from Los Angeles into lucrative trade with these countries; (2) start numerous foreign-based projects, such as manufacturing firms; (3) create wide-ranging educational and cultural programs; and (4) establish conditions in the business and education sectors to provide needed expertise for various trade projects.

A liaison attorney working with this project, Howard Manning, Jr., asserted that several U.S. firms are working on foreign trade projects that could result in millions of dollars and extensive benefit to Los Angeles's minority firms. He stressed that blacks must become more internationally conscious. Manning cited some specific needs of African countries that minority entrepreneurship could well fulfill, for example, that Tanzania needs a plant for manufacturing spare parts for vehicles.[15]

More recently Mayor Bradley has led a task force to the Ivory Coast seeking trade and other connections with that country. The adaptation that follows is a report of minutes of one meeting between this delegation and officials of that country. Participants in this meeting were Minister of State, Camille Alliali; Minister of Agriculture, Denis Bra Kanon; Mayor N'Koumo Mobio Ernest of Abidjan; GGOCI Ambassador to U.S., Charles Gomis; Ambassador Dennis Kux; Mayor Thomas Bradley; William Elkins, Los Angeles Staff;

Wilfred Marshal, Los Angeles Staff; Mr. Waite Smith, Businessman; Mr. Jona Goldridge, Businessman; Mathew Rooney, political office of the Mayor.

Adaptation VIII

DATE & PLACE: Wednesday, January 21, 1987. Presidential Palace, Abidjan Plateau. SUBJECT: Mayor Thomas Bradley of Los Angeles makes presidential call on Felix Hophouet-Boigny, President of the Republic at 12:00 p.m.

African-American Delegation In Africa

Presidential Palace, Abidjan. The president began with an exposition of his views on commodity speculation and the damage it causes to the Côte d'Ivoire's orderly development. These points were raised by the president in all of the meetings he has had in the past few weeks with American officials and are by now well known: the faceless speculator who ruthlessly manipulates prices for coffee and cocoa and other commodities, while the farmer who produces them sees his labor go unrecompensed. The president reiterated his desire that the United States not view the Côte d'Ivoire as a private hunting ground of any nation, especially France. These points came up again in conversation over lunch.

The mayor responded with a description of the composition of his group and their purpose in coming. Two of the businessmen were present, Jona Goldridge and Waite Smith, and the mayor asked them to describe briefly to the president their impressions and the results of their trip.

Mr. Goldridge began by outlining his experience in the field of low-cost government-subsidized housing, and went on to sketch impressions of the way things are done in Côte d'Ivoire. In his view, "affordable" housing was still too expensive for the quality, whether because of too-high guaranteed profit margins, he did not know. Further, he felt that the French standards were being imported, and he commented that in his experience French low-cost housing was the poorest quality in the Western world. This standard, he said, will be outmoded in ten to fifteen years. Housing is not like other commodities; it should last 100 years. As the country evolves, people will become dissatisfied with their housing long before it has worn out. The mayor interjected to ask about lowering the price, and Mr. Goldridge said that this could be done, and output speed increased, all with a higher standard, by adopting the American system. Although housing is not subject to export and must be done on the spot, the technology was available and could be exported. The mayor asked if Mr. Goldridge's firm was prepared to put its experience at the disposal of the Ivorians. He replied that his intention was to send a representative to Côte d'Ivoire to study the problem in consultation wih the government and/or private housing entreprenuers. He commented lastly that he thought the tax on housing, which, he had been told, ranged up to 30 percent, was too high and should be lowered, at least for low-income housing. The mayor said that his group had come to offer whatever expertise it had as the Ivorians deemed appropriate.

The president replied that the Ivorians were well aware of the American superiority in this domain. Every nation, he said, has its moment, and we had seen the Greek epoch, the Roman, then the European. Now was surely the American epoch. Not just in building, but in singing, dancing, movies.

And what, said the president, have we noted? In building, for example, we note that Europe continues to build with load-bearing walls, although the Americans have moved to internal structures that are stronger and more solid. This is why my assertion that we have started from zero is so key: while Europe struggles over whether and how to adopt new methods—and the past cannot beat the present, let alone the future—we, starting with nothing, have nothing to lose from abandoning an outmoded way of doing things.

Our means are limited, but we must find ways to live at a decent standard with them as our nation evolves. You mentioned that a home has a social function in your country; for us it also has an economic function. For ours is a fundamentally agricultural country and we must find ways of keeping the farmer on the land. Therefore, we must bring some of the amenities of the town to the village. Homes in the villages must be healthy, with running water and electricity. How can we do this if the efforts of our farmers are not justly recompensed? It is thus that we appreciate all you can do for us where commodities prices are concerned.

The mayor then spoke, saying that it was not the Los Angeles group's purpose to criticize any country and especially not France, only to offer a second opinion. As a doctor, Mr. president, you can understand the value of a second opinion before starting to operate. The mayor described the interest of one of his members as strictly humanitarian, that of Dr. Marc Rose, a prominent ophthalmologist from Los Angeles who had come in the hope that he could demonstrate and teach the latest methods. He had visited some clinics and found the training excellent—this followed the French system—but felt that the equipment and techniques were outmoded. Therefore, the Los Angeles group hoped only to offer advice and expertise where the Ivorians felt it would be of value. The mayor then introduced Mr. Smith, of New Horizons Export Trading Co., and asked him to describe some of his products.

The mayor added that one of the firms on the mission represented some thirty U.S. manufacturers of farm equipment, which among them produced highly efficient lightweight equipment, some of which could be operated by one person. This firm, said the mayor, planned to stay in Aibidjan up to sixty days to continue its contacts. He then asked Mr. Smith to speak briefly about his companies' products and activities.

Mr. Smith stated that New Horizons represented 30 U.S. manufacturers, of which 25 were in agricultural implements business. Further, New Horizons had on its staff David Ray, an agricultural specialist who had managed his family's 5,000-acre cotton plantation. They had contacts in the academic world as well, and pledged to ascertain that equipment they proposed to sell in Côte d'Ivoire was appropriate for the job. Mr. Smith went on to say that they had studied the Ivorian Rural Development Plan of 1985 and had made an effort to find appropriate implements. For example, he had a portable water-well pump that could be operated by one person, "even a lady." For more permanent installation, they had a wind-powered pump and a solar one as well. He handed the president a list in French of his firm's products and offered the president a sample. Finally, he said he looked forward to lending his firm's expertise to the Côte d'Ivoire.

The mayor said that he wanted the president to know that, even though the United States government sometimes seems to reward countries that were manifestly not its friends and whose governments were certainly not stable, he appreciated the Côte d'Ivoire's sharing our philosophy of government and its many achievements in 26 years of independence.

He also wanted the president to know that the United States private sector was interested in helping. In this spirit, he said, surely other communities in the United States have similar resources to offer and these are offered in the spirit of helping. The mayor went on to introduce Wilfred Marshal, the director of the Office of Small Business Assistance of the City of Los Angleles, who had brought together this diverse group in the spirit of good faith. The mayor concluded by expressing his admiration for the president as a friend and a world leader, and said he and his colleagues looked forward to working with him and his government.

The president spoke of examples of cooperation with other countries, saying that Côte d'Ivoire fully appreciated the need for this. For example, he said, "At independence, we signed agreements with France under which they were to help modernize and mechanize our agriculture. After one year, I had to stop importing machinery from France. They said to me, 'you are not following through on your agreements.' I said, 'look, you have no more forest to clear, and your soil has been tilled for centuries. Your farm machinery is designed accordingly: it can't clear land or till packed soil that has never been tilled before.' So I turned to the United States, which was still clearing land and breaking new soil and whose machinery is designed accordingly. That is why, today on our roads and in our fields, you will see Caterpillar and other American machinery. We are not inhibited in this area."

"Take Abidjan," the president continued, "a city built for the colonial era. It is not suited to the modern era, with its twisting narrow streets and cops directing traffic at every corner. I admire Washington, but much prefer the simplicity of New York: broad, straight streets intersecting at right angles, where streetlights instead of cops impose discipline. I have been to Los Angeles, and I saw the impressive complex of highway interchanges. You might have noticed that we are building a modest one here, down by the lagoon. They started to build one out of a mountain of earth, but I made them take it down. No more mountains of earth, I said, those are too dirty and hard to maintain. We shouldn't be building with earth when we have steel and concrete. Why not build like they do elsewhere? That is why, if you go to the interior towns and cities, you will see broad, straight streets. Twisting streets are pretty, but outmoded, (and) we have the room.

"We must change with the times," the president continued, "and America has proven itself. We shouldn't be
using steam now, we would never get anywhere. Having
been through the Industrial Revolution, we must now leap
into the computer age; we must look ahead without looking
back. This is why we have an open door and open mind to
learn all we can, now, and in the future, from those who
have preceded us."

The mayor thanked the president, then spoke of an item
he had overlooked earlier: the key importance of agribusi-
ness in southern California. The interest of one firm, that had
almost sent a representative on this trip, in exporting Ivorian
produce, especially pineapples to the United States. This
firm also had expertise in development of special strains
which, for example, had very long shelf lives. This, said the
mayor, is another example of the lively interest Americans
had in the Côte d'Ivoire.

The president invited us to go to the next room for
lunch, where the conversation continued along similar lines.

End of Adaptation

The federal government also is actively promoting overseas private investment with Third World countries and en-
couraging minority participation in the process. For ten
years the government has owned a small, little known,
profit-making corporation called the Overseas Private Investment Corporation (OPIC), which was headed by a black
American attorney, J. Bruce Llewellyn. The mandate of OPIC
is to promote small business investments overseas. It does
this by requiring that a large percentage of its funds be
loaned directly to small business, and use of its profits on
loaned funds (up to 50 percent) to further subsidize services
and promote programs to assist small business investment
overseas. Although the agency does not keep records on the

racial background of its borrowers, it is reported that at least two have been black. The first minority loan was to TAW International Leasing, a black-owned firm that leases heavy automotive equipment owned by Jake Henderson, Jr., which had expanded its operation into ten African countries by 1973.

Opportunities for small business investment in Africa are abundant, and there are expanded opportunities for minority participation in this development. To paraphrase Peggy Shepard, author of the report on OPIC and minority participation: OPIC's new push toward small business involvement is giving black business a better chance to participate in international business, but there is a learning process inherent in this. The key thing is expertise, not capital, says Henderson.[16]

These examples suggest a kind of link between blacks and Third World development that is clearly of benefit to blacks in providing employment and a sense of valued participation in meaningful enterprise. For the developing countries, the reward is the high technical skill and expertise as well as a meaningful and dignified cultural connection within which to carry out national development. For the United States as a whole, the value of this liaison is immense, both in terms of the new roles and elevated status that American blacks thus become heir to and in terms of providing a creative way for the white supremacy mythology to die a deserved, nonviolent, unnoticed, and relatively painless death.

Questions for Review and Further Study

1. Explain the concept of perspective and how it applies to the study of race relations in the United States.

2. What are the three suggested perspectives found in black American communities?

3. What is the meaning of castelike as used in this chapter? How does this differ from the meaning of *caste,* for example, as it exists in India?

4. Explain the meaning of colonialism and of imperialism and indicate how they are said to relate to racism in the United States and world.

Notes

1. Additional reasons, or factors, leading to the same goal and relating to the social structure of the society itself have been suggested by Talcott Parsons. See his "Full Citizenship for the Negro American: A Sociological Problem," *The Negro American,* ed. with Kenneth B. Clark (Boston: Houghton Mifflin, 1966).

2. See Tamotsu Shibutani, *Society and Personality, An Interactionist Approach to Social Psychology* (Englewood Cliffs, N.J.: Prentice-Hall, 1961). See especially discussion on pp. 118-27. I have made use of the concept in an attempt to distinguish degrees of commitment to delinquent norms among a group of juvenile hall detainees. See "Varieties of Juvenile Delinquency," *British Journal of Criminology* (January 1962), pp. 251-61.

3. See W. I. Thomas, *The Polish Peasant in Europe and America,* with Florian Znaniecki, (New York: Knopf, 1927), pp. 1846-49; see also Thomas, *Primitive Behavior* (New York: McGraw-Hill, 1937), p. 8.

4. Joseph A. Gobineau, *Inequality of the Human Races,* trans. by Adrian Collins (London: Heinemann, 1915).

5. For a dramatic account of this great time based on actual events and written by a master storyteller, see

Howard Fast, *Freedom Road* (New York: Duell, Sloan and Pearce, 1944).

6. This is implied in Adrianne Koch, *The American Enlightenment: The Shaping of the American Experiment and a Free Society*, (New York: Braziller, 1965).

7. Robert Park's stage of assimilation (discussed earlier) bears some resemblance to what can be expected as proportional representation is reached. However, in my characterization assimilation is one among other options, though doubtless one that is increasingly utilized.

8. An excellent account of this process can be found in Frank Tannenbaum, *Slave and Citizen, The Negro in America* (New York: Knopf, 1946). The position of Tannenbaum that slavery in the United States was more severe than in Latin America has been challenged by a number of scholars in recent years. See discussion in August Meier and Elliott Rudwick, *From Plantation to Ghetto* (New York: Hill and Wang, 1976), pp. 69-75.

9. The term imperialism is given a variety of meanings. In the words of Hans Daalder the term is entirely at the mercy of its user. My use of it here denotes the aggressive expansion of the European powers into non-European societies and establishing hegemony therein by force and violence. It should be pointed out that although the version of it of concern in this analysis is associated with capitalism as a form of socioeconomic organization, it is by no means exclusive to capitalist systems. See the discussion by Hans Daalder, "Imperialism," *Encyclopedia of the Social Sciences*, ed. David Sills, vol. 7 (New York: Macmillan, 1968), pp. 101-8. English imperialist expansion, as it relates to race and color, is ably described by Robert Huttenback. See his *Racism and Empire, White Settlers and Colored Immigrants in the British Self-Governing Colonies, 1830-1910* (Ithaca, N.Y.: Cornell University Press, 1976).

10. Rupert Emerson, *From Empire to Nation: The Rise of*

Self-Assertion of Asian and African Peoples (Cambridge, Mass.: Harvard University Press, 1960), p. 3.

11. Aime Cesaire, *Discourse on Colonialism*, trans. by Joan Pinkham (New York: Monthly Review Press, 1972), p. 21.

12. Rudolph Van Albertini, *Decolonization: The Administration and Future of the Colonies 1919-1960*, trans. by Francisca Garvie (New York: Doubleday, 1971), p. 523.

13. A point made some years ago and which it is important to reemphasize. See Sethard Fisher, "Essay Review: Negro Life and Social Process," *Social Problems* (Winter, 1966), pp. 343-53.

14. *Black Enterprise*, February 1978, p. 38.

15. Ibid., May 1979, p. 15.

16. Ibid., March 1979, p. 40.

10
PROLETARIAN VANGUARD OR INTEREST GROUP

We now come to the important question of strategy and tactics. I have argued that black Americans are now in the process of achieving upward mobility in the United States at an unprecedented rate when viewed historically. I further claim that the process is not likely to be halted and reversed as has been the case historically. Major reasons for this change in the historical pattern are the emergence of new and more positive definitions about blackness and being black among blacks themselves, and the recent rapid decline of colonialism throughout the world. It was stressed, however, that the decline of racism in the United States is not a predestined matter. Awareness and intelligent struggle must be guided by strategic and tactical thinking best suited to the situation within which the struggle is taking place. The issues of strategy and tactics are taken up in this chapter.

A number of different influences are competing for dominance in directing the course of the black equality movement. There are separatist influences that prescribe detachment by blacks from whites and the buildup of a separate society. There are liberal, or pluralist influences that advocate interest group formation among blacks and other minorities as the most viable means of achieving racial equality. There are Marxist influences that suggest a need to view the strug-

gle for racial equality as part of a broader process of social class change. Each of these options or tendencies is part of already existing approaches to social change that are alive in the broader society and world. Two of them, because of their rather broad appeal within the black equality movement, are discussed and assessed in this chapter.

Marxism and the liberal approach to the problem of racism are discussed in order to determine which is better suited as the basis for tactics and strategy to guide the growth and prosperity of the black equality movement. Each of these approaches is both ideologically based and theoretically rooted in the history of ideas of the Western world. Attention has already been given to theoretical aspects of these approaches. What do they suggest by way of tactics and strategy?

One important change within the black community, mentioned earlier, is an emphasis on black pride. This represents cultural change. There are now new and healthy feelings emerging among black people in the United States about blackness that are profoundly different from the conditioning about blackness traditionally inculcated in the surrounding White Anglo-Saxon Protestant American culture. Testimony to the new exuberance and feelings of worth are legion in the writings of young black students who are now moving in large numbers on to college campuses throughout the country. For example, Rhonda Leonard writes of pride,

> Now, almost overnight a new sense of pride has swept over black people. The seeds for this new feeling were sown during the reign of the King, Martin Luther King. He drew black people together.

> There is a new sense of beauty, magnificent, powerful, bare of

phoniness. Get white ideas of beauty out of your head and you will feel it.

I personally wish I could put the feelings it gives me on this paper, but the only word I can think of is magnificent. Magnificent is wild, free, beautiful and untamed, to me.[1]

Clearly, the emphasis on black pride and dignity is a healthy trend; its very health being the affront it offers to the traditional white supremacist imagery. It stands to reorient American culture in an important way (black and white alike) to recognition of beauty in blackness and to recognition of a pridefulness and pleasure in being black in America.

However, to endure and represent basic change in the United States, such widespread changes in cultural definitions must become institutionalized. The new surge of pride in blackness among black people, and the new and positive acquaintance with blackness by white Americans must not be a fitful, short-lived episode in history, but a permanently changed condition of existence. To endure, cultural definitions require structural support, which means that this new sense of dignity and pride must be carried into the wider community with skill and determination. This change will survive and prosper only if it can be buttressed with social power, prestige, and influence. This means that the current focus of the black movement must be on the tactics and strategy for achieving social power, prestige, and influence. One important tactic for their achievement, influential among some black youth organizations, stems from the tradition of the revolutionary left.

The tradition of revolution as a means for social change has given rise to some notable human achievements. In 1776, the colonists declared their independence from England and drafted a declaration setting forth the rationale for revolution and a view of what is proper between the governed and those who govern. Then in France in 1789, revolution as a means of social change deposed a corrupt French aristocracy. In 1917, in Russia, Czar Nicholas II was overthrown by an insurgent group and a new set of rulers emerged with a drastically different policy direction.

In the interval between these eighteenth- and twentieth-century revolutions, a series of ideas and programs about revolution as a tactic for social change appeared and have enjoyed wide popularity among oppressed peoples throughout the world. These ideas attempt to explain the social origins of oppression and to suggest techniques for ending it. Important among these have been the writings of Karl Marx, Frederick Engels, and Vladimir Ilyich Lenin. Today, the keenly felt sense of oppression of subject peoples is widely influenced by ideas of revolutionary change particularly as oppressive institutions and peoples fail to meet the just demands of oppressed groups.

The connection between the black movement and revolution has been discussed by several spokesmen. According to Harold Cruse, not himself of revolutionary persuasion,

> The theory and practice of revolutionary Marxism in America is based on the assumption that white labor, both organized and unorganized, must be a radical, anticapitalist force in America and must form an alliance with Negroes for the liberation of both labor and the Negro from capitalist exploitation.[2]

George Breitman, of the Socialist Worker's party, and an ideological antagonist of Cruse has also made the case in his *How a Minority Can Change Society*. In the concluding sections of this statement he writes,

> And so today many of us, I am sure, will be able to grasp and act on the concept of Negroes as leaders of the workers' revolution not just as a possibility, but as a probability. I shall not try, because that is a job for the whole movement, to work out

or complete everything that flows from this concept, except to say that much does, and that all of it seems to be a cause for optimism.[3]

First (as stressed by Cruse) it must be clearly seen that revolutionary theory has as its objective broad social change, i.e., change from one kind of social system to another. Generally, this corresponds to a change from capitalism to socialism. For example, Claude Lightfoot, long associated with the American Communist party and author of *Ghetto Rebellion to Black Liberation*, argues: "Since capitalism is the source of the inferior status of black people, it would follow that only with the elimination of the system can Negroes gain equality." [4] This is to say that black equality is not the basic aim of revolutionary change; rather its primary aim is destruction of the system that gave rise to racism, namely, capitalism. An important assumption here is that racism will disappear with this change. Lightfoot continues,

> Thus racism was specifically a product of capitalist society, serving as a cloak behind which to mask the drive for profits. Profits and super-profits, this is the rationale behind the oppression of the black people. Therefore, the removal of the economic incentives which give birth to this ideology is the main way to destroy it.[5]

Second, as stressed by Breitman, the specific role of black people in this overall process of system change is that of vanguard or catalyst. It is from black people, and their dissatisfactions and revolt, that the stimulus for the broader movement will presumably come. Recognizing the failure of white workers to respond according to the expectation of revolutionary Marxist theory, subsequent modifications of this theory have focused on the black movement, seeing it as a precursor to the larger proletarian revolution. The vanguard role is taken seriously by many black students who function in leadership roles on college campuses. They have

come to envision the Marxist idea of class conflict as fundamental to black subordination and to assume that the road to
black equality is through a black-led proletarian uprising
and seizure of power.

Logically, this development leads to a heavy emphasis
on the revolutionary left vision among subsequent generations of black leaders, and followers, and may thus implant
to a significant degree a revolutionary orientation in the
black community. Evidence that this process exists among
blacks is provided by the following open letter, written by
Nathan Hare. In the 1960s he was the center of a major controversy over Black Studies at San Francisco State College.

February 26, 1975

AN OPEN LETTER ON MY RESIGNATION AS
PUBLISHER OF THE BLACK SCHOLAR

After almost six years as publisher of *The Black Scholar*,
since its conception and inception in the late fall of 1969, I am
resigning and severing all association with it and its activities. This decision comes with considerable regret, but it does
not come suddenly. I do so with a gnawing sadness, but also
with resolute satisfaction that in doing so at this crucial time
in our history I may contribute my part in preventing the
black movement from making an untimely mistake and getting sidetracked and further decimated for perhaps another
generation.

I have had the rare opportunity to watch firsthand a
black Marxist takeover and seizure of an organization, in this
case *The Black Scholar*. At the same time I have been engaged
in a serious study of Marxism since 1965, receiving informal
tutelage and official instruction from some of the best Marxist minds. My study came after a Ph.D. in sociology from the
University of Chicago and simultaneously but not always in

connection with my activity in the black movement. My active involvement in the black movement began with SNCC (the Student Nonviolent Coordinating Committee), on through RAM, the Revolutionary Action Movement, and The Black Panther Party (though I never officially joined these organizations) and as the subject of two stormy political firings (at Howard University in 1967 and in the first and longest black studies strike at San Francisco State College in the year 1968-69).

Although I came to appreciate the basic insights of Marx and their potential contribution to black struggle, I also saw that they need to be almost totally revamped (as no doubt Marx would do if he were alive as a brilliant social scientist who always tried to tie his analysis to the historical context).

Anyway, *The Black Scholar* was launched with the expressed aim of providing a vehicle, an open forum for debate, study, and analysis among black intellectuals and activists of all persuasions, toward evolving a new and viable black ideology that could rally black people and their allies at large for a sustained and victorious struggle for liberation. I saw and still see that struggle as one of both class and color. The challenge was to find some way, somehow, to combine them. But the unfortunate fact is that most militants strive instead to emphasize one and reject the other. The majority of American Marxists, for their part, see black revolutionary change primarily, even totally, as a class struggle, and seek accordingly to minimize the relevance of color. Their motives are sometimes ideological, sometimes grow out of political rivalry, sometimes personal or ego dilemmas, sometimes a combination of these.

There is much that I could say about that, but I only want to say that I have reached the point of no return and can no longer endure their strategy and tactics. These included a narrow devotion to conventional Marxist interpretations and an ironclad intolerance for and resistance to opposing views. They do not see this as a policy of self isolation. If you are not with the people, in a certain sense you are against them. A vanguard without a base is not a true vanguard but an elite. Now and again they will feign to change their isolationist ways, and actually appear to do so, but it is true that a leopard cannot change its spots; it can only camouflage them. Thus, *The Black Scholar* which initially had been widely acclaimed as one of the most significant black publishing events of recent times in intellectual and movement circles, has increasingly come to be regarded as locked in a deadly vice of progressive deterioration.

This is largely because instant black Marxists are seldom their own men or women, let alone their own original opinion makers. This is in part due to the sociological fact that most people are basically conformist, even those who identify with radicalism. I have known and wrestled with this agonizing fact since the Howard rebellion of 1967. The radicals merely cling to a popular or conventional fad or fashion in radicalism. I have watched it close-up and it appears to be a form of religious conversion. Their fanaticism, however, does not bring undying devotion to their cult. Instead they switch allegiance from one group (and its ideology) to another according to popular fad or their own intermittent regroupings and reconversions.

The Black Scholar under the umbrella of the Black World Foundation was incorporated as a non-profit organization with by-laws and a board of directors, with all policy decisions to be made by majority vote of the board members. That was supposed to be in the spirit of revolution, but it was my first mistake. That majority is now black Marxist, and I soon found my contribution sabotaged and almost liquidated. It was much like the problems Dr. W.E.B. Du Bois had with the old NAACP of the Walter White era before Du Bois left that group. The particulars are of course different, but the problems remain the same.

But, I hung on feeling that my own personal satisfaction was secondary to a chance to help black people. I stood perplexed, but I felt that much of the current ideological conflict and bickering between narrow Marxists and ultra-nationalists was spurious and eventually would pass away, that somehow there would emerge a metamorphosis in black thought which would transcend the narrow dictates and interpretations of both of them.

Meanwhile, I began to withdraw temporarily to prepare myself for a later contribution to the understanding of the black condition on which that new transcendence could be based. And so I returned to school and in August of this year I am to receive my second Ph.D. (this one in clinical psychology, with special emphasis on psychotherapy). I intend to wed both fields (sociology and psychotherapy) as instruments for the understanding and interpretation of the black condition; not as ends in their conventional selves or in the service of whatever dogma. This has left me with increasingly less time to devote to *The Black Scholar*, and it is clear now that my new direction was the first stage of my leaving *The Black Scholar* and moving to a higher level of involvement in the black movement. That is all I can say at this time. Thank you for listening and I remain yours,

For our freedom,
Nathan Hare,
February 26, 1975

Consequences of the wide development of this process will be to increasingly identify the revolutionary left with the cause of black people, and to nourish the rise to massive polarization and containment tactics. A widespread alliance between the black equality movement and the revolutionary left will further the gap between the black and white communities and incalculably increase the hostility and fear of the one for the other. To the extent that inroads to the wider society have been cut off, the power, prestige, and influence needed in the black community will be increasingly impossible to achieve. If the revolutionary left vision is inappropriate, what approach to black equality is better suited to accelerated gain?

The lethargy and reluctance of power holders in the United States can be drastically changed, not by a total investment by blacks in the tactics and strategy of the revolutionary left, but by a posture of militant civil disobedience combined with interest group strategy and orientation. This approach allows the black movement to utilize the widespread and increasing legitimacy of its aims (among black and white) to its advantage, and also to make use of the continuing responsiveness of American institutions to effective group pressure.

The tradition of civil disobedience is generally associated with the life and works of Henry David Thoreau. In fact, his widely read essay *Civil Disobedience*, was written while he was in jail for refusing to pay poll taxes. He held, accurately, that this tax was promoted by a few slaveholders who were using the government as their tool for extending slavery into new territory. This doctrine, of course, did not originate with Thoreau, but his particular formulation of it has had wide appeal and wide effectiveness against various kinds of tyranny. Gandhi's movement in South Africa and India and the freedom riders from all over the United States have made effective use of this important tradition of revolt. As a current tactical and strategic option for the black community it has infinitely greater value than the tactics and strategy issuing from the revolutionary left. Perhaps the most recent effective use of the approach was made by Reverend Martin Luther King, Jr.

The tradition of civil disobedience poses the problem of racism in terms that are essentially different from those stemming from the vision of the revolutionary left. The main difference is that it depicts racism as not simply a matter of capitalism versus socialism (its origin being clearly associated with the rise of capitalism), but also as a matter of justice and injustice. This is an important difference because it is primarily issue rather than system oriented. It recognizes the important fact that the social system can change without a significant change in the racist status quo. Several implications can be drawn from this view.

An issue-oriented view of racism suggests, first, that black inequality is an autonomous, real evil to be resisted as such rather than a condition that will automatically disappear once capitalism is destroyed as envisioned by the revolutionary left. Black equality cannot wait for overall change of the social system from capitalist to socialist or to some other form. Its aims are straightforwardly those of spreading black Americans throughout the stratification system in proportions equal to their numbers under conditions of pride and dignity. This is not to say that black equality is antithetical to concerns for broader social change, but that the interest in black equality at this point cannot be subordinated or sacrificed to broader concerns.

Second, allies of the black movement must be dedicated to the goals of black equality rather than participate in the black movement as exploitative agents of other movements. The strategy of the revolutionary left, which is to promote revolutionary change using the black movement as a vanguard, cuts off large numbers of potential allies who fall on the liberal to conservative side of the political spectrum. Allies in the interest of black equality must be sought across the spectrum of political affiliation, excluding only the racists. Can the revolutionary left offer blacks assurances that the widespread change that it promises, once achieved, will end racism? It seems entirely possible that racism and the new society of the revolutionary left could coexist. A hard focus now on racism will provide greater assurance that the need for such coexistence will not arise.

Third, black protest action should be geared to black gains (power) in specific existing institutions rather than to destroying these institutions. The black community must set certain pragmatic goals to be achieved over a specific time, and must mobilize itself and its white allies to achieve these goals. Primary among these must be proportional political representation and economic participation. Black people must count their numbers and ensure proportional representation at local, state and federal levels of government, as well as in the industrial labor market. The plan for reform should coordinate building skills and capabilities within the black community with the expansion of opportunity in the wider society. This means an emphasis on acquiring the skills necessary for effective functioning as politicians, businesnesmen, and professors, according to the freely chosen dispositions and talents of black students. The ultimate goal of this plan would be proportional distribution of black Americans in the class structure of the society.

The achievement of political power by ethnic groups is explained by Chuck Stone as follows:

> The dominant fact of ethnic political power, more specifically the political power of the Irish, Italians, Jews, and Poles, is the ability of these groups to control a higher proportion of the high elective and appointive offices than their percentage in the population warrants. They all have perfected the mechanics that control the theory of proportional equality.[6]

Perfection of the mechanics of proportional equality, as Stone calls it, must become a major aim of the black movement in all areas of a sizable black population.

John Kenneth Galbraith describes the process by which the competitive advantage of disadvantaged groups is strengthened as the development of countervailing power.

Historically, such groups as labor, businesses, and associations whose market power was weak have developed a pattern of internal organization for purposes of greater advantage in competition against holders of original market power. Galbraith sees some groups in American society as having a kind of competitive advantage based on their position with reference to the production and distribution of goods and services in the society. Others he sees as distinctly disadvantaged. A process of internal organization and the development of adequate strategy and tactics, he argues, have been the traditional manner by which countervailing power has been mobilized and increased market advantage achieved by formerly powerless groups. He argues: "There are still millions of Americans who are without any organized expression of market power and whose standards of living and welfare are categorical evidence of the consequences. These include, for example, some two million hired farm workers, the truly forgotten men of American life."[7]

He further argues that

> The group that seeks countervailing power is, initially, a numerous and disadvantaged group which seeks organization because it faces, in its market, a much smaller, and much more advantaged group. This situation is well calculated to excite public sympathy and, because there are numerous votes involved, to recruit political support. [8]

Galbraith also stresses the increasingly important role of government in the development of countervailing power:

> In fact, the support of countervailing power has become in modern times perhaps the major domestic peacetime function of the federal government. Labor sought and received it in the protection and assistance which the Wagner Act provided to union organization. Farmers sought and received it in the form of federal price supports to their markets , a direct subsidy of market power. Unorganized workers have sought and

received it in the form of minimum wage legislation ... These measures, all designed to give a group a market power it did not have before, comprised the most important legislative acts of the New Deal.[9]

In his brief sketch of the concept of countervailing power, Galbraith has essentially charted the effective developmental course for the realization of power for black Americans. It is precisely the development of internal strength and organization and the use of these to demand government assistance in boosting their competitive capability that black Americans must seek. In fact, the major legislative actions in the civil rights area represent precisely this process. School desegregation legislation, fair employment and fair housing legislation, legislative prohibitions against discrimination in places of public accommodation, and so on, are indeed actions that add to the competitive capability of black Americans. It is drastic acceleration of this process that must be a goal in the coming years by those who seek black equality in American society.

Finally, this approach, as is also true of the revolutionary left approach, recognizes the need for black solidarity (though not for purposes of racial chauvinism, black nationalism, or as a revolutionary vanguard) but for the ultimate purpose of upward mobility in the stratification system. Upward mobility for ethnic groups in the contemporary United States seems to involve at least the following three conditions:

❖ Ethnic concentrations in specific politically relevant geographic areas. Boston and New York are areas of high Irish concentration and of considerable Irish political influence and control. New York and Connecticut are states with high Italian populations. In Newark, New Jersey, and Hartford, Connecticut, Italians are a predominant influence in city government.

The recent increase in the number of black mayors is a reflection of the massive black migration to the central cities of the major metropolitan areas.

❖ The buildup of rituals and groups and associations designed to maintain ethnic solidarity and group welfare. Jewish organizations of great national prestige and influence, such as the Anti-Defamation League and B'nai B'rith, are well known. Such national groups, combined with the local community support from which their legitimacy derives, are powerful forces in influencing election of local and state politicians and in influencing national policy. Ethnic networks of this kind can also be found among the Irish, Italians, and Poles, though they vary in extensiveness and effectiveness from group to group, place to place, and time to time.

❖ Forging of functional links in the wider society in the process of which stable patterns of political and economic participation and gain emerge.

Ethnic concentrations and ethnic networks that fan throughout the society are necessary but not sufficient conditions for proportional reward to an ethnic group. There is, in addition, the highly competitive and entrepreneurial process by which the historical and cultural resources of ethnic groups are brought into play for purposes of competitive advantage. This process leads to relatively stable patterns of accommodation of these groups to one another and of each group to the surrounding world. Typical career patterns and dominant patterns of relatedness to the institutions of the wider society are laid down within this context. Nathan Glazer and Daniel Patrick Moynihan comment on this process as it applies to the Irish: "The Irish controlled the political machines and city administrations, and Irish wealth developed in construction, contracting, trucking, and public utilities, on the basis in part of this political link."[10] Jews have been prominent in the manufacture of clothing, in ownership of department stores, and in entertainment. In more recent times they have become prominent in light manufacturing, real estate, and building.

The ability of an ethnic group to carve out opportunity structures successfully depends on a range of factors. One set of such factors can be envisioned as largely internal to the group itself. They tell of the degree of capability within the group for coming to terms with the external world. Such features of group life as level of education, extent of professional skill, and self-conceptions are of major importance here. Although for analytic purposes these characteristics may be seen as internal, they do not operate independent of external conditions. One major internal task of the black movement is the elaboration of a model for bringing unity and greater organizational effectiveness to black communities throughout the country. Such a model must be one that both unifies and at the same time encompasses the vast diversity of views, opinions, and situations among black people. John Monroe's idea of a national black union is suggestive. Using an analogy with labor, he argues,

What white America respects is not weakness but strength; America respects not rational pleas for help, but rather any serious threat to vital parts of the system; and most particularly any threat to profits and sacred property. I am old enough to remember the great national labor struggles in the 1930's. We learned then that our great industries, Ford, General Motors, big steel, were not responsive to the needs and concerns of the individual workers, until the workers, with a prolonged, brutal effort, pulled their thing together, and developed the institutional strength to stop the great factories and shut off their profits. Then the working man got attention, and he got respect. He became then a respectable threat; an organized, institutional threat. The American black community will start making real progress in the United States when it discovers the analogy between its own position and the position of unorganized labor a half century ago. It will not work in our society to think of the black community as a separate nation: the metaphor is just wrong. But it will work to think of the black community as a great, national, black union ... Whereas labor unions were in a position to command respect and attention because they could and did close down factories, the black community is in a position to command respect and attention because it can shut down great cities. That threat strikes a nerve in the power structure: it makes its money in the great cities.[11]

The idea of a national black union is a strategic suggestion. It comes closest to the kind of organizational vehicle needed for promoting an indigenous black equality movement. It makes possible a movement that aggressively challenges racism unencumbered by the fetters of the revolutionary vision. This movement would have a legitimacy that could gain and maintain a broad base of support in the wider society.[12]This condition is absolutely essential to its success.

The potential for accelerated gain to the black community exists in the ever increasing numbers of black youth moving onto college campuses throughout the nation. However, realization of this potential depends on the extent to which this movement results in significant increments of skill and capability among black people. Given a rapid increase in professional, craft, administrative, and other skills, there exists the real prospect for unprecedented change in the status of black Americans. It is this possibility that makes the current emphasis on the revolutionary vision among black leadership on college campuses of special concern to the entire black community. Because of their disastrous consequences, several tactics currently employed by some campus leaders of the black movement should be avoided. This leadership must not

❖ See itself as in the service of the revolutionary left, but as in the service of black equality that recognizes visions other than those of the revolutionary left as both relevant and necessary.

❖ Avoid involvement and excellence in conventional curriculum areas and insist on entirely black or "soul" courses. They must promote academic excellence along conventional lines as well as innovation.

❖ Demand separation in public institutions, but pridefully take the dignity of blackness into the white world to further dispel myths of white superiority.

❖ Use threat, intimidation, and subterfuge to manipulate opinions among black students, but promote dialogue, discussion, and resolve diverse opinions through freely emerging consensus, and recognize the necessity of tolerating differences and simultaneously maintaining unity.

Further, strategy among black people (campus leadership included) must seek as an overall goal proportional representation in the political, economic, and social life of the United States. To achieve this goal two targets must be clearly kept in the mind: (1) constant and accelerated expansion of opportunities for black people; and (2) constant and accelerated preparation of black people to effectively, and in dignity, make use of these opportunities. Through a vehicle such as a national black union, effective demands could be made on government, industry, and political institutions for proportional representation according to an agreed-upon timetable. Such a change can be stimulated only through the militant, creative, strategic, and tactical efforts of black people themselves.

Turning now to factors more external to interest groups, how amenable is the larger society to the self-interested actions of black Americans? To the extent that the image of the group in the wider society is one of negativism and subordination, external barriers will prohibit group advancement and welfare. Some decline of the traditional recalcitrance of white racism to black prosperity is an important new change in the external world of great importance to blacks.

The school desegregation process, combined with the emphasis now given minority employment (in particular affirmative action legislation) symbolize this decline. To be sure, this is all too slow and all too insufficient. Nevertheless, it means that the second and third stages of the above cited process can now get underway with high prospects of success.

The previously suggested economic, political, and social autonomy of the nonwhite African, Asian, and Latin American peoples are additional external factors that facilitate this decline. Japan is now a recognized power and China has rapidly developed to the same stature. Africans are now the undisputed rulers of the African continent with the important exception of South Africa, which in time will also become ruled by black people. Thus, by dint of the demise of colonialism, the emerging Third World offers support, sympathy, and some degree of influence in efforts to achieve racial equality in the United States.

Accompanying this massive changeover of power and authority is the growth of new and happier visions about themselves among formerly oppressed peoples (internal factors) that also facilitate this decline. Myths of white superiority nurtured by the colonialist cultures are fast fading as the pride and arrogance of freedom take hold of nonwhite peoples throughout the world. This new reality has special implications for black Americans. Their condition in the United States is a bellwether of the capability of the country to come to terms with the newly emerging equality and independence of black and brown peoples throughout the world.

It must be noted that there remain powerful external forces, particularly the Radical Right and its lunatic violent fringe, which are in chronic opposition to equality for black and other minority Americans. The threat of such groups was emphasized in Adaptation VII from the Southern Poverty Law Center. This organization takes as its special mission careful monitoring of the illegal activities of the Radical Right, especially the Klan.

It is important to note that to date, confinement of the violent wing of the Radical Right is a matter of constant vigilance and prosecution of its illegal activities. The following adaptation emphasizes the chronic nature of the threat and the turmoil generated in efforts to curtail it.

Adaptation IX

This adaptation comes from the Los Angeles Times, April 20, 1991. It was written by Times staff writer Ronald L. Sobel. The struggle to keep law enforcement free of lunatic radical right influence is constant. This adaptation tells of the effort in Los Angeles.

Klan's Attempt to Recruit Police Probed

Racism. LAPD confirms some officers received KKK mailings. Gates says he would seek dismissal of any officer who joined the hate group.

Attempts to recruit Los Angeles police officers into a militant Ku Klux Klan group are being investigated by the LAPD's Anti-Terrorist Division, according to police officials.

A two-page application from the Kansas City, Mo. based White Knights of the Ku Klux Klan has been received by some LAPD divisions, department spokesman Cmdr. Robert S. Gil confirmed. The investigation was launched after copies of the recruitment literature was shown to the Los Angeles Police Commission on Tuesday.

Lt. Fred Nixon, another department spokesman, said the inquiry was initially launched by the LAPD's Internal Affairs Division, but it was then handed over to the anti-terrorist squad because of the nature of the klan.

"It's very distasteful," Gil said of the KKK mailers. "It represents everything we don't stand for .... We don't know if any officers are taking it seriously."

Chief Daryl F. Gates said through a spokesman that if any LAPD officer joins the Ku Klux Klan, "I would charge him with misconduct and I would do my best to fire him." The White Knights unit, which was organized in 1989, is "armed, super-militant" and has "a potential for serious trouble making," according to a report released this year by the Anti-Defamation League of B'nai B'rith, a Jewish civil rights group headquartered in New York.

According to an intelligence report issued this month by Klanwatch, another KKK watchdog group based in Montgomery, Ala., the White Knights leader, or Imperial Dragon, Dennis Mahon, has been promoting "a heightened stance of militancy."

In a telephone interview from his Tulsa, Okla. office, Mahon did not deny his group has the potential for violence. "We're the most violent klan in America," he said. "We are trained in counterinsurgency."

Mahon, 40, said his group, which wears white berets but no robes, has 400 members, more than twice as many as a membership count conducted by the ADL and Klanwatch. The White Knights, he said, mailed the recruitment applications a couple of weeks ago to several LAPD divisions, to individual officers at the stations and to some officers' homes.

Thus far, Mahon said, he has received about 50 responses from officers asking for more information. "A handful," he said, actually returned filled-in applications.

Moreover, he said, "if [cops] see [Police Chief Daryl F.] Gates hammered, you're gonna see a lotta guys join up." Mahon was referring to the controversy over whether Gates should resign after the beating of black motorist Rodney G. King by four white LAPD officers.

Mahon's claim that he has received inquiries prompted ADL and Klanwatch officials to question whether Mahon was attempting to attract publicity.

Irwin Suall, the ADL's fact-finding director in New York, said he was "very dubious" about any claims Mahon makes about recruiting police officers. Mahon's group, he said, has been very weak in California.

Danny Welch, director of Klanwatch, said a handful of

officers in relatively small police departments have joined KKK units, but added he "would find it hard to believe" that LAPD officers would even correspond with the White Knights.

End of Adaptation

The demise of colonialism and reduction of racism in our society is part and parcel of a more widespread change in the modern world, namely, change in capitalism as a dominant mode of socioeconomic organization. It is toward acceleration of this change in the United States that the revolutionary left incites the black movement. There is, however, an alternative view of this decline more in keeping with the dynamics of social change in large-scale industrial societies. Robert Heilbroner views organized knowledge and its applied counterpart, scientific technology, as an irresistible force in modern times that will ultimately change capitalism. In discussing the corrosive effect of science and technology on capitalism in America, he argues,

> The incursion of technology has pushed the frontiers of work from the farm to the factory, then the factory to the store and the office, and now from store and office into a spectrum of jobs whose common denominator is that they require public action and public funds for their initiation and support. The employment-upsetting characteristics of technology thus act to speed capitalism along the general path of planning and control down which it is simultaneously impelled by the direct environment-upsetting impact of technological change.[13]

Notable in the Heilbroner account of the demise of capitalism in America is its divergence from the vision of this demise forecast by the traditional revolutionary left. For Heilbroner, the central agents in the decline of capitalism are new knowledge and technology rather than the mobilized opposition of an organized black revolutionary cadre. This new society, independent of the class background of its power wielders, will depend heavily on science and technology as essential ingredients in its political and social life. This emphasis, though not diametrically opposed to that of the revolutionary left, suggests different options for those currently oppressed by capitalism. Rather than irrational militancy against the system, a major effort must be made to acquire the scientific and technological skills that the post capitalistic era will require. Rather than a detached black-separatist withdrawal, there must be creative nurturing and growth of those qualities and capabilities that will ensure black survival in dignity and equality in a society greatly dependent on science and technology.

Indeed, as the Marxists claim, there is a relationship between the black equality movement and class-based change in the broader society. However, I believe that analyses by both the revolutionary left as well as those of conventional academic spokespersons have assessed the relationship improperly. Neither group has given to racism the priority it deserves in the ordering of social, political, and economic life in the United States. Neither assessment has properly attributed to racism the status of independent variable in discussions of stability and change in the wider society. It is precisely this degree of influence that appears to me warranted due to the depth of racist pathology in the United States.

Questions for Review and Further Study

1. How would you distinguish a Marxist approach to the problem of racial equality from a liberal approach?
2. What are the strengths and weaknesses of each of the approaches cited above?

3. What is the meaning of proportional representation of racial/ethnic groups by class?

4. What is the meaning of "perfecting the mechanics of proportional equality"?

5. Explain the concept of countervailing power.

6. What are the suggested three steps required for black upward mobility?

7. What are the factors "internal" to ethnic groups that facilitate upward mobility?

8. What is your assessment of the suggestion by Monroe that the situation of blacks today is similar to that of unorganized labor a half-century ago? What is Monroe's suggestion for change?

9. How is the decline of racism related to changes in U.S. capitalism?

10. What is the difference between the Heilbroner view of race change and the view of it stemming from the revolutionary left?

Notes

1. Rhonda Leonard, "Pride," *Together* (Black Student Union, University of California: Riverside, 1968-69), p. 32.

2. Harold Cruse, *Marxism and the Negro Struggle* (New York: Pioneer Publishers, 1966), p. 30.

3. George Brightman, *How a Minority Can Change Society: the Real Potential of the Afro-American Struggle* (New York: Pathfinder Press, 1965).

4. Claude Lightfoot, *Ghetto Rebellion to Black Liberation* (New York: International Publishers, 1968), p. 87.

5. Ibid., p. 136.

6. Chuck Stone, *Black Political Power in America* (New York: Bobbs-Merrill, 1968), p. 147.

7. John K. Galbraith, *American Capitalism* (Boston: Houghton Mifflin, 1956), p. 149.

8. Ibid., p. 136.

9. Ibid.

10. Nathan Glazer and Daniel Patrick Moynihan, *Beyond the Melting Pot* (Cambridge, Mass.: MIT Press, 1970), p. 210.

11. John Monroe, "Escape from the Dark Cave," *Nation* (October 1969), pp. 434-39. For an extended discussion of this idea see Appendix D.

12. That such legitimacy is possible is suggested by recent findings regarding racial attitudes that bring the old Bogardus studies up to date. Nationwide studies of racial attitudes utilizing the Bogardus Social Distance Scale were initiated by Emory Bogardus as early as 1926. This scale was utilized in 1946, 1957, 1966, 1977, to determine change in attitudes of ethnic groups toward one another. Thirty ethnic groups within nationwide college student populations were ranked based on their performance on the scale. In 1926, blacks ranked 26; in 1946 they ranked 29; in 1956 they ranked 27; and in 1966 they ranked 29. In the 1977 replication of the study they jumped to 17. These findings were taken to mean a large positive change in attitude toward blacks in American society. See Carolyn A. Owen, Howard C. Eisner, and Thomas R. McFaul, "A Half Century of Social Distance Research: National Replication of the Bogardus Studies," *Sociology and Social Research* (October 1981), pp. 80-98.

How generalizable these findings are is not certain because they were based on college student populations. They are, however, supported by other recent survey results. In their 1972 study for the National Opinion Research Center, "Attitude Towards Racial Integration, The South 'Catches Up,'" (unpublished) Andrew M. Greeley and Paul B. Sheatsley, found impressive changes in attitudes toward blacks over the past three decades. They used acceptability of public school integration as their criterion measure and reported that acceptance by the public had gone from 30 percent in 1952, to 49 percent in 1956, to 63 percent in 1963. By 1970, acceptability had climbed to 74 percent and by 1972 it had reached 86 percent.

13. Robert Heilbroner, *The Limits of American Capitalism* (New York: Harper & Row, 1966), p. 123.

11

NONWHITE EQUALITY AND SOCIAL TRANSITION

In the ongoing preoccupation among social scientists with
such grand issues as stability, instability, and change in the
American social system, racism is a much neglected factor.
Yet, observation clearly shows racism to be an influential
matter in the daily lives of ordinary citizens. Our lives are
influenced regularly and profoundly by racism in a multitude
of ways: fear and turmoil between blacks and whites in
inner-city ghetto areas; anxiety about affirmative action issues; worry over the integration of elementary and high
schools as well as colleges. It seems strange that a matter of
such clear and obvious relevance to the average citizen should
not more meaningfully engage the attention of sociological
theorists.

Marxist students of the race problem are an exception to
this tendency. They do, in fact, link racism and the overall
dynamics of U.S. society. They claim that racism and capitalism are inextricably tied. Yet, the Marxist view is not sufficiently tempered by a full appreciation of the autonomy of
cultural factors in relation to economic factors. Such an
appreciation is found in the contributions of Max Weber to
social science. Neither the traditional omission of race, nor a
subordination of race to class, is an appropriate assessment of
the enormous influence of this form of oppression on our

245

national life.

There is, of course, a connection between racism and social class, and a very important one. The unraveling of this connection and articulation of an alternative to the Marxist vision are the tasks undertaken in this final chapter. I shall argue that the castelike perspective, and the tyranny of coercive racism have been chronic stabilizing forces within the working class that have thwarted proletarian-based efforts at social change and the development of working-class politics.[1]

I shall further argue that only as upward mobility, in significant measure, is achieved by blacks will it be possible for the kind of working-class politics that have developed in other capitalist countries to emerge in the United States. By this assessment, increased racial equality is a precondition for the achievement of further class equality in the United States.

The characterization of contemporary American society as capitalist means several things, among which the following are central[2]: private ownership of the means of production; production primarily for profit; and a legitimating ideology rooted in liberal individualism, currently expressed as social Darwinism.[3] A formidable resistance to the capitalist ethic developed along with the full emergence of capitalism in Europe during the eighteenth century. Today, even in a major capitalist country like the United States, one finds exceptions to the above characterization. There is some public influence on private ownership. There is some control on private profit making. There is considerable opposition to the heritage of liberal individualism. These exceptions, among other realities, are often claimed to indicate that world capitalism is in a state of transition, change, or decline.

Joseph Schumpeter, a non-Marxist economist, made such a claim. Although Schumpeter disagreed with Marxist theory in many essentials, his overall conclusion about capitalism coincided with that of Marx. Both agreed that capitalism is destined to disappear as a dominant form of socioeconomic organization. In *Capitalism, Socialism, Democracy*, Schumpeter wrote,

> Can capitalism survive? No. I do not think it can.... The thesis I shall endeavor to establish is that the actual and prospective performance of the capitalist system is such as to negate the idea of its breaking down under the weight of economic failure, but that its very success undermines the social institutions which protect it, and "inevitably" creates conditions in which it will not be able to live and which strongly point to socialism as the heir apparent.[4]

As noted earlier, Robert Heilbroner, a former student of Schumpeter, is also of the opinion that capitalism will undergo severe change. In his *The Limits of American Capitalism*, he argues,

> Thus, in a manner not entirely dissimilar from the way in which the steady monetization of feudal life weakened the relevance and effectiveness of manorial ties, the incorporation of technology into the working mechanism of the capitalist system also renders less relevant and effective the market ties on which that system is ultimately founded. Partly because of the social disturbances it creates in an urban industrial environment, partly because of the progressive compression of the need for human effort in the provisioning of society, the steady entrance of technology into capitalism forces new social structures of control and supervision to rise within and over the marketplace.[5]

Concerning the nature of the antagonism between capitalism and technology, Heilbroner writes,

> The conflict does not lie on the surface, in any clash between the immediate needs of science and those of capitalism. It lies in the ideas that ultimately inform both worlds. The world of

science, as it is applied by society, is committed to the idea of man as a being who shapes his collective destiny; the world of capitalism to an idea of man as one who permits his common social destination to take care of itself. The essential idea of a society built on scientific engineering is to impose human will on the social universe; that of capitalism to allow the social universe to unfold as if it were beyond human interference.[6]

These several statements suggest a broad movement in U.S. society from its capitalist past and present to a system that limits private profit, that modifies private ownership of production with an eye for the greater public good, and that humanizes the availability of resources. In other words, this is a movement toward a system that attempts to remedy the more blatant ravages of capitalism. There is disagreement about the timing of this change and about the precise areas within the current social structure where it will first, and decisively, appear. For example, Schumpeter suggested the possibility of a paralysis, or "equilibrium," of the present system at some level of output and employment less than maximum. This would slow the "decomposition."[7] In addition, Schumpeter differed from Marxists as to the source of capitalism's decline. His analysis pointed to the social and cultural destruction caused by the "economic engine" rather than the functioning, or malfunctioning, of economic institutions. Further characterization of the transition is provided by Heilbroner:

> The new institutions of social and economic control will appear only slowly and sporadically amid the older forms, and will lack for some time an articulate conception of a purposively constituted and consciously directed social system. The old ideas of the proper primacy of economic aims will linger together with newer ideas of the priority of scientific interests. And no doubt the privileges of the older order will endure side by side with those of the new, just as titles of nobility exist to this very day, some assimilated to the realities of capitalism, some adorning doormen or taxi drivers. It is

conceivable that violence may attend the displacement of power and responsibility from one elite to another, but more probably the transfer will be imperceptible; managed, as in the case of the English aristocracy, by the sons of the old elite entering the professions of the new.

Before the activist philosophy of science as a social instrument, this inherent social passivity of capitalism becomes archaic, and eventually intolerable. The "self-regulating" economy that is its highest social achievement stands condemned by its absence of a directing intelligence, and each small step taken to correct its deficiencies only advertises the inhibitions placed on the potential exercise of purposeful thought and action by its remaining barriers of ideology and privilege. In the end capitalism is weighed in the scale of science and found wanting, not alone as a system but as a philosophy.[8]

In spite of the many scholarly disquisitions regarding the fate or the decline of capitalism, to date they have been grandly defied by the operation of the capitalist process in the United States. The degree of misery of the masses, calculated by Marx to increase with the rise of capitalism, has apparently maintained a relatively constant level since the turn of the century. Gabriel Kolko, in a study of social class and income distribution in the United States, tells us that, "A radically unequal distribution of income has been characteristic of the American social structure since at least 1910, and despite minor year-to-year fluctuations in the share of the income tenths, no significant trend toward income equality has appeared."[9]

Looked at from the vantage point of social class and income, the degree of misery has been constant for a number of years. Strangely, this rather extensive degree of inequality has not called forth a corrective response in the society, at least, not in the form that such response has taken in other major capitalist countries. It has not called forth a labor-based, socialist, or communist political party in which the interests and aspirations of the proletariat are invested. This is a deviant pattern of capitalist development if we consider political developments in other major capitalist countries, such as England, France, or Germany. In these countries the response to social class inequality was the formation of labor-based political parties as a means of bringing remedy to important working-class grievances. Why the difference in the social and political unfolding of capitalism in the United States?

A number of explanations have been offered to explain this divergence. One claim is that the deviation is due to the enlightened self-interest of the capitalist class itself. This class is said to have recognized the needed improvements in working-class life and to have allowed the more important of them to be realized within the existing social and political boundaries. Another explanation is that the very high level of affluence in the United States has itself curtailed the severity of need and unrest within the working class. By this reasoning the degree of severity of grievances has been insufficient and/or insufficiently widespread to generate a working-class political movement and party. Certainly these and several other factors must be part of any exhaustive explanation of the stability of the two-party system, and the bourgeois central tendency of our social and political life. One factor that would seem of the very highest salience in explaining the matter, namely, racism, to my knowledge has not been seriously considered in recent academic dialogue on the question.

I shall now consider two different junctures in American history that illustrate the manner in which racism relates to class-based change, or lack of change, in our society. The first instance is drawn from colonial history; the second is modern.

American historians have been challenged recently by other disciplines whose interests are to trace the history of oppression, exploitation, and racism. As Morgan[10] notes, this challenge has caused American historians to examine more directly the role of slavery in early American history. Until recently, noting especially the exception of Staughton Lynd,[11] slavery was dealt with as a taken-for-granted natural circumstance. Yet, at the time of the American Revolution, slaves were twenty percent of the population and always there was restlessness and aspirations for freedom among them. Morgan cites the paradox of a society imbued with ideas of freedom and equality but run by slaveholders. Benjamin Franklin, Thomas Jefferson, James Madison (all major American men of the Enlightenment) were slave owners throughout their lifetime.

Morgan explains the paradox in terms of Jefferson's vision of the good society, a vision taken more generally as the prototype of the Enlightenment vision.[12] This explanation illustrates the crucial role of racism in social class stability in American society. What was Jefferson's vision of a viable republic? What kind of society was best suited to bring about human happiness and well-being in his view?

Independence was seen, by Jefferson, as a condition necessary to a virtuous life. This meant, above all, the absence of debt. He believed that debt leads to subservience and subservience to venality. Jefferson also believed that property ownership, especially small rural landholdings, was necessary to virtue. Land ownership gave one a stake in society that brought forth virtuous and constructive behavior. Jefferson was a staunch advocate of widespread ownership of land. He had great fear of those who were indebted and of those who were landless. This fear was widely shared by many of the colonists. The growth of an indebted and landless population in the developing colonies was a matter of grave concern to the Founding Fathers, including Jefferson.

This was a vision carried over from England where large numbers of landless, unemployed, men roamed the countryside and towns in search of food, shelter, and employment. Many were jailed or were confined as insane; others simply drifted and threatened the peace and security of the propertied, more affluent, stable elements of English society. They were roundly hated and were the objects of numerous scholarly tracts that, generally, attributed their destitution to idleness. As Morgan suggests, their failure to show the deportment, zeal, and circumstance of a successful practitioner of the Protestant Ethic was never thought to lie outside of their behavior, was never considered as caused by other than their idleness and personal depravity.

The same hatred of the destitute and landless was carried over to the colonies where thrift, industry, and property were also signs of virtue. This meant that the newly released freedmen (both white and black) who increasingly populated colonial America came to be objects of suspicion and derision. This was especially true as they became more numerous and as it became impossible for many of them to be clear of indebtedness and acquire property. Once their activities came to threaten the propertied, as eventually happened, the problem of control of the growing landless, indebted populace loomed ominously before the colonists.

Successful attempts were made to extend their terms of bondage. Yet the problem grew, and the seriousness of their threat to the propertied became a nightmare. The fear of organized rebellion loomed. Shays's Rebellion and Bacon and Ingram's Rebellion were the kinds of uprisings most grievously feared by the colonists. The thought of enslaving the white vagrants, drifters, and landless was rejected in that it would cause great outcry in England itself and generate more trouble than it would solve.

The solution came to be seen in the blacks. To keep them in bondage for life would cause no international outcry, yet it would do away with the need for ever greater numbers of white bondsmen. This would in turn so reduce the numbers of white propertyless freedmen that they would no longer threaten the propertied. It would allow those remaining few to be taken into the ranks of the propertied in numbers sufficient to stem their dissatisfaction, yet not destroy or infringe on the existing prerogatives of the propertied. As Morgan states it,

> With the freedman's expectation, sobriety, and status restored, he was no longer a man to be feared. That fact, together with the presence of a growing mass of alien slaves, tended to draw the white settlers closer together and to reduce the importance of the class difference between yeoman farmer and large plantation owner.[13]

Blacks, then, and slavery, served the function of thwarting the growth and development of a political expression and remedy for lower-class discontent. Stability of the colonial system rested, according to this view, on the progressive dehumanization of blacks. The important point here is that this was not a spurious development, but has remained the functional role of racism in the American system ever since.

The inability of the dispossessed under capitalism in the United States to mount an effective political response to their legitimate grievances according to patterns established in other major capitalist countries now more clearly can be seen as a function of racism. This explains the inability of black gains to reach their proportionate measure and the oscillation of black history.[14] Had they reached proportionate measure earlier, the stage would have been set for a more fundamental change process than ever could be achieved by protest efforts of blacks alone. Thus, the racist confinement of minorities in America must be seen as a stabilizing force in existing class inequalities. The following consideration of blacks in the class structure, in 1960, will show essentially the same picture as during colonial times. It is, however, a rapidly changing picture and, as I have argued, is likely to continue changing at an even more rapid pace.

A class view of the discrepancy between blacks and whites in the stratification order is shown in the following tables based on 1960 census figures.[15]

TABLE 11.1
Nonwhites and Whites in the Upper Class

	Socioeconomic Status of the Population by Color, for the United States, 1960		
SES Status Score	Total Population (%)	White (%)	Nonwhite (%)
90 to 99	5.4	5.9	0.7
80 to 89	7.8	8.6	1.5
70 to 79	11.2	12.2	3.5
Actual totals (%)	24.4	26.7	5.7

Nonwhite underrepresentation (%): 21 (4,398,240).

In Table 11.1 the top three-tenths of the socioeconomic status ranking contains 26.7 percent of the white population, but only 5.7 percent of the nonwhite population. Nonwhites are underrepresented at this "class" level by 21 percent, or roughly 4,398,240 persons. In Table 11.2 the next four-tenths along the same scale identifies a rough equivalent of the middle class. Here, there is an underrepresentation of nonwhites by 14.5 percent, or roughly 3,036,880 persons.

TABLE 11.2
Nonwhites and Whites in the Middle Class

| SES Status Score | Socioeconomic Status of the Population by Color, for the United States, 1960 | | |
	Total Population (%)	White (%)	Nonwhite (%)
60 to 69	13.6	14.8	4.6
50 to 59	15.1	16.1	7.6
40 to 49	14.0	14.1	12.8
30 to 39	11.6	11.0	16.5
Actual totals (%)	54.3	56.0	41.5

Nonwhite underrepresentation (%): 14.5 (3,036,880).

TABLE 11.3
Nonwhites and Whites in the Lower Class

| SES Status Score | Socioeconomic Status of the Population by Color for the United States,1960 | | |
	Total Population (%)	White (%)	Nonwhite (%)
20 to 29	9.3	8.3	18.0
10 to 19	7.6	6.2	18.8
0 to 9	4.3	2.8	15.9
Actual totals (%)	21.2	17.3	52.7

Nonwhite overrepresentation (%): 35.4 (7,331,400).

Considering now the lower class, see the area of extreme overrepresentation of nonwhite peoples in Table 11.3. While only 17.3 percent of whites occupy this class level, more than half (52.7 percent) of the nonwhites in the country are located at this class level. This was the situation in 1960.

These tables reflect two important aspects of black American reality. First, they clearly indicate enormous historical gain since slavery when practically the entire black population was located in the bottom tenth of the SES stratification hierarchy. The gradual achievements by blacks in income, education, jobs, and other resources, have led to a degree of upward mobility that these tables show as of 1960. And yet much of the gain reflected since 1900 has been a quite recent achievement. The Kolko study referred to earlier stated that,

> The Negro's economic position compared to the white improved sharply from 1939 to 1947, primarily due to the end of unemployment, which hit the Negro harder. In 1947, the Negro male's annual median wage was 54 percent of the white's; ten years later that figure was one percent higher or virtually no change at all. And despite the highly touted shift upward in Negro occupations, which presumably would produce higher incomes, the segment of Negro men who were unskilled or service workers dropped only from 56 percent to 52 percent in the twenty year span from 1940 to 1959.[16]

Much the same picture is presented by Herman P. Miller's study of national income for the Social Science Research Council. His study claims that the situation for blacks was so unequal in 1940 that a black college graduate earned less, on the average, than the white who did not complete grammar school. By 1950, there had been change: "Between 1940 and 1950 there was some improvement in the kinds of jobs available to non-white men; however, the fact remains that the non-white industrial worker still finds himself (as of 1950) generally restricted to the lower paid jobs in our economy."[17]

From 1940 to 1950, increasing gains are accounted for by opportunities made possible during World War II. Yet the following quote by Kolko highlights an important second aspect of black American reality in 1959: "It is still a rule of thumb that the number of Negroes in the lowest income classes and in poverty situations is twice the number of whites."[18]

This is an important reminder that, while there has been gain to blacks, there has been as much or more gain to whites in some areas. This means that not much change has occurred in the relative standing of blacks in the class structure. My argument is that the slow incremental gains (involving periodic loss) have now reached sufficient quantity that qualitative changes in both black culture and the society as a whole are an important consequence. Nonwhites are rapidly gaining the technical, educational, and other necessary abilities to protect and further their interests within American society. In addition, the international situation is no longer such that the welfare of American nonwhites can be suppressed and neglected without serious negative national consequences. As I have emphasized earlier, this is because of the rise of nonwhites to positions of international leadership throughout the world, and the decline of colonial domination of nonwhite societies.

These changes in the social situation of nonwhite Americans indicate the beginning of a shift in class position: an end to their traditional deprivation. Such changes signal, over time, broad class-based proportional differentiation within each nonwhite group, similar to other ethnic groups as they made the same upward transition over generations. It also means superseding ethnic identity with class identity in considerable measure. In the case of nonwhite Americans, however, this shift is more than a simple absorption into the fabric of the society. It is more than a spurious equalization of creature comforts between nonwhite and white Americans. This shift is also a necessary and sufficient precondition for significant class-based, or qualitative, change in the broader society. The reasoning behind this conclusion is as follows, and reflects again the stabilizing function of racism for class relations.

We have already seen (Chapter 3) that roughly one-third of the working class in 1960 was nonwhite (30.3 percent). From the same data, here presented in Table 11.4, we see that the very bottom tenth of the SES hierarchy contained nearly as many blacks as whites (41.6 percent compared with 58.4 percent). Here we see in greater refinement than in Chapter 3, the disproportionate numbers of black Americans at the very bottom of the SES ladder and the severe disproportion of blacks in the working class. Thus, the proletariat is significantly split on a race basis just as we have established was the case in colonial times. This distinctive and fateful constituency of the traditional proletariat, or working class, in the United States is clearly revealed.

When translated into actual numbers of persons, the meaning of these figures becomes clear. Given a total white population of 169,163,000 and a total black population of 20,944,000, specific numbers can be estimated.[19] On this basis the working class or proletariat (bottom three-tenths of the SES hierarchy) in the United States consists of 10,890,880 blacks and 28,757,710 whites. This means that the American working class consists of roughly one black person for every two-plus whites. This numerical assessment makes the retarding influence of racism on working-class solidarity readily apparent. Some additional evidence of this racist retardation is provided by a series of attitudinal studies of race and class that show the greater intensity of working-class racism.

Frank Westie and Margaret Westie interviewed randomly selected persons in Indianapolis in 1957.[20] Samples were drawn from the upper, middle, and lower socioeconomic levels; their findings were presented in the form of a social distance pyramid (see Figure 11.1).

TABLE 11.4

Percent Distribution of the Population, by Color
within Socioeconomic Status Categories, for
the United States, 1960

Socioeconomic Status Score	Total	White	Nonwhite
90 to 99 (high)	100.0	98.5	1.5
80 to 89	100.0	97.9	2.1
70 to 79	100.0	96.5	3.5
60 to 69	100.0	96.2	3.8
50 to 59	100.0	94.4	5.6
40 to 49	100.0	89.8	10.2
30 to 39	100.0	84.1	15.9
20 to 29	100.0	78.5	21.5
10 to 19	100.0	72.4	27.6
0 to 9 (low)	100.0	58.4	41.6
Total population	100.0	88.8	11.2

Source: Current Population Reports. See Figure 3.3.

This pyramid reveals the amount of social distance expressed by blacks from whites, and by whites from blacks, at each economic level. The data from the figure show that (1) The greatest social distance is maintained by lower-status whites and lower-status blacks; (2) The least social distance is maintained by upper-status whites and upper-status blacks; (3) At all three levels the distance preferred by whites from blacks is greater than that preferred by blacks from whites. Thus, from these data, racist attitudes increase as one descends the hierarchy of social classes. Racist attitudes were most strongly expressed by the working class.

An earlier study, by Bruno Bettelheim and Morris Janowitz, was conducted among male veterans in Chicago. Only Caucasians were interviewed, and they represented several occupational groups. An important finding was that

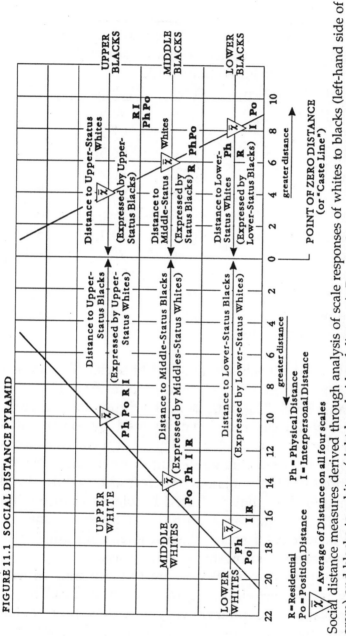

FIGURE 11.1 SOCIAL DISTANCE PYRAMID

R = Residential   Ph = Physical Distance
Po = Position Distance   I = Interpersonal Distance
x̄ = Average of Distance on all four scales

Social distance measures derived through analysis of scale responses of whites to blacks (left-hand side of diagram) and blacks to whites (right-hand side of diagram). Respondents are classified according to occupational rank.

Source: Frank and Margaret Westie, "The Social Distance Pyramid: Relationships Between Caste and Class," *American Journal of Sociology,* September, 1957, pp. 190-96.

the most intolerant persons were located in the occupational category that is distinctively working class (unskilled and semiskilled workers). These data are consistent with findings from a nationwide survey in September 1970, by Louis Harris. Clearly, evidence suggests that the proletariat is the least likely of all strata to work cooperatively with blacks. A situation that, as previously suggested, goes back to colonial America and slavery.[21]

What, then, happens to prevent the development of class consciousness and a labor-based political party in a society with a long history of caste-race oppression? The Leggett study of Detroit autoworkers provides a good example. Black workers were mainly semiskilled or unskilled laborers with little education, often unemployed, lacked influence on the job when employed, and were racially isolated. This group faced many problems, but unions and union membership were of little value in understanding and resolving them. The group relied on the ethnic subcommunity: its churches, lodges, associations, and so on. All of this had no value as a political resource from a labor perspective.

As for the white workers, they were mainly northern European, better educated, with regular contact with the middle class, and they were more skilled. Leggett, in a telling passage, adds,

> Along with these advantages and mainly because they were white, these workers had better relations with the white middle class. At the same time, racial prejudice and segregated work places limited the number and closeness of contacts between white and Negro workers. White workers in auto, steel, and chemical unions did have contact with Negroes on the job, but social relations generally stopped there. Seldom did they extend to neighborhood, school, church, or family.[22]

Thus, racism, by means of segregation and of the social estrangement, ignorance, and fear it engenders, makes cooperative collective action within the working class difficult if not impossible to achieve. Cooperation and collective action among workers is an essential element in the buildup and maintenance of a working-class political movement and party.

Given the broad ranging and comprehensive pattern of change within the society forecast by Schumpeter, Heilbroner, and others, we can connect the relationship of this tendency of system change to racism in American society. As Heilbroner's analysis implies, broad system change in American society does not depend on the direct efforts of the black community to destroy capitalism after the directives of the revolutionary left. The dynamics of this more basic change process spring from science and from new technology and information. The most important contribution to be made by black Americans to this important process is achievement of equality in the forms of proportional representation and participation in the wider society.

Paradoxically, only as this goal is achieved to a significant degree, which means proportional distribution of blacks within the class structure of the society, is the American working class increasingly released from its historic paralysis. Within the interest group frame of reference, then, certain specific, conventional, and entirely legitimate objectives must be sought by nonwhites. Achievement of these objectives, however, will make possible a more widespread activation of the American working class. This thesis deserves further brief elaboration.

The history of the rise of working-class movements in the Western industrial capitalist world has involved, at minimum, the following three developmental stages: significant numbers of urban unemployed, propertyless, and aggrieved; a sharing by the aggrieved of grievances and banding together to achieve job security, higher wages, and other necessary and desired benefits; and formation of an independent labor-based political party that competes for power in society. Data cited above clearly indicate the enormous schism within the American working class. This is a schism due to racism, which has paralyzed the free mobilization of a working class, or labor, movement in the United States. The second stage in the process has been realized only imperfectly, partially, and inadequately. The third stage has not been realized at all. Racism occupies a central place in social and political change in the United States, a place that is largely ignored in scholarly discourse on change in the social system.

More typical in scholarly circles is the work of Seymour Martin Lipset, who has argued that the rise of radical (working-class) socialist or communist politics in the Western countries is a result of the rate of industrialization.[23] Where this process was rapid, causing extreme discontinuity between the preindustrial lifeways and industrialization, there emerged a radical working-class response in the form of socialist or communist parties. Where the transition was slow, radical left politics did not emerge. The absence of radical left parties in the United States and Canada, he argues, is due to the gradual pace of industrialization here, combined with the fact that both countries industrialized late.

The pace of industrialization and the timing of the process are no doubt relevant to the rise of radical politics, yet according to the foregoing analysis these factors are not sufficiently explanatory. They neglect the central place of the specific social conditions and processes within the proletariat of Canada and the United States themselves. Only as these conditions and processes are given a central analytical place can the failure of left politics be adequately understood.[24]

Contrary to most white, Western European countries, the United States had within its institutional framework an expansive system of slavery. Large numbers of black and other nonwhite peoples in America lived a life of subordination, humiliation, and degradation of the most inhumane kind. Negative and demeaning definitions of these groups emerged and crystallized as cultural norms that became societywide in their recognition and social impact. This fact has been significant in the failure of development of a corrective response to the class-based victimization of U.S. capitalism. That is, it has been important in restraining the rise of radical or left-wing politics. The crucial retarding element is that a working class, or a lower class, made up roughly of two-thirds virulent racists and one-third objects of a racist ideology, cannot generate sufficient rapport, organizational acumen, and stability to launch a countermovement. White lower-class leadership can always be enticed in sufficient numbers into patterns of upward mobility made possible by existing institutional arrangements within a white supremacist framework. Typically, such leadership makes political gain for itself by further exploitation and depression of the social situation of nonwhites, especialy blacks and Mexican-Americans. The racist political campaigns of southern politicians, and the racial exclusion of labor unions are ready examples.

A more important explanation of the failure of radical labor-based politics to emerge in the United States is that an inordinate amount of the devastation of being lower class is absorbed by traditionally pariah or castelike groups, that is, nonwhites. This leaves intact the prospect of realization of the American dream via existing racist avenues of upward mobility for significantly larger numbers of white Americans. This prospect greatly reduces their need and potential for radical change. As blacks, in fact, emerge to ethnic status in the society and achieve proportional representation in the class structure, greater pressure will be felt by lower class whites to initiate class-based change. It is this process that will get underway as nonwhite peoples secure proportional class representation. For this reason the achievement of nonwhite equality is an essential aspect of what has been referred to above as the transition, or change, of capitalism. The question may now be raised as to how this process is likely to develop. The answer, I believe, takes us to ethnic politics of the urban environment.

Traditionally in U.S. society necessary commodities such as food, shelter, and medical care (basic human needs) have been allocated through a mechanism of private control and profit, accompanied by charity toward those insufficiently cared for. The emerging controversy over these services reflects widespread recognition of the inadequacy and failure of this traditional model. The extravagance of private profit in areas of basic human need is now more commonly recognized as an intolerable luxury that leaves many chronically in need and others in superfluous affluence. Demands are being made by significant numbers of citizens for increased access to basic goods and services, such as housing and medical care, unregulated by private interests, private control, and private profitability. Uncertain efforts are now being made to realize a mechanism of production and allocation that rests on need primarily, unencumbered by excesses of private profit-making and control.

Because cities are increasingly inhabited by those who have been victims of the exploitation of unregulated or inadequately regulated profit-making in such industries as housing, they are likely to become centers of a corrective process as the politicization of urban nonwhites and poor increases. They may be seen as areas of important experimentation in search of new ways to meet the growing urban crises caused by the systematic and unnecessary human deprivation endemic to capitalist resource allocation. This is the framework within which urban nonwhite politics can be seen. This is the rationale and, I suggest, likely direction of ethnic politics in urban America.

The goal of urban nonwhite ethnic politics must be basic

change in selected institutional areas and especially change in patterns of production and resource allocation to various segments of the population. Urban nonwhite ethnic political strategy must seek to take such industries as housing and medical care, out of the hands of private profit makers and convert them into responsible public institutions. Only in this way can the constituency of urban (increasingly black) politicians be best served. These constituencies can be expected to articulate and militantly demand that their interests be better served. Urban nonwhites (and the white poor) are likely to become an effective force whose interests are reflected through the new nonwhite political presence now emerging in the United States. This, at least, is the rational direction for the racial equality movement, because, as Bayard Rustin has cogently, and correctly, argued,

> While most Negroes in their hearts unquestionably seek only to enjoy the fruits of American society as it now exists, their quest cannot objectively be satisfied within the framework of existing political and economic relations. The young Negro who would demonstrate his way into the labor market may be motivated by a thoroughly bourgeois ambition and thoroughly "capitalist" consideration, but he will end up having to favor a great expansion of the public sector of the economy. At any rate, that is the position any movement will be forced to take as it looks at the number of jobs being generated by the private economy, and if it is to remain true to the masses of Negroes.[25]

The politics of urban nonwhite Americans can, and I believe will, become the catalyst through which the full transition from caste to class status is achieved. Simultaneously, this will mark the beginning of a more self-conscious class politics in America.

Questions for Review and Further Study

1. What is the suggested connection between racism and social class?

2. What is the importance of social status to class for Max Weber?

3. What function has racism served traditionally in U.S. society?

4. What class changes are suggested as the decline of racism progresses?

5. What was Joseph Schumpeter's view of change in capitalism?

6. What is Heilbroner's view of change in capitalism? How does it differ from the view of Marx?

7. What two historical events illustrate the dynamics of racism in U.S. society and its function for class stability?

8. What does the Westie and Westie study of racial attitudes suggest about black-white relations?

9. What is the importance of this finding for class-based social change?

10. What was the point in presentation of the study by John C. Leggett?

11. Where and how is the transition of U.S. capitalism likely to occur?

Notes

1. This point was noted by Marx and Engels. In a letter to Fredrick A. Sarge, December 2, 1893, Engels comments on some important obstacles to the emergence of a working-class party in the United States. He writes:

"Then, ... immigration, which divides the workers into two groups: the native-born and the foreigners, and the latter in turn into (1) the Irish; (2) the Germans; (3) the many small groups, each of which understands only itself: Czechs, Poles, Italians, Scandinavians, etc. And then the Negroes. To form a single party out of these requires quite unusually powerful incentives." (See Karl Marx and Friedrich Engels, in Lewis Feuer, *Basic Writings on Politics and Philosophy* (Garden City, N.Y.: Doubleday, 1959), p. 485.

Karl Marx also noted that racial differences would have a damaging effect on the growth of a labor party and movement in the United States. See Karl Marx and Friedrich Engels, *The Civil War in the United States* (New York: Citadel Press, 1961), pp. xiv, 280-81. This reference is reported in a study of working-class consciousness in the Detroit auto industry. John C. Leggett, *Class, Race and Labor: Working Class Consciousness in Detroit*, (New York: Oxford University Press, 1968), p. 216-17. Observations on the role of race and ethnicity in relation to a working-class movement in the United States have been neglected by scholars who concern themselves with social change in the society. Marxist scholars and others who do emphasize racism as a major evil in the society have, nevertheless, improperly assessed the role of race in relation to social change, as subsequent discussion will suggest. The recent book by William Wilson, *The Declining Significance of Race* (Chicago: University of Chicago Press, 1978), is a good example. For an extended discussion of Wilson's book see Appendix C.

2. For extensive discussion of the classic model of capitalism and its legitimating rationale see Ludwig Von Mises, *The Free and Prosperous Commonwealth* (Princeton: Van Nostrand, 1962). For a discussion of changes in this model in the present-day United States, see Robert Heilbroner *The Limits of American Capitalism*, (New York: Harper & Row, 1966); and his *Between Capitalism and Socialism*, (NewYork: Random House, 1970).

3. See Richard Hofstedter, *Social Darwinism in American Life* (Boston: Beacon Press, 1959); see also Sethard Fisher,

Power and the Black Community (New York: Random House, 1970).

4. Joseph Schumpeter *Capitalism, Socialism, and Democracy* (London: Allen & Unwin, 1961), p. 61.

5. Heilbroner, p. 125.

6. Ibid., p. 132.

7. See Schumpeter, Ch. VI.

8. Ibid., pp. 131-33.

9. Gabriel Kolko, *Wealth and Power in America: An Analysis of Social Class and Income Distribution* (New York: Praeger, 1962), p. 13.

10. Edmund S. Morgan, "Slavery and Freedom: The American Paradox," *Journal of American History* (June 1972), pp. 5-29.

11. See Staughton Lynd, *Class Conflict, Slavery and the United States Constitution: Ten Essays* (Indianapolis, Ind.: Bobbs-Merrill, 1967).

12. For a discussion of the writings and ideas of several American Enlightenment figures see Adrienne Koch, *The American Enlightment: The Shaping of the American Experiment and A Free Society* (New York: Braziller, 1965).

13. Morgan (1972: p. 28). This is to emphasize the deep and tenacious economic roots of slavery. As David Brian Davis expressed it, the American colonists' Enlightenment rhetoric of freedom "was functionally related to the existence, and in many areas to the continuation of Negro slavery." See his *The Problems of Slavery in the Age of Revolution, 1770-1823* (Ithaca, N.Y.: Cornell University Press, 1975), p. 262. Davis correctly takes issue with Winthrop D. Jordon, who seems to underestimate the tenacity of the institution by naively assuming that the end of slavery appeared to be within reach during the final quarter of the eighteenth century. Jordan calls it a time of missed opportunity for American society. No such opportunity ever existed, insists Davis, and the assumption that it did "distorts our understanding

of the forces that maintained slavery and of the kind of struggle that abolition required" (Davis, 1975: p. 256). See also Winthrop D. Jordon, *White Over Black, American Attitudes Toward the Negro, 1550-1812* (Chapel Hill: University of North Carolina Press, 1968), p. 374.

14. There are several scholarly formulations on American racism that hint at the major thesis presented here regarding blacks and the function of racism in the society. Comments by Marx and Engels presented earlier are an example, as well as those by Robert E. Park. See also Sterling D. Spero and Abram L. Harris, *The Black Worker* (New York: Atheneum, 1974). As we have seen, the Marxist literature emphasizes race quite extensively in the interest of class-based social change.

15. My assessment of the extent of over- and under-representation at the three class levels is based on U.S. Census Reports: *U.S. Census of Population, 1960, PC(2) 8 Series, 5C, Socioeconomic Status.* Table 1 of this document lists a total U.S. population (all ages and all races) as 179,310,655. It lists 158,814,132 as the total white population (all ages and all races). The nonwhite total population figures used in my assessment are the difference between these two population figures, or 20,4096,523. In another Census Bureau document using 1960 data (Current Population Reports, Technical Studies Series, No.12, July 31, 1964:p. 23) *Socioeconomic Characteristics of the Population, 1960)* socioeconomic status rankings by race from high to low on a ten-interval scale are provided. The top three rungs on the scale contain 26.7 percent of the white population and 5.7 percent of the nonwhite population. Thus, nonwhites are underrepresented by 21 percent, or 4,304,269 persons. By the same calculation the adequacy of representation in the middle class (middle four-tenths) was assessed, and so on.

16. Kolko, p.93.

17. Herman P. Miller, *Income of the American People* (New York: Wiley, 1955), p. 47.

18. Kolko. There are several good discussions of gain to blacks in recent years that are somewhat different from the view of Kolko. For example the study by Elliott Rudwick and August Meier, *From Plantation to Ghetto* (New York: Hill and Wang, 1976); Bart Landry, "The Economic Position of Black Americans," in H. Roy Kaplan, *American Minorities and the Opportunity Structure*, (Ithaca, N.Y., Peacock, 1977), pp. 50-108.

19. These are 1969 population figures taken from a U.S. Census report of that year. The SES calculations are based on 1960 data and come from a U.S. Census report as indicated above. For an extended discussion of black stratification, see James E. Blackwell *The Black Community: Diversity and Unity*, (New York: Dodd, Mead, 1975), Ch.3.

20. Table adapted from Frank Westie and Margaret Westie, "The Social Distance Pyramid: Relationships Between Caste and Class," *American Journal of Sociology* (September, 1957), pp. 190-96.

21. Bruno Bettelheim and Morris Janowitz, *The Dynamics of Prejudice: A Psychological and Sociological Study of Prejudice* (New York: Harper and Brothers, 1950). Some studies of ethnic prejudice have suggested the importance of mobility, of orientation toward mobility, and of working-class consciousness in socioeconomic variations of it. See Joseph Greenbaum and Leonard I. Perlin, "Vertical Mobility and Prejudice: A Sociopsychological Analysis" in Reinhard Bendix and Seymour Martin Lipset (eds.) *Class, Status, and Power* (Glencoe, Ill.: Free Press, 1953), pp. 480-91; Fred B. Silberstein and Melvin Seeman "Social Mobility and Prejudice," *American Journal of Sociology* vol. 65 (1959), pp. 258-64; John C. Leggett, *Class, Race, and Labor: Working Class Consciousness In Detroit* (New York: Oxford University Press, 1968), pp. 91-95; Louis Harris, *The Harris Survey Yearbook of Public Opinion 1970: A*

Compendium of Current American Attitudes (New York: Louis Harris and Associates, 1971), p. 222.

The incomparability of data on which these studies are based suggests the need for caution in generalizing from them. None of them, nor others that I have found in the literature, presents empirical evidence contradicting the findings of the Westie and Westie study.

22. John C. Leggett (1968), p. 99.

23. See Seymour Martin Lipset, "Socialism Left and Right, East and West," *Confluence* 7, No. 2 (Berkeley: The Institute of Industrial Relations, University of California, Summer 1958).

24. This view is consistent with the argument advanced by Herbert Blumer, "Industrialization and Race Relations," found in Guy Hunter (ed.), *Race Relations and Industrialization* (New York: Oxford University Press, 1965). He would argue that industrialization need not have the uniform effect suggested by the Lipset formulation. Social forces of this magnitude are always mediated through a pattern of existing social institutions and customary activities that have a highly determinative effect.

25. Bayard Rustin "From Protest to Politics," *Commentary* 39, No. 2 (February 1965).

APPENDIX A:
Blacks and the Radical Left

The limited analysis of the black American situation in the writings of Marx has already been mentioned. Yet, by the time of the Russian Revolution of 1917, the issue of colonial domination by capitalist countries, and nonwhite minorities within these countries, had become important to Lenin and the Bolsheviks. This included the blacks in the United States, former Africans forcefully subjected to slavery and dehumanization in much the same manner as other colonial peoples. The American Communist party from that time took up the black issue in America as a central ingredient in its program. Specific directives and guidelines for doing this were formulated in Moscow in 1928.

The origins of the revolutionary program for blacks came from two distinct sources (which show some variation in approach). One was basically influenced by Stalin. The other was largely a product of discussions with Leon Trotsky. A version of the Stalinist view, or the official view, on the black question in the United States and its development is found in a recent (1978) publication by a black American who became a Bolshevik several years ago. Harry Haywood, in his *Black Bolshevik*,[1] describes the meeting of the Sixth Congress of the Comintern held in Moscow in July and August of 1928 as approving and subsequently promoting a distinctive view of the black situation in the United States. The policy was formulated and adopted in the worldwide communist movement. This was a time when U.S. Communists began to take a new departure in their union activities, emphasizing increased union organizational activities rather than continuing to work through existing conservative labor organizations (Haywood, p. 246).

A number of commissions were formed at the Sixth Congress to look into, debate, and formulate resolutions on issues important to world communism. These resolutions were then presented before the entire congress for official action, thereby making them official policy, with the backing of the worldwide communist movement. One such commission was the Negro Commission which was, in fact, a subcommittee of the Colonial Commission. Resolutions from the Negro Commission were included in the final draft of the congress's thesis on the revolutionary movement in the colonies. Establishment of the Negro Commission August 6 at the twenty-third session of the congress, was described by Haywood as a remarkable day, particularly for us black communists, a day to which we had all looked forward (p. 259). This meant full-dress treatment of the black question by a wide range of delegates from throughout the world.

Two basic positions emerged from early debate and discussion. One view, forwarded by two black delegates particularly, emphasized that U.S. blacks were a racial minority. The blacks' interests and those of white Americans were essentially the same, the major problem being racial barriers set up by the bourgeoisie based on skin color. In this view, these barriers should become the objects of attack in the working class and in the society. Communist strategy should direct itself to this goal.

The other view held that blacks, especially in the South, were an oppressed nation. It stressed their right, therefore, to self-determination. Supporters of this view claimed that to see blacks simply as an oppressed racial group diminished the revolutionary implications of the black equality struggle, that it reduced the goals of the black movement to simply integration and amalgamation. As Haywood saw it,

What was clear to me was that our thesis of self-determination had correctly elevated the fight for Black rights to a revolutionary position, whereas the (other) theories attempted to downgrade the movement, seeing it as a minor aspect of the class struggle. Our thesis put the question in the proper perspective: that is as a struggle attacking the very foundation of American imperialism, an integral part of the struggle of the American working class as a whole (p. 264).

The final resolution coming from the Sixth Congress represented a new line on the Afro-American question. It rejected assimilationist race theories, which had previously been the basic party line on the black question. It defined the black movement as a national revolutionary movement in its basic character. This was largely due to the concentration of blacks in the Black Belt and to their utter and absolute oppression there. It called for resistance to petty bourgeois nationalism such as Garveyism. Finally, it insisted that the U.S. Communist party strengthen its work and activity among black proletarians and fight for acceptance of blacks by unions, many of which barred blacks. This new line committed the party to the slogan of the right of self-determination, and this seems to have meant separate government and alliance with the white, communist-led proletariat. Exactly how these ideals were to be put into practice was not spelled out. Yet, from this basic vision has come a wide range of tactical and strategic activities among American blacks and others involved in the racial equality movement. Of course, from this first early effort, additional refinements of the communist, or Stalinist, approach to American racism have been made. The basic slogan and image of separation, of self-determination, and of joint white-black proletarian liaison has been maintained. The view expressed by Lightfoot (quoted in Chapter 7) is essentially compatible with that of Haywood and a number of others in the communist movement U.S.A. who have adhered to what is basically a view growing out of the works and orientation of Joseph Stalin. Stalin's views, of course, are claimed by him to be in the tradition of Lenin and Karl Marx.[2]

From another developmental source has come the view on the black question expressed by the followers of Leon Trotsky. This view too, however, is within the Marxist-Leninist, or revolutionary, tradition. The view of the black question held by the Socialist Workers party (SWP) stems from several discussions of an American group of followers of Trotsky with their mentor in Prinkipo, Turkey, in 1933, and again in Coyoacan, Mexico, in 1939.[3] C. L. R. James (referred to in Chapter 2), a black Marxist, used some notes from these 1939 discussions to prepare a statement for discussion and possible adoption by the Socialist Workers party.

In these discussions, Trotsky was disturbed that the party had not done more work among American blacks. He argued that if work among them failed to get underway the party would degenerate. Blacks were viewed as the most dynamic element of the working class, or the group most capable of revolutionary activity, and destined to become a vanguard of the working class.

James was not enthusiastic in these discussions regarding advocacy of the right of self-determination for blacks. Although he upheld that right, he felt that American blacks, unlike Africans and West Indians, want to be American citizens. In James's words,

> The danger of our advocating and injecting a policy of self-determination is that it is the surest way to divide and confuse the workers in the South. The white workers have centuries of prejudice to overcome, but at the present time many of them are working with the Negroes in the Southern sharecropper's union, and with the rise of the struggle there is every possibility that they will be able to overcome their ageless prejudices. But for us to propose that the Negro have this black state for himself is asking too much from the white workers, especially

when the Negro himself is not making the same demand
(James, p. 41).

Trotsky's response to James was essentially sympathetic,
feeling that the SWP should support but not advocate self-
determination among blacks. Trotsky commented,

It seems to me that the Communist Party's attitude of making
an imperative slogan of it was false. It was a case of the whites
saying to the Negroes, you must create a ghetto for yourselves.
It is tactless and false and can only serve to repulse the
Negroes. Their only interpretation can be that the whites want
to be separated from them (Trotsky, pp. 47-48).

At its national convention of 1939, held in New York
City, the SWP Committee on Negro Work presented a program of action plus two resolutions. The first resolution, entitled, "The SWP and Negro Work," was adopted without
opposition. This resolution proposed that black members of
the SWP, aided and supported by the party, take the initiative and collaborate with other militant blacks to form a
mass organization devoted to the struggle for black rights.
This organization was to consist of large numbers of black
workers and farmers and was to work out a program corresponding to their daily struggles. This resolution, proposed
by James, was adopted by the convention on July 3, 1939.

The second proposal forwarded by the Committee on
Negro Work was entitled, "The Right of Self-Determination
and the Negro in the United States of North America." Two
members of the committee had differences with this
proposal and presented them to the convention. These
minority reports received little support, and the resolution
was adopted as a basis for a final draft resolution that would
be incorporated into a more general resolution dealing with
many aspects of the black situation.

This resolution suggested that because of the severity of

oppression in America, blacks may demand the right of self-determination, that is, the formation of a Negro state in the South. Thus,

> The question of whether the Negroes in America are a national minority to which the slogan of self-determination applies will be solved in practice. . . . Should the masses of Negroes raise the slogan, the SWP, in accordance with the Leninist doctrine on the question of self-determination . . . will pledge itself to support the demand.

> The SWP, while proclaiming its willingness to support the right of self-determination to the fullest degree, will not in itself, in the present stage, advocate the slogan of a Negro state in the manner of the Communist Party of the USA. The advocacy of the right of self-determination does not mean advancing the slogan of self-determination. Self-determination for Negroes means that the Negroes themselves must determine their own future (Trotsky, pp. 77-78).

Within the SWP this issue is yet not firmly settled. In a 1978 publication, R. S. Frazier challenges George Breitman's characterization of the Negro question within the framework of "the colonial and national questions."[4] Frazier contends that Trotskyism must tear the Negro question in the United States away from the national question and establish it as a separate and autonomous political problem. This, of course, is a tendency somewhat opposed to that taken by Trotsky in the above-mentioned discussions with James and others, of the American delegation in Mexico, even while the Trotsky position remains different from the official communist position.

NOTES

1. Harry Haywood, *Black Bolshevik: Autobiography of an Afro-American Communist* (Chicago: Liberator Press, 1978).

2. See *Questions and Answers to American Trade Unionists: Stalin's Interview with the First American Trade Union Delegation to Soviet Russia* (New York: Workers Library Publishers, 1927).

3. See Leon Trotsky, *On Black Nationalism* (New York: Pathfinders Press, 1978).

4. See *What Strategy for Black Liberation, Trotskyism vs. Black Nationalism* (New York: Sparticist League, 1978), pp. 2-16.

APPENDIX B:
The Meaning of Third World

My reference to the Third World generally follows the description given by Pierre Jaleé.[1] He distinguishes between those countries with a capitalist system and those with a socialist system, and argues that there is a wide gulf between the underdeveloped and subject countries and the developed and dominant countries within the capitalist group. These African, Asian, and Latin American countries, the underdeveloped and subject countries within the capitalist world, are the Third World countries. This is similar to the classification used by the United Nations. Specifically, they are America (excluding the United States, Canada, and Cuba), the whole of Africa, Asia (excluding the socialist countries, Japan, and Israel), and Oceania (excluding Australia and New Zealand).

Population in the Third World is unevenly distributed, two-thirds being in Asia, 20 percent in Africa, and 15 percent in Latin America. Per capita income among the socialist, capitalist, and Third World countries shows important and fateful variation. Excluding those in Asia, the socialist countries have a per capita national income about one-third lower than the advanced capitalist countries. Third World peoples of Asia and Africa have a per capita income about one-tenth to one-eleventh of that in the advanced capitalist countries. Latin American per capita income is about one-fifth of that of the advanced capitalist countries.

The Third World, which amounts to about half the world population, had only 11.5 percent of the world total gross domestic product in 1965, while one-fifth of the world population (the advanced capitalist countries) had about 60

281

percent of it. This means that 650 million persons produced five times the wealth generated by 1,500,000,000 other persons. The United States alone produces nearly two-and-one-half times what all underdeveloped countries of Asia, Africa, and Latin America combined produced. These countries have a combined population eight times larger than that of the United States.

Among the Third World countries themselves, inequality exists. Latin America is the least poor, with a gross domestic product of $77 billion (1961) for 235 million people. Africa is next, but is more than twice as poor as Latin America, with $50 billion for 310 million people. And underdeveloped Asia is by far the poorest of all, with just $103 billion of gross domestic product for nearly a billion people.

One important meaning of these conditions is that the move toward independence and self-rule that swept through the colonized countries after World War II has, as yet, not led to very much change in the relative standing of these countries in terms of domestic prosperity. Data on Third World production in agriculture show that production is poor in spite of the fact that in every Third World country the main occupation is agriculture. The level of productivity in animal husbandry among Third World countries appears to be as low or lower than in agriculture. Furthermore, the level of productivity in these areas since 1958 suggests that agricultural productivity up to 1964 was expanding more slowly than before 1958. Between 1958 and 1964 total agricultural production in the Third World increased more rapidly than in the United States and Canada, but per capita production fell slightly for the Third World though remaining stable in the United States and Canada.

Part of the explanation of the lack of productivity in agriculture in the Third World is that a large percentage of its product is not for domestic consumption, but goes to the large industrial countries. So, although the Third World actually produces all or nearly all of the world's coffee, cocoa beans, bananas, jute, natural rubber, and palm kernels, more than 70 percent of the world's tea, ground nuts, and timber, nearly 60 percent of the world's rice and 40 percent of its cotton, "The final destination of almost all of these products is the markets and factories of the developed countries." (Jaleé, p. 21).

The situation with minerals, of which Third World countries extract large quantities, is similar to that of agriculture, and animal husbandry. Between 1958 and 1965 there was a greater expansion in the production of minerals in Third World countries than in the advanced capitalist countries, although they are still modest producers of materials extracted from the subsoil. The strategic importance of Third World subsoil extraction is that its extractions are in many instances essential to the industries of the advanced capitalist countries. The Third World's share of iron ore production increased from 13 percent of the world total in 1956 to 23 percent of the world total in 1964. The Third World's share in world production of antimony between 1956 and 1964 decreased, but over the same period its share of world bauxite production increased from 57 to 59 percent. Africa holds about one-third of the world's bauxite reserves, though Africa's proportion of world production of the metal is low.

Between 1956 and 1964 world production of chrome ore declined, but the Third World's contribution rose from 89 to 94 percent. The Third World's contribution to world copper production during this period rose from 42 to 44 percent; its share of manganese ore production rose from 42 to 45 percent; and its share of world cobalt ore production rose from 69 to 72 percent.

Generally, the Third World has made progress in the extractive industries in the recent past, with its share of production growing and expected to continue. This is happening while deposits in the advanced capitalist countries are declining in a number of important areas. In this way the increasing dependence of the advanced industrial countries, and especially the capitalist countries is starkly revealed. A small number of Third World countries hold strategic mineral and petroleum reserves that are absolutely essential to the economies of the advanced capitalist world.

Manufacture, too, further reveals the nature of the interdependence between the Third World and the advanced capitalist countries. Here, again, the picture is not unlike what has already been described. First of all, the Third World's share in world manufacturing is considerably less than its share in agricultural production. In 1965, manufacturing industries of the Third World represented about 6.5 percent of world production, whereas in agricultural production the figures were 29 to 30 percent. Underindustrialization is a major problem in these countries. They have practically no industrial capacity to separate important minerals from the ores that they extract abundantly. Almost none of the minerals and raw materials are used in factories of the Third World. Some limited use is made of its raw materials in the textile industry and in the iron and steel industries, but in either case the percentage of world total production is quite low. On pages 51 to 52 of his book Jaleé suggests,

> Under present conditions of characteristic imperialist exploitation of Third World raw materials, the fact that a Third World country possesses a given raw material does not necessarily lead to related industrial activity. This is the exact opposite of the pattern of industrialization which occurred in what are now the developed capitalist countries.

The initiation of this more elaborate industrial process, beyond initial extraction of ores, depends on infusions of capital from the developed capitalist countries. In spite of large increases in productive activities in Third World countries in recent years, enormous population growth reduces the value of this activity on a per capita basis when comparisons with the more industrialized countries are made. This means the gap between the advanced industrialized countries is not being narrowed by the increased industrial activity in Third World countries.

We see, then, that enormous dependencies remain between the Third World countries and the advanced capitalist countries. This is essentially the kind of dependence that was spawned by many years of colonial and, later, imperialist rule by the white Western European world. There is now, however, an important new ingredient in the interdependence: The Third World countries, mainly the nonwhite areas of the world, hold strategic resources that are absolutely essential to the white-majority capitalist Western world. However, full ownership of these resources is now in the hands of indigenous nonwhite leaders and political systems. It is this reality that makes the Anglo-Saxon mythology about the white race and its presumed superiority, what Ashley Montagu has called humankind's most dangerous myth.[2]

Nonwhite Americans have an exceedingly strategic role to play in facilitating the decline of white racism by assuming important intermediary roles involving a kind of diplomacy as well as technical expertise that would be difficult for even well-trained diplomats with a white supremacist viewpoint to assume. The white supremacist American is too costly a luxury when no less than vital interests and national well-being are at stake.

Official awareness of the need for cooperation, alliance, and diplomacy regarding the Third World predates the recent Mideast petroleum crisis. As far back as 1956, President Lyndon Johnson's close academic adviser, W. W. Rostow, gave the following testimony before hearings of the Subcommittee on Foreign Economic Policy of the Joint Economic Committee, 84th Congress of the United States:

The location, natural resources, and populations of the under-developed areas are such that, should they become effectively attached to the Communist bloc, the United States would become the second power in the world. . . . Indirectly, the evolution of the underdeveloped areas is likely to determine the fate of Western Europe and Japan, and therefore the effectiveness of those industrialized regions in the free world alliance we are committed to lead. If the underdeveloped areas fall under Communist domination, or if they move to fixed hostility to the West, the economic and military strength of Western Europe and Japan will be diminished, the British Commonwealth as it is now organized will disintegrate, and the Atlantic world will become, at best, an awkward alliance, incapable of exercising effective influence outside a limited orbit, with the balance of the world's power last to it. In short, our military security and our way of life as well as the fate of Western Europe and Japan are at stake in the evolution of the underdeveloped areas. We evidently have a major national interest, then, in developing a free world coalition which embraces in reasonable harmony and unity the industrialized states of Western Europe and Japan on the one hand, the underdeveloped areas of Asia, the Middle East, and Africa, on the other.[3]

Certain vital interests of the United States clearly depend on the quality of its relations with the nonwhite peoples of the world, and the success of this effort surely will involve the nonwhite American communities in very considerable measure. Such a requirement for national security clearly demands the rapid demise of the Aryan and Anglo-Saxon mythology of white supremacy. Jaleé has argued that "Though the contradiction between capitalism and socialism seems to be essential and fundamental in present conditions, it is concretely subordinate to the resolution of the contradiction between imperialism and the Third World" [emphasis added] (p. 115). Similarly, the burden of this volume has been to suggest that this contradiction is also subordinate to resolution of the problem of racism within the United States.

NOTES

1. Pierre Jaleé, *The Third World in World Economy*, trans. by Mary Klopper (New York: Monthly Review Press, 1969), pp. 3-4.

2. Ashley Montagu, *Man's Most Dangerous Myth* (New York: Oxford University Press, 1974).

3. Reported in Harry Magdoff, *The Age of Imperialism, The Economics of U.S. Foreign Policy* (New York: Monthly Review Press, 1969), p. 54.

APPENDIX C:
The Significance of Race Controversy

The recent controversy over William Wilson's *The De-clining Significance of Race* has aroused comment from a variety of divergent sources, some favorable and some highly unfavorable.[1] Nathan Glazer has referred to the book as an important statement, not because its message is new but because this is the first time that this message has been publicized by a black academic. Thomas F. Pettigrew, who reviewed the book for *Contemporary Sociology* comments on its brevity and cites the limited theoretical value of the book.[2] Kenneth Clark, the well-known black New York psychologist, expresses concern that the book will suggest to government and other officials that their support of blacks is no longer needed. C. V. Willie, a black sociologist who teaches at Harvard, has criticized the book on academic and scholarly grounds, suggesting that Wilson's main claim, that the significance of race is declining, is not properly supported with data. In addition, the Association of Black Sociologists issued a formal statement denouncing the volume, showing special concern for the invitation they feel the volume extends to those who would adopt a benign neglect attitude toward the condition of blacks in American society. This brief characterization of the controversy is by no means definitive of its range or intensity.

The extent of the controversy over Wilson's book indicates both the intensity and continuing volatility of the race issue in U. S. society. Wilson's statement is a brief, impressionistic, and interesting excursion. He has examined aspects of Marxist theory, mentioned earlier as one important theo-

289

retical orientation regarding racism, as it pertains to racial oppression and found the theory not completely satisfactory. He suggests an alternative to the Marxist view, yet giving recognition to the manner in which the empirical reality of race relations did indeed fit this view during distinctive historical intervals. However, he finds it inadequate in explaining today's reality of race relations, especially the progressive rise and prosperity of a black middle class. Neither the older traditional Marxist appraisal nor the newer split labor market theory adequately explains this development. This failure, he argues, is because there has emerged a new phase of growth called corporate capitalism, a phase that has a distinctively different effect on race than the other two phases. He sees the social forces of production as giving rise to a theoretically unanticipated reality for some blacks, namely, progressive prosperity, although he acknowledges that the segment of the black population at the very bottom of the stratification order is undergoing progressive emiseration as older Marxist interpretations would suggest.

Today, Wilson argues, education is the key to economic success because of the high technology needs of the economy. Both blacks and whites who are better educated will receive greater rewards. Race is not a significant obstacle here. Equally so for the uneducated. They will increasingly and equally reap the devastation of the society because of their loss of a functional role in the economy. Corporate capitalism needs, seeks, and rewards the highly educated and the technologically capable.

According to Wilson's assessment, about one-third of the black population remains below the poverty income level (1974), and this group constitutes roughly one-third of the population referred to as the underclass. For this segment of the black population and the white also he argues that there has been little advancement. In his words: "As we begin this last quarter of the twentieth century, a deepening economic schism seems to be developing in the black community, with the black poor falling further and further behind middle- and upper-income blacks" (p. 152). And, "At this point there is every reason to believe that talented and educated blacks, like talented and educated whites, will continue to enjoy the advantages and privileges of this class status" (p. 153). The cause, argues Wilson, of this new reality is to be found in "the deleterious effect of basic structural changes in modern American economic growth, increasing technology and auto- mation, industrial relocation, and labor-worker segmenta- tion" (p. 154).

The disproportionate representation of blacks in the un- derclass is primarily a matter of the cumulative effect of past racism. The blocking of access to job opportunities, charac- teristics of past phases of American economic life, accounts for the overrepresentation of blacks in the American under- class, a group so distant from current opportunities as to be literally doomed to significantly diminished life chances.

Yet, at the other end of the economic spectrum, the highly educated and talented are rapidly achieving upward mobility. The growth of a large black urban population and the expansion of job opportunities following World War II (called the modern industrial period) are developments cor- related with the emergence of a black middle class and thus with significant class division within the black community. The modern industrial phase of American economic life (cor- porate capitalism) will continue to reward education and technological expertise largely independent of race, says Wil- son. It is on the basis of this assumption that Wilson rests his claim that race is increasingly declining as a significant factor determining the life chances of American citizens and is be- ing superseded in importance by class.

If Wilson's work is taken to be an exploratory descrip- tive analysis of black-white relations, as I take it to be, the work can be seen as a provocative and thought-provoking exercise. It clearly challenges the commonly held vision of American capitalist society as forever racist, a vision that supports the view discussed in previous chapters that capitalism and racism are inseparable. It is a provocative idea, well worth debate and study in intellectual and academic circles that appear to be dominated by the Marxist perspective that racism's demise is possible only with the destruction of capitalistic society. Wilson's analysis raises another prospect. There are, of course, other critical issues regarding Wilson's study to be addressed. This requires a careful assessment of his analysis, especially of his analytic units.

Wilson makes use of analytic units that derive basically from Marxist theory itself, though he makes a different use of these units than most contemporary Marxist theorists and tacticians. In the Marxist vision of social life the most powerful forces influencing human beings and their behavior are to be found in the economic sphere. Economic variables as units are determining, or independent, variables. This means that as they change there is also corresponding predictable change in several other interconnected areas of social life.

A basic analytic unit in the economic sphere is ownership, that is, owners of the means of production, and those who do not own the means of production. In our era, that of capitalist society, these groupings would correspond to the capitalists, or bourgeoisie, and the proletariat, respectively. A second analytically important unit within the economic sphere is the means of production itself. This refers to the level of technological development of the instruments and techniques used in the production of goods and services in a social system. In fact, social change occurs, in Marxist analysis, by a process called revolution in the means of production. As new technologies and strategies are developed that change the production process (the forces of production), this produces change in the patterns of social relations in the society (the relations of production). Wilson puts great emphasis on one element of the relations of production, namely, the laws and policies of the state. He argues that these laws and policies provide constraints that shape the structural relation between racial and class groups and which thereby produce different patterns of intergroup interaction (p. 9).

Wilson's three-stage historical classification is based on what he envisions as distinctive variations in the interplay of the two variable forces of production and the social relations of production; that is, the laws and policies of the state and consequent patterns of black-white relations. Together these constitute what he calls the system of production. Wilson says that the term 'system of production' not only refers to the technological basis of economic processes or the forces of production, but also implies the social relations of production, that is, the interaction (for example through employment and property arrangements) into which men enter at a given level of the development of the forces of production (p. 12).

Thus, in his view, different systems of production impose constraints on interaction between racial groups. Each of his three historical categories is based on what he envisions as distinctive variations in the system of production. In his words,

> My central argument is that different systems of production and/or different policies of the state have imposed different constraints on the way in which racial groups interact, constraints that have structured the relations between racial groups and produced dissimilar contexts not only for the manifestation of racial antagonisms but also for racial groups' access to rewards and privileges (p. 22).

The different stages of race relations, he argues, are structured by the unique arrangements and interactions of the economy and polity. Both elements of the system of production, Wilson suggests, must be seen as in dynamic interaction rather than one being (as in the Marxist scheme) a dependent variable of the other:

> Although I stress the economic basis of structural racial inequality in the preindustrial and industrial periods of race relations, I also attempt to show how the policy more or less interacted with the economy either to reinforce patterns of racial stratification or to mediate various forms of racial conflict (p. 3).

And for the modern period he says,

> I try to show how race relations have been shaped as much by important economic changes as by important political changes (p. 3).

The earliest stage referred to by Wilson is called the preindustrial stage. In the antebellum South, a plantation economy generated a paternalistic rather than competitive form of race relations. This form involved close symbiotic relationships marked by dominance and subservience, by extensive social distance, and with clearly symbolized rituals of racial etiquette. Economically, the southern white aristocracy created a split labor market along racial lines by enslaving blacks to work more cheaply than white free laborers. The form of race relations during this period was not based on the actions of white laborers, who were powerless to bring about racial change, but on the structure of relations established by the aristocracy. Stage 1 coincides with antebellum slavery and the early postbellum era, and Wilson calls this the period of plantation economy and racial-caste oppression.

Stage 2 starts, Wilson says, in the last quarter of the nineteenth century and ends at roughly the New Deal era. He calls this the period of industrial expansion. Periods 1 and 2 have one common ingredient: During these periods there were overt efforts of whites to solidify economic racial domination (ranging from the manipulation of black labor to the neutralization or elimination of black economic competition) through various forms of juridical, political, and social discrimination (p. 4). He views racial problems in these two periods as mainly conflict over economic resources. Thus, says Wilson, economic theories of racial antagonism and conflict are readily applicable here. Such theories are not as readily applicable to the third stage.

Stage 3 began during the 1960s and 1970s. Formally, he calls it the modern industrial period of American race relations. During this time fundamental economic and political changes have made economic class affiliation more important than race in determining black prospects for occupational advancement. This period may be characterized as the period of progressive transition from racial inequalities to class inequalities (p. 3).

During Stage 3 the policies of the government have become much more autonomous and favorable toward black interests than during earlier periods. This assistance has, Wilson argues, significantly changed the racial balance of power (p. 18). Since the early 1940s the black population has steadily gained political resources and with the help of sympathetic white allies, has shown an increasing tendency to utilize these resources in promoting or protecting its group interests (p. 18).

Wilson is essentially correct when he contends that race is declining in significance as a factor regulating life chances of black Americans. His correlated point that social class is more important than race on black life chances is more questionable. Yet both points deserve further study. Although I agree with the general direction of Wilson's thought on the matter, I hold important differences with his view.

My position is that race is in the process of being replaced by class as a significant determiner of black life chances, but this process is not as far along nor as certain as

Wilson suggests. In fact, at this point in time race is essential to the progress (upward mobility) now being achieved by some blacks. These achievements result from the increased use of ethnic status by blacks. They are the product of efforts by black, black-run, and/or black-influenced groups that operate to protect and enhance black well-being. The NAACP, the Urban League, and the Congressional Black Caucus are typical among these. It is the fact of ethnic status (strategy and tactics among blacks as during the civil rights effort) that accounts for the new governmental, or state, promotion of black interests that Wilson seems to attribute to corporate capitalism.

Corporate capitalism does in fact account for one aspect of what Wilson accurately describes, namely, the irretrievable drop to the very bottom by large numbers of lower-class blacks, what he calls the underclass. But corporate capitalism should not be credited with the upward achievements that blacks have made in recent years. These achievements were not because of, rather they were in spite of, corporate capitalism. The civil rights movement forced corporate capitalism to accommodate, to a limited extent, the needs of blacks. This was largely through governmental action on the spectrum of agencies and agents that dispense jobs in significant numbers. Furthermore, even in the face of threat of governmental penalty, the dominant corporations of corporate capitalism are the most recalcitrant and reluctant units to respond favorably to affirmative action directives.

An important related point is that without struggle there is no reason to believe that the gains made under corporate capitalism will continue. Corporate capitalism is not a stable entity with a predetermined and automatic direction regarding racial equality. Under an ultraconservative state apparatus, corporate capitalism could readopt the white supremacist hiring practices of the recent past.

Wilson's approach gives one reason to assume a confluence of events that link corporate capitalism automatically with a positive governmental policy regarding blacks. This is an important error, an error to which Herbert Blumer time and again has alerted the sociological community.

It is difficult for Wilson to entertain the prospect of loss of recent gains made by blacks because of the powerful political and social movement against job discrimination (p. 153). This reflects a failure to assess properly the social movement to which he refers. It is not a constant and uniform entity but a wavering, insubstantial, now-latent, now-active element of the sociopolitical order. There is no assurance at all that the equal employment imperatives now somewhat operative within the corporate structure of the society will continue to be upheld. Recruitment of talented whites to replace talented blacks would make the task of hiring easier for the American corporate structure. Only as corporate capitalism shares a sociopolitical arena wherein allegiance to the democratic process is maintained, along with the several freedoms guaranteed by the Constitution, will the corporate structure become and remain nonracist. Furthermore, the democratic process and its traditional associated freedoms must be supplemented by a widespread cultural awareness of, and commitment to, racial equality as a way of life.

Without these two basic conditions, corporate capitalism will in all likelihood revert to the standard operating procedure that has held for most of our past history racial segregation and subordination. For this reason I agree with those of Wilson's critics who are concerned about the meaning of his message to American policymakers. Special and remedial programs for blacks will continue to be necessary until proportional representation in the economic, political, and social life of the country has been achieved.

One final comment, which in some tangential way is related to the above criticism of Wilson's improper use of corporate capitalism as an analytic unit. Throughout his book there is no mention of Robert Ezra Park or his writings on race. Park's importance does not reside in his being a founding member and chairperson of the sociology department of which Wilson is, these many years later, a member. Nor does it reside in the fact that Park was one of the, if not the, foremost students of race and culture in the world, and that his writings took black Americans as an object of direct focus. Although these attributes would seem to qualify him for attention, they do so less imperatively than the fact that it was Robert Park who first enunciated the proposition of which Wilson's thesis is a variant. Park saw the centrality of racial oppression for class relations many years ago as some years before him it had been adumbrated by Marx and later articulated by Lenin. In Park's view class problems and issues would in the long run replace race problems and issues as blacks passed through the same cycle as other ethnic groups in the United States. Wilson's unique and distinctive contribution then, if any, is to suggest in an interesting though unconvincing way that what Marx and Lenin hoped for and developed strategy to achieve and what Park worked for and vaguely predicted, has in his opinion at long last come to pass.

APPENDIX D:
Tactics and Strategy

I have suggested devising tactics and strategy furthering the cause of Afro-American equality within a liberal rather than a revolutionary left framework. In addition, I have suggested that racial equality rather than power to the proletariat be the goal of strategic and tactical formulations. Formation of a nationwide Afro-American membership group, somewhat after the suggestion of Monroe cited in Chapter 6, could be a central element in this process. In this appendix I shall expand briefly on this idea, its importance, as well as on the direction that might be taken in its implementation.

The primary purpose of a national organization of Afro-Americans would be to add an important resource to and by blacks to increase and accelerate progress toward proportional representation in the class structure of the society.The fact that enormous gains have been made in the recent past, and at an accelerated pace, should not obscure the fact that continued and severe racial inequality remains that requires much more extensive change. The deeply entrenched Aryan and Anglo-Saxon myths make recent gains to black Americans tenuous at best. These gains must be stabilized and enormously expanded if proportional representation is to be realized in fact. This realization will in large part depend upon capitalizing on the resources and energies of blacks themselves.

A national and representative organization of Afro-Americans would once again set the black population in motion in its own behalf. It would engage blacks in important

299

activity related to their own survival and well-being. Provided the organization is sufficiently representative, that is to say, a mass organization, and sufficiently well run, it would become a meaningful validation to blacks of the "system" and a source of pride and dignity. It would be a clear instance of reward based on individual initiative and self-help. Such a mass organization must be essentially self-supporting, widely representative of the class composition of the black community, and provide regular organized, intelligent, and disciplined efforts in each local black community throughout the nation.

Financing a national black organization must become a matter to which each and every Afro-American citizen contributes directly. This means of all age and income levels. The contribution of each person should be in the same amount. Given a black population of over 22 million and a $1 yearly contribution by each person to the organization, one would expect a minimum budget of more than $22 million. Of course, contributions to the organization by friends and associates would increase this considerably. Yet, $22 million a year is entirely sufficient for a number of important goals to be achieved by such an organization.

In addition to self-support, the character of representation on its governing board is important. It will function effectively if there is a deliberate effort to make this board representative of the entire spectrum of social classes. A formula of four persons from the working, or blue-collar, class, four from the middle or white-collar class, and another four selected at large is illustrative. Board members must have staggered terms of sufficient length to provide continuity of functioning of the organization but sufficiently short to prevent the rise of oligarchy. A governing body of broad class representation will increase the range of appeal by the organization among blacks as well as the relevance of its program to blacks.

Self-support and broad class representation achieved, there arises the issue of providing meaningful activity on local levels throughout the nation. These activities should tie directly into the broad goals of the organization, as each community works out the several activities through which these goals are best achieved under local conditions. This will vary from location to location. The overall goal of achieving proportional class representation of Afro-Americans suggests at least the following as important activities that would be an aspect of most local programs and activities:

❖ Providing and publicizing information about black life, history, and experience, with special emphasis on positive achievements and contributions. Such information and interpretation from a black viewpoint is sorely needed in American society because of the long history of racist propaganda that has severely distorted the positive features of black life and history among both blacks and whites.

❖ Providing public exposure about and generating counteraction regarding important local and national grievances that persist from the remains of white supremacy in the social structure and culture. Private industry is known to be much more resistant to affirmative action mandates than governmental agencies, yet they are the primary source of employment in the nation. In fact, some large private industries as well as areas of higher education appear deliberately defiant in utilization of qualified blacks. Racist practices in such industries and educational establishments must become widely known throughout the nation and they must be appropriately penalized. These are matters to be initiated in local communities throughout the country.

❖ Devising special programs and strategies to induce

change in instances of structural, or institutional, racism as reflected in underemployment of blacks or lack of access to (and preparation for) higher education. Local communities must take the initiative in monitoring places of employment, educational establishments, as well as the activities of renegade violent racists, and so on, in the interest of protecting and enhancing black well-being in the society. They must also see that blacks are increasingly prepared to function effectively at all levels of education and employment. The needs of very low-income blacks in each community will require special attention. Representation of blacks in business activities, such as banking, finance, industrial, and commercial areas, is extremely important and must be closely monitored and increased. Regular contacts must be established in each local community to achieve this monitoring, and avenues must be developed to publicize and remedy persistent racist resistance. Needless to say, close monitoring, in cooperation with local law enforcement, of the potential violence of disconsolate white supremacists must be a matter of serious and ongoing attention in each local community.

❖ Establishing and maintaining ties of solidarity and support with allied groups and organizations also concerned to eliminate racial oppression from national life. Chicano, Asian, Jewish as well as a variety of white religious groups and organizations (to cite a few) are natural allies of blacks and must be so considered and treated. Such groups will be essential in black efforts to pass needed legislation, to establish ties in the business community, and to participate in protest marches. Their willingness to cooperate in such ventures in large part depends on the kind of tact, diplomacy, and concern that have been utilized locally in allying them with the new national organization.

❖ Establishing and maintaining ties with Third World countries both for purposes of mutual solidarity and moral support and for purposes of technical assistance where possible. See discussion in Appendix B as well as Chapter 6. An additional concern here must be efforts to initiate change in those Third World countries where blacks are, as in the United States, still victims of white supremacist practices. This refers especially to certain Caribbean and Latin American countries that were heavily involved in the slave trade and slavery. A national organization of Afro-Americans could provide information, support, and solidarity with groups and individuals in such countries, seeking to change the racist status quo toward racial equality.

Special-interest groups of various kinds already exist in the black community, several of which already have national stature. The NAACP and Urban League are perhaps the oldest among these. Newer groups are the Congressional Black Caucus, the National Black Economic Development Conference, and the Congress on Racial Equality. Overall, these are positive developments, provided there can emerge from the mélange a broad and widely representative body that unifies these special efforts in an assertive, democratically run, and Afro-American-controlled national organization.

The pivotal significance of the black community to the national welfare of the United States has already been mentioned. Recognition of this fact among white Americans is clearly seen in the many agents and agencies among them that seek to direct and/or influence the direction of the black community. Marxist-Leninists seek self-determination and a nationalist direction for blacks. Unrelenting white supremacists seek a return to Jim Crow and slavery for Afro-Americans. Liberal groups seek a more pluralist and integrationist course. The several competing options, in light of the utter fatefulness of the issue for blacks and for the country, demand that the matter become widely discussed among blacks and that some consensus be achieved in open and public forums. A national black union of the kind suggested here would provide such a forum and keep the fate and direction of the black community within the larger society largely in the hands of blacks themselves, a circumstance obtaining with other ethnic groups for a considerably longer time.

Index

abolition, 10–12, 66
Academy of Sciences, 16
affirmative action, 145–46, 153, 155–56, 160–61, 235, 296, 301
African Methodist Church, 69
African Slavery in America, 14
African Task Force, 204
Afro-Americans, 42, 48, 90, 99, 299, 301, 303
    history, 54
Alabama
    blacks in politics in, 69
    disenfranchisement, 81
    runaways, 59
Alarcón, Hernando de, 57
American Communist party, 221
American Revolution, 13–15, 39
Anglo migrants to California, 95
Anti-Defamation League, 231, 238
Aquinas, St. Thomas, 5
Argentina, 11
Arkansas
    blacks in politics in, 70
Association of Black Sociologists, 289

B'nai B'rith, 231, 238
Baltzell, E. Digby, 16, 20
Baptists, 8
Barzun, Jacques, 27, 46
Battle of Long Island, 65
Battle of Monmouth, 65
Bentham, Jeremy, 8, 19

Bergman, Peter M., 57, 79, 86
Black Belt, 48, 80
Black Scholar,The, 222–25
blacks, 2, 19, 35, 50, 89, 95, 142, 144–46, 149, 160–61, 179–81, 183, 190–91, 194–99, 203–4, 212, 217, 222, 226–27, 235, 241–42, 260, 289–91, 294, 296–304
blacks and Hispano Californians, 90
blacks in California, 89
blacks in early California, 94
blacks in regions of the U.S., 89
blacks in San Francisco, 96
blacks, and poverty, 146
blacks, income gains, 147
blacks, men's incomes, 147
Blauner, Robert, 35, 47
Blumer, Herbert, 18, 297
Bolivia, 11
bourgeoisie, 34, 39, 292
Boxton, Thomas F., 7
Bradley, Thomas, 204–6
Brazil, 11
Breitman, George, 220
Burgess, Ernest, 28, 46
Burke, Edmund, 14, 18
Burnett, Peter H., 95
Bury, John B., 23, 46

Cabeza de Vaca, Álvar Núñez, 57
California, 99–100, 203–4, 211, 238, 241
California black population growth, 97
California Real Estate Association, 98
Canada, 281–82
capitalism, 21, 36, 202, 214, 221, 227, 239–41, 286, 290–92, 296–98
Cardozo, Francis, 70

Carnegie, Andrew, 83
Carolinas
    disenfranchisement, 79, 81
    runaways, 59
    segregation, 80
    slavery in, 57
Carry, Lott, 66
castas, 90
caste groups, 38
Caucasians, 191
Cesaire, Aime, 201, 215
change, 7–8, 22, 37, 48–49, 144, 161, 180–84, 195, 198, 203,
    210, 217–21, 223–24, 226–27, 233–35, 239–42, 282, 291–
    92, 294–95, 299, 302–3
change in California race relations, 94
China, 25, 235
Civil Rights Act of 1964, 153
civil rights movement, 45, 145, 193, 296
Civil War, 2, 8, 27, 150
Clark, Kenneth, 289
Clarkson, Thomas, 6, 8
colonialism, 180, 199, 201, 203, 213, 217, 235, 239
Colored Citizens Convention, 97
Columbia, 100
Common Sense, 13
Communist Manifesto, 33–34, 47
Congress, 15, 98, 286, 296, 303
Congress on Racial Equality, 303
Congressional Black Caucus, 296, 303
Connecticut, 15, 230
Constitution, 297
Contemporary Sociology, 289
Continental Congress, 65
Convention of Colored Citizens, 96
Coronado, Francisco Vásquez, 57

corporate capitalism, 290–91, 296–98
Council of Fourteen, 5
coyotes, 90
Crane, Verner, 15
Crisis, 14
Cruse, Harold, 220, 241

de Ayllón, Lucas Vásquez , 57
de Las Casas, Bartolomé, 4
de Montesinos, Antonio, 3
de Oro, Siglo, 18
de Saint-Pierre, Abbé, 24
de Sepúlveda, Juan Ginés, 4, 18
Deane, Silas, 14
Declaration of Human Rights, 36
Declining Significance of Race, The, 289
Delaware, 15
Delmatier, Royce, 93, 96, 99–100

Ecuador, 14
Emancipation Proclamation, 196
Emerson, Rupert, 200, 214
employment, 141, 145, 160–61, 198–99, 212, 230, 235, 239,
    293, 297, 301–2
employment, agricultural, 150
Encyclopedists, 24
Enlightenment, 3, 9, 16, 24–25, 27, 196, 214
Españoles, 90
Ethiopia, 200
ethnicity, 35, 161, 180, 195
evolutionary philosophy, 28, 33

Fifteenth Amendment, 97
Florida
    blacks in politics in, 70

Forbes, Jack, 89
France, 3, 8–11, 14–16, 18, 196, 200, 206, 208, 210, 220
Franchise League, 96
Franklin, Benjamin, 13, 15, 20
Frazier, E. Franklin, 39, 49
Frye, Hardy, 94, 100
Fuller, Leonard, 203

Galbraith, John Kenneth, 228
Gandhi, 226
Garvey, Marcus, 197
Georgia, 193
    blacks in politics in, 70
Ghetto Rebellion to Black Liberation, 221, 241
Glazer, Nathan, 231, 242, 289
Gobineau, Joseph, 191
Goode, Kenneth, 41, 49
Great Britain, 3, 13, 200
Greeks, 23

Haiti, 11
Handlin, Oscar, 45, 50
Hare, Nathan, 39, 49, 222, 225
Hawkins, Augustus F., 97
Heilbroner, Robert, 239, 243, 247–48, 262, 268
Helvétius, 24
Hispaniola, 3
d'Holbach, 24
Howard University, 223
Hughes Helicopter Company, 203

identity, 36, 39, 143, 199
imperialism, 200–1, 213–14, 286
inbreeding, 31
indentured servants, 42, 94

India, 4–5, 19, 90–91, 183–86, 189, 213, 226
Industrial Revolution, 17, 200
industrialization, 284
Inequality of the Human Races (Gobineau), 191, 213
integration, 32, 242, 304
internal colonialism, 13
Irish, 228, 230–31
Italians, 228, 231

Jaleé, Pierre, 281, 287
James, C.L.R., 10, 19
Jamestown, 41
Japan, 161, 235, 281, 286
Jatavs, 184, 186–90
Jats, 184–85, 187–90
Jim Crow, 43, 50, 78, 80–82, 179–80, 196, 303
Johnson, Lyndon, 285
Junto, 16

Kant, Immanuel, 25
Kenya, 204
Klein, Herbert, 6, 18–19
Klingberg, Frank, 7, 19
Ku Klux Klan, 77, 237

Lamarck, 26
Larkin, Thomas, 93
Law of Burgos, 5
Leidesdorff, William Alexander, 93
Leonard, Rhonda, 218, 241
Liberia, 200
Limits of American Capitalism, 243
Locke, John, 8, 19
Luther, Martin, 218, 226

Machiavelli, 23, 46
Maryland, 42
Mead, George Herbert, 46
Mehrana, 184–86, 189
Memmi, Albert, 36, 47
mestizos, 90–91
Methodists, 8
Mexican rule in California, 93
Mexican-Americans, 161
Mexico, 14
Middle Ages, 23
mobility, 161, 181, 198–99, 217, 230, 241, 291, 296
mobility, socioeconomic, 52, 55, 72, 85
Mongoloids, 191
Monroe, John, 232, 242
Montagu, Ashley, 285, 287
Moynihan, Daniel Patrick, 231, 242
mulattoes, 90–91

NAACP, 44, 74, 83, 197, 224, 296, 303
Narváez, Pánfilo, 57
National Association for the Advancement of Colored
    People (NAACP), 44, 74, 79, 83
National Black Economic Development Conference, 303
natural law, 28
natural selection, 26–27, 30
Nazis, 192
Negroes, 39, 44, 48, 100, 144, 220–21
Negroids, 191
New Jersey, 230
Nigeria, 204

Origin of Species, The (Darwin), 26–27, 33
original sin, 23
Oro, Siglo de, 6

Overseas Private Investment Corporation (OPIC), 211

Paine, Thomas, 13–15, 18, 20
Paley, William, 8, 19
pardos, 90–91
Park Robert E., 22, 28
Pennsylvania, 16, 18
Pettigrew, Thomas F., 289
Plato, 23
Portugal, 200
Powell, Gen. Colin, 72
Presbyterians, 8
progress, 3, 13, 15–16, 23, 27, 145–46, 160, 184, 199, 224, 232,
    283, 290, 295–96, 299
proletariat, 34, 292, 299
protest, 1, 44, 188–89, 228, 302
Protestant Establishment, The, 16, 20
Protestantism, 8

race relations cycle, 30
race relations in California, 91
racism, 1, 21, 28, 35, 37, 181, 193, 213, 217–18, 221, 227–28,
    233, 235, 239–41, 285, 287, 290–92, 302
racism in early California, 95–96
Randolph, A. Philip, 197
Reconstruction, 43–44, 196
Redemption, 78
Reflections on Negro Slavery, 10
Reflections on the Revolution in France, 14
Republican party, 69, 79, 82, 96
Revolutionary Action Movement (RAM), 223
Rey, Francisco, 93
Rhode Island, 15
Rights of Man, 14
Roman Catholicism, 5

Rome, 23, 185
Rumford, William Byron, 98

San Domingo, 10
San Francisco State College, 222–23
Sartre, Jean-Paul, 36
Schapiro, J. Salwyn, 9, 19
segregation, 41, 45, 80, 97, 181, 230, 235, 297
Sharp, Granville, 8, 19
Shepard, Peggy, 212
Siglo de Oro, 6
Skinheads, 192–93
slavery, 3, 6–9, 11, 16–19, 39–40, 43, 179–80, 182, 191, 194–
    96, 199, 201, 214, 226, 294, 303
Smith v. Allwight, 85
Smith, Adam, 8, 15, 19
Social Contract, 9
Socialist Worker's party, 220
Society for Effecting the Abolition of the Slave Trade, 6
Society for the Mitigation and Gradual Abolition of Slavery
    Throughout the British Dominions, 7
sociology, 22, 28, 222, 225, 298
Solberg, Curtis, 91
South Africa, 203, 226, 235
Spain, 3, 6, 18–19
Spanish rule in California, 92–93
status groups, 40
Stone, Chuck, 228, 241
Student Nonviolent Coordinating Committee (SNCC), 223
Supreme Court, 98

Tanzania, 204
Tapia, Jose Bartolomé, 93
TAW International Leasing, 212
Third World, 180, 203–4, 211–12, 235, 281–87, 303

Thomas, W. I., 182, 213
Thoreau, Henry David, 226
Treaty of Guadalupe Hidalgo, 93

unions, 233
University of California, 204, 241
University of Chicago, 19, 22, 46, 223
Urban League, 197, 296, 303
Uruguay, 11

Valladolid, 5
Van Albertini, Rudolph, 201, 215
Vann Woodward, C., 50
Venezuela, 14
vigilantes, 52
Voter Registration Project, 128

Washington, Booker T., 83, 197
Wealth of Nations, The, 15, 19
Weber, Max, 21, 38, 46, 48
Wesley, John, 8, 19
Wesleyans, 8
West Indies, 8, 43
Westie, Margaret, 260
White Walter, 224
Wilberforce, William, 6, 8
Willie, C.V., 289
Wilson, William, 289

Zambia, 204

About the Author

SETHARD FISHER received his bachelor's, master's, and Ph.D. degrees in sociology from the University of California at Berkeley. He also received an MSW degree from the same institution and is a licensed clinical social worker. He has taught sociology in Canada and in the United States, and has lectured in Europe, Latin America, and throughout the United States. Race relations, especially black-white relations, has been one of Dr. Fisher's primary areas of interest for a number of years. He has developed a challenging, provocative, and seldom-enunciated thesis on race relations. It is that fundamental and irreversible changes toward racial equality are well along among black and white Americans, that the demise of capitalism is not a precondition for this change, and that once achieved, this change will itself precipitate a more fully developed class politics in the United States.